Digital Transformation and the Economics of Banking

The book provides deep insight into the processes of digital transformation of banking according to economic, institutional, and social dimensions. Together with the transformation of incumbent banks, the processes result in changes in the scope of existing banking services. Moreover, new entities (FinTech firms) partner with incumbent banks and reshape the banking sector and its financial environment.

The far-reaching transformation of banks and the banking sectors is accompanied by some institutional and socioeconomic processes. Regarding institutional processes, the book provides insight into the digitalization of the banking sector from a legal point of view. Traditionally, banking is strongly regulated by norms and rules and this status should be maintained when new entities are entering the sector and/or when new technological solutions contribute to the provision of banking services. Regarding socioeconomic processes, it must be highlighted that digitalization is exerting a powerful impact on societies. One significant example, among others, is the increase in the financial inclusion of disadvantaged groups (especially customers either underserved by the traditional financial sector or unbanked). The socioeconomic aspect, however, has a much greater dimension and its selected aspects are described in this book.

The principal audience of the book will be scholars in the fields of banking and finance, but also other related disciplines in the social sciences that are of particular relevance to the banking sector's digital transformation. This includes legal science, management, and psychology. The book also targets professionals in the financial industry interested in the impact of new financial technologies on banking sectors and bank services, particularly with a main focus on legal and socioeconomic dimensions.

Piotr Łasak is Associate Professor at the Institute of Economics, Finance and Management, Jagiellonian University in Krakow, Poland.

Jonathan Williams is Professor of Banking and Finance in the Department of Finance and Accounting and Centre for Sustainable and Explainable FinTech at Surrey Business School.

Routledge International Studies in Money and Banking

Activist Retail Investors and the Future of Financial Markets
Understanding YOLO Capitalism
Edited by Usman W. Chohan and Sven van Kerckhoven

Banking, Risk and Crises in Europe
From the Global Financial Crisis to COVID-19
Renata Karkowska, Zbigniew Korzeb, Anna Matysek-Jędrych and Paweł Niedziółka

Inflation Dynamic
Global Positive Economic Analysis
Weshah Razzak

COVID-19 and European Banking Performance
Resilience, Recovery and Sustainability
Edited by Paul Wachtel and Ewa Miklaszewska

The Cryptocurrency Phenomenon
The Origins, Evolution and Economics of Digital Currencies
Gianni Nicolini and Silvia Intini

Ethical Finance and Prosperity
Beyond Environmental, Social and Governance Investing
Ugo Biggeri, Giovanni Ferri, Federica Ielasi, Pedro Manuel Sasia

Alternative Acquisition Models and Financial Innovation
Special Purpose Acquisition Companies in Europe, and the Italian Legal Framework
Edited by Daniele D'Alvia, Ettore Maria Lombardi and Yochanan Shachmurove

For more information about this series, please visit: www.routledge.com/Routledge-International-Studies-in-Money-and-Banking/book-series/SE0403

Digital Transformation and the Economics of Banking

Economic, Institutional, and Social Dimensions

Edited by
Piotr Łasak and
Jonathan Williams

Routledge
Taylor & Francis Group
LONDON AND NEW YORK

First published 2024
by Routledge
4 Park Square, Milton Park, Abingdon, Oxon OX14 4RN

and by Routledge
605 Third Avenue, New York, NY 10158

Routledge is an imprint of the Taylor & Francis Group, an informa business

British Library Cataloguing-in-Publication Data
A catalogue record for this book is available from the British Library

Library of Congress Cataloging-in-Publication Data
Names: Łasak, Piotr, editor. | Williams, Jonathan (Professor of banking and finance), editor.
Title: Digital transformation and the economics of banking : economic, institutional, and social dimensions / edited by Piotr Łasak and Jonathan Williams.
Description: 1 Edition. | New York, NY : Routledge, 2024. |
Series: Routledge international studies in money and banking | Includes bibliographical references and index.
Identifiers: LCCN 2023024803 (print) | LCCN 2023024804 (ebook) |
ISBN 9781032374932 (hardback) | ISBN 9781032374956 (paperback) |
ISBN 9781003340454 (ebook)
Subjects: LCSH: Banks and banking—Technological innovations. | Financial services industry—Technological innovations. | Information technology—Management.
Classification: LCC HG1708.7 .D554 2024 (print) | LCC HG1708.7 (ebook) |
DDC 332.10285/46—dc23/eng/20230714
LC record available at https://lccn.loc.gov/2023024803
LC ebook record available at https://lccn.loc.gov/2023024804

ISBN: 978-1-032-37493-2 (hbk)
ISBN: 978-1-032-37495-6 (pbk)
ISBN: 978-1-003-34045-4 (ebk)

DOI: 10.4324/9781003340454

Typeset in Sabon LT Pro
by codeMantra

Contents

Illustrations

Figures

Tables

Preface

This book offers a deep insight into the processes of digital transformation in banking according to economic, institutional, and social dimensions. It focuses on the impact of new financial technologies on incumbent banks and highlights the advantages and disadvantages of bank transformation. Together with the transformation of banks, the processes of digitalization result in changes to the scope of existing banking services. Moreover, new entities (FinTech firms and BigTech firms) are partnering with incumbent banks in ways which are reshaping banking sectors and their environments.

The far-reaching transformation of banks and banking sectors is accompanied by some institutional and socioeconomic processes. Regarding institutional processes, this book provides insight into the digitalization of the banking sector from a legal point of view. Traditionally, banking is strongly regulated by norms and rules and this status should be maintained when new entities enter the banking sector and/or when new technological solutions contribute to the provision of banking services. Such solutions such as central bank digital currencies (CBDC) and other forms of electronic money need consideration from a legal point of view. Apart from exerting a direct impact on the regulatory issues which accompany the digital transformation of banking, the application of new technological solutions also impacts the mechanisms and frameworks of internal governance within banks and related banking services. In this context, a leading question is whether traditional forms of governance might be replaced by a new type of blockchain governance.

Regarding socioeconomic processes, it must be highlighted that digitalization is exerting a powerful impact on societies. One significant example, among others, is the increase in the financial inclusion of disadvantaged groups (especially customers either underserved by the traditional financial sector or unbanked). Financial inclusion has a much greater dimension than just widening access to banking services because it is associated to a significant extent with the psychological aspects of human behaviour. It is also important in this context to consider the ethics and other features of the new technologies being applied in the financial sector. The incorporation of

FinTech firms and new financial technologies into banking activity should enhance the sustainability of banking development and address salient issues such as gender disparity, climate change, and other Environment, Social, and Governance (ESG) issues.

These issues are considered by the authors of the chapters in this book. While the principal audience of this book will be banking and finance scholars, it will also interest financial industry professionals interested in the impact of the digital transformation in banking.

Acronyms and Abbreviations

ADIs	Authorized Deposit-Taking institutions
AFS	Alternative Financial Services
AI	Artificial Intelligence
AIS	Account Information Service
AISP	Account Information Service Provider
AML	Anti-Money Laundering
API	Application Programming Interface
ASPSP	Account Servicing Payment Service Provider
ATM	Automated Teller Machine
BaaS	Banking-as-a-Service
BigTech	Big Technology Firms
BNPL	Buy-Now-Pay-Later
CBDC	Central Bank Digital Currency
CCD	Consumer Credit Directive
CCR	Climate Change Risk
CDP	Carbon Disclosure Project
CEO	Chief Executive Officer
CFO	Chief Financial Officer
CMU	Capital Markets Union
CRD/CRR	Capital Requirements Directive/Capital Requirements Regulation
CSC	Common and Secure Communication
CSR	Corporate Social Responsibility
DeFi	Decentralized Finance
DLT	Distributed Ledger Technology
EB	Embedded Banking
EBA	European Banking Authority
ECB	European Central Bank
EIOPA	European Insurance and Occupational Pensions Authority
EmFi	Embedded Finance
ESG	Environment, Social, and Governance
FCA	Financial Conduct Authority
FDA	Food and Drug Administration

FHA	Federal Housing Administration
FP	Field Partner
FinTech	Financial Technology Firms
FII	Financial Inclusion Index
FIs	Financial Institutions
FMSA	Financial Market Supervision
FSB	Financial Stability Board
GFC	Global Financial Crisis
GHG	Greenhouse Gases
GRI	Global Reporting Initiative
GS	Google Scholar
INFE	International Network on Financial Education
InsurTech	Insurance Technology
ITS	Implementing Technical Standards
KYC	Know Your Customer
ML	Machine Learning
MSMEs	Micro Small- and Medium-sized Enterprises
NGO	Non-government Organizations
NIS	Network Information Systems
OB	Open Banking
PFSA	Polish Financial Supervision Authority
PIS	Payment Initiation Service
PSA	Payment Services Act
PSD	Payment Services Directive
PSM	Propensity Score Matching
P2P	Peer-to-peer
RegTech	Regulatory Technology
RTS	Regulatory Technical Standards
SaaS	Software-as-a-Service
SASB	Sustainability Accounting Standards Board
SCA	Strong Customer Authentication
SDGs	Sustainable Development Goals
SFDR	Sustainable Finance Disclosure Regulation
SMEs	Small and Medium-sized Enterprises
SREP	Supervisory Review and Evaluation Process
SupTech	Supervision Technology
TCE	Transaction Cost Economics
TCFD	Task Force on Climate-Related Financial Disclosures
TPP	Third Party Provider; Third (payment) Party (service) Provider
UN	United Nations
VCs	Value Chains
WHO	World Health Organization
WoS	Web of Science

Notes on Contributors

Danilo Abis, University of Turin. Danilo Abis is PhD candidate in Business and Management in the Department of Management, School of Management and Economics, University of Turin, Italy. He started his academic career as a teaching assistant on the *Financial Markets and Intermediaries* courses in the School of Management and Economics in Turin. He was also a visiting postgraduate researcher in the Department of Finance and Accounting at Surrey Business School in the academic year 2022/2023. His research interests centre on the banking and financial industry and include FinTech, Asset Management, Private Banking, Securities Markets, sustainable finance, and behavioural finance.

Jan Byrski, Cracow University of Economics. Jan Byrski (PhD, Hab.) is Associate Professor in the Department of Public Economic Law and Labour Law at the Cracow University of Economics. He is Graduate of the Faculty of Law and Administration of the Jagiellonian University, and the School of German Law of the Jagiellonian University, University of Heidelberg, and the University of Mainz, as well as the School of Austrian Law of the Jagiellonian University and the University of Vienna. He is scholarship recipient at the Ruhr-Universität Bochum (a scholarship awarded by the Foundation for Polish-German Cooperation), Ernst-Moritz-Arndt Universität Greifswald, Johann Gutenberg Universität Mainz, and Max-Planck-Institut für Immaterialgüter-und Wettbewerbsrecht. He is author and co-author of numerous academic and popular-science publications, including the monograph "Tajemnica prawnie chroniona w działalności bankowej" (Legally Protected Secret in Banking Operations), which earned him the top award in the Scientiae Legis Excellentia contest for the best PhD dissertation on economic law organized by the National Bank of Poland, as well as the habilitation dissertation "Outsourcing w działalności dostawców usług płatniczych" (Outsourcing in the Activities of Payment Service Providers) (C.H. Beck 2018).

Stefano Cosma, University of Modena and Reggio Emilia. Stefano Cosma is Full Professor of Banking in the Marco Biagi Department of Economics, University of Modena and Reggio Emilia, where he is vice-Dean, a member of Academic Council of Doctoral Research Course in Labour, Development and Innovation, and a member of the Board of the International Doctoral Research School in Labour Relations – Marco Biagi Foundation. Stefano is a member of CEFIN (Center for Studies in Banking and Finance), ADEIMF (Association of Teachers in Economics of Financial Intermediaries, Markets and Corporate Finance), AIDEA (Italian Association of Business Administration), and European Association of University Teachers in Banking and Finance. He is a member of the scientific committee of the Foundation for Financial Education and Saving Plans (FEDUF) and Chairman of Sella Personal Credit (Sella Group), Smartika (P2P Lending FinTech, Sella Group), and Nephis (Sella Group). In the field of sustainability, he is a member of the Board of Directors of Holostem Advanced Therapies (a biotech in stem cell-based Regenerative Medicine) and the National Center for Gene Therapy and Drugs. His recent research topics include Consumer Credit, Retail Lending, Digital Transformation in Financial Intermediation, and Sustainable Finance.

Timothy King, University of Vaasa. Timothy (Tim) King is Professor of Finance in the School of Accounting & Finance, University of Vaasa. He also serves as an external examiner for the University of Glasgow and Heriot-Watt University. Previously, he worked at the University of Leeds and the University of Kent where he also served as Director for the Centre for Quantitative Finance. His research is in the areas of banking, FinTech, Corporate Governance, Corporate Finance, CSR, and ESG. He has published in leading journals including the *Journal of Corporate Finance* and the *British Journal of Management*. Tim is also the lead editor as well as a contributor to the book *Disruptive Technology in Banking and Finance: An International Perspective on FinTech* published by Palgrave Macmillan. He regularly disseminates his work at leading conferences and invited talks as well as contributing and interacting directly with industry – for example, he has acted as an expert judge for UK banking sector awards and contributed regularly to industry-focused reports. He holds an undergraduate degree in Business Studies and Economics, a master's degree in Banking and Finance, and a doctorate in Banking and Finance – all from Bangor University.

Grzegorz Kuca, Jagiellonian University. Grzegorz Kuca is Professor at the Faculty of Law and Administration and a member of the Centre for Interdisciplinary Constitutional Studies at the Jagiellonian University in Kraków. He has acted as an advisor and senior advisor – an assistant of a judge of the Constitutional Tribunal. Currently, he is an attorney-at-law at Legal Skills International Business Lawyer EEIG, a member of the Krakow Bar Association and the Polish Association of Constitutional Law, and a fellow of the European Group of Public Law. He has completed research internships in Belgium (KU Leuven), Switzerland (University of Luzern), and the Czech Republic (Charles University). He is author and co-author of several publications concerning Polish and comparative constitutional law. His research interests include constitutional law, electoral law, and public finances.

Piotr Łasak, Jagiellonian University. Piotr Łasak (PhD, Hab) is Associate Professor at the Institute of Economics, Finance and Management, Jagiellonian University in Krakow, Poland. His research, publication, and teaching activities focus on banking, corporate finance, and international finance. The main research topics are financial markets development, banking regulation and supervision, mechanisms of economic, financial and currency crises, and shadow banking system development. Among his research interests is the development of the Chinese financial market. His current main research area concerns FinTech and the transformation of the banking sector as a direct consequence of digitalisation and the influence of financial technologies. He is the author of several publications on this subject.

Michał Nowakowski. Michał Nowakowski (PhD) is a legal counsel; lawyer specializing in financial innovation (FinTech) and new technologies with professional experience in regulatory and supervisory bodies and financial institutions. He has participated in numerous legislative processes for the financial sector, including financial safety. He has advised on the implementation of technical solutions for financial institutions, including in the context of anti-money laundering and counter-terrorist financing and data analytics. He is the author of the book "FINTECH - Technology, Finance, Regulation. A practical guide for the financial innovation sector" and numerous scientific publications. He is a lecturer and trainer in FinTech, RegTech, and data management and artificial intelligence.

Anna Omarini, Bocconi University. Anna Omarini is Researcher with tenure in financial markets and intermediaries in the Department of Finance at Bocconi University (Italy) where she is also course director for the undergraduate course *FinTech for Digital Transformation in Banking* and for the graduate course *Bank and Fintech: Vision and Strategy*. She is a member of faculty and the Knowledge Group in Banking and Insurance, at SDA Bocconi School of Management. Anna's expertise is in bank strategy and management, FinTech, open banking, and digital banking. She is the author of several articles, papers, and books which examine issues related to these fields. Anna is a reviewer, an editorial board member for several journals, a member of numerous associations, organizations, and scientific committees, and a speaker and chairperson in conferences. She graduated in Business Administration, with specialization in Banking and Financial Markets, from Bocconi University, and obtained an ITP (International Teachers Program) degree at the Stern Business School, New York University. She has also been an independent board director for banks and other financial institutions.

Daniela Pennetta, University of Modena and Reggio Emilia. Daniela Pennetta is Research Fellow at the Marco Biagi Department of Economics, University of Modena and Reggio Emilia, where she is also subject expert in Economics and the Management of Banks. She holds a PhD in Labour, Development and Innovation from the Marco Biagi Foundation, Modena, Italy. She is a member of ADEIMF (Italian Association of Teachers in Economics of Financial Intermediaries, Markets and Corporate Finance). Her research interests include Banking and Digital Transformation in Financial Intermediation. In detail, recent research topics include FinTech, the bank–FinTech relationship, Open Banking and banking platforms, sustainability, and the financing of medical research.

Patrizia Pia, University of Turin. Patrizia Pia is Associate Professor of *Financial Markets and Intermediaries* in the Department of Management, University of Turin, Turin, Italy. Professor Pia is the leader of courses in Financial Markets and Intermediaries, Private Banking, Financial Markets, and FinTech. Her research interests mainly focus on Asset Management, Private Banking, Commercial Banking, Securities Markets, Derivatives, FinTech, and ESG investment. She is the author of several papers and books. Patrizia is also a member of the Italian Private Banking Association (AIPB), and she participates actively in the internal education programs of several banks.

Błażej Prusak, Gdańsk University of Technology. Błażej Prusak is Associate Professor in the Management and Economics Faculty of Gdańsk University of Technology, Poland. He is Head of the Finance Department. His main research interests are corporate finance, corporate bankruptcy prediction, institutional aspects of corporate bankruptcy, business valuation, investment projects, financial analysis, and risk management. Currently, he is an Editor of *Research on Enterprise in Modern Economy - Theory and Practice (REME)* journal, as well as a representative of the Editorial Board of the *Intellectual Economics* journal. He is author or co-author of several monographs about corporate bankruptcy, financial analysis, stock recommendations, and market ratios. He has also published in several international journals including *International Insolvency Review*, *Economic Research*, *Risks*, *International Entrepreneurship and Management Journal*, *International Journal of Management and Economics*, *Intellectual Economics*, and *Environmental Science and Pollution Research*.

Robert Rybski, University of Warsaw. Robert Rybski is Assistant Professor at the Faculty of Law and Administration, University of Warsaw, Poland, where he also acts as Head of "Sustainable Finance – Postgraduate Studies in Law and Finance". He is also expert in the Market Surveillance and Infrastructure Department at the Polish Financial Supervision Authority (KNF) and previously worked as a lawyer specializing in climate and energy law for ClientEarth. For voluntary work, he acts as the University of Warsaw Rector's Plenipotentiary for Environment and Sustainable Development.

Michał Synowiec, Cracow University of Economics. Michał Synowiec (PhD) is a Doctor of Law at the Jagiellonian University in Cracow. He is Graduate in Law and Administration from the Jagiellonian University in Cracow, Faculty of Law and Administration, Kraków Intellectual Property Law Summer School run by the Jagiellonian University, Winter School on European Business Law run by Julius-Maximilians-Universität Würzburg (Germany), and the School of American Law of the Catholic University of America in Washington, Columbus School of Law, and Jagiellonian University. He is scholarship recipient at the Julius-Maximilians-Universität Würzburg scholarship and Jagiellonian University. He is speaker at Polish and international academic conferences on payment services law, personal data protection, intellectual property law, and civil law. He is author and co-author of academic and popular-science publications on payment services law and economic law.

Łukasz Wacławek, Gdańsk University of Technology. Łukasz Wacławek works as an Analyst in the advisory at PwC Poland. He is currently studying Finance and Accounting at Warsaw School of Economics. He is a highly motivated, ready for new challenges enthusiast of economics. His main research interests are FinTech, banking, and the management and application of innovative technology in finance. He devoted his first thesis to the role and importance of the FinTech sector in Poland and globally and plans to devote his next thesis to a scientific extension of the subject.

Krzysztof Waliszewski, Poznań University of Economics and Business. Krzysztof Waliszewski is Associate Professor in the Department of Money and Banking, Institute of Finance, Poznań University of Economics and Business, Poland. His research focuses on personal financial planning and management, financial intermediation, personal financial advice, PFM applications, FinTech, and robo-advice. He is a laureate of the prestigious prize of the Presidency of the Polish Academy of Sciences for outstanding scientific achievements in the field of finance for the habilitation monograph. He is a member of the Presidium of the PAN Financial Finance Committee, director of undergraduate studies of Banking and Financial Advisory and Financial Technology (FinTech), and a member of the Finax Advisory Board.

Jonathan Williams, University of Surrey. Jonathan Williams is Professor of Finance in the Department of Finance and Accounting at Surrey Business School, and its Centre for FinTech – the Centre for Sustainable and Explainable FinTech. A banking and finance specialist, he is also Visiting Professor at the University of Turin, the University of Malta, and Zhejiang University of Finance and Economics. Professor Williams is the chair of the European Association of Teachers of Banking and Finance (The Wolpertinger Group), treasurer of the Financial Markets and Institutions Special Interest Group of BAFA (British Accounting and Finance Association), and a member of the Chartered Banker Institute's Quality and Standards Committee. His works have been published in leading international journals including the *Journal of Corporate Finance*, *Journal of Banking and Finance*, *Journal of Financial Stability*, and *Regional Studies* among others. He has presented his research at institutions including The World Bank and Deutsche Bundesbank and at conferences and universities in countries across the world. His current research interests include executive compensation and corporate governance, financial deregulation and competitiveness, and FinTech. He is co-author of *Disruptive Technology in Banking and Finance: An International Perspective on FinTech* (2021).

Paweł Marek Woroniecki, Jagiellonian University. Paweł Marek Woroniecki is a Doctor of Legal Sciences at the Faculty of Law and Administration, Jagiellonian University in Kraków. His research interests include the legal aspects of the functioning of government and local government finances, regulations connected with the functioning of entrepreneurs in the economic system, particularly their legal situation, conditions, and forms of conducting economic activity, in addition to normative grounds of public administration's activity.

1 Introduction

Piotr Łasak and Jonathan Williams

1.1 Introduction

While the digital revolution is unprecedented in many ways, such as its velocity and scope, arguably most important is the power of digitalization to facilitate wholesale transformations of systems of production, management, and governance. Despite the potential benefits, it is fair to acknowledge that, for many firms, the process of digitalization is a disruptor and constitutes a significant challenge to incumbents. Digitalization is impacting banks, banking sectors, and the financial system at large as newly unleashed competitive forces necessitate incumbents to reassess opportunities and threats, and strengths and weaknesses, all leading to a transformation of business models. The challenges facing finance *per se* underscore the pivotal role that a digitally enhanced financial services sector is expected to perform in the Fourth Industrial Revolution.

A brief synopsis of salient developments in finance following the 2008 Global Financial Crisis (GFC) serves to illustrate the transformative nature of the digitalization process. The emergence of and rapid growth in the application of new technologies to financial services was deemed to be game changing, a disruptor to facilitate the decentralization of market structures by unbundling traditional banking services. While uncertainty precludes a definitive assessment of likely competitive conditions in the financial services industry, various scenarios have been suggested (BCBS, 2018). In the market for financial services, the main protagonists are incumbents like banks and technology firms. The latter cohort comprises small, agile financial technology (FinTech) firms and very large, big technology (BigTech) firms. What is certain is the nature of competition in financial services will evolve. While one scenario sees the end of banks amid complete phantomization of financial services, other scenarios envisage a robust competitive response by banks the bedrock of which is the digitalization of banking.

Initially, banks perceived FinTech as a disruptor. Reasons for this view included the small size of FinTech startups that explained their attention to payments and settlements and some segments of retail banking. In comparison with FinTech's customer-friendly apps, the legacy IT infrastructure and

DOI: 10.4324/9781003340454-1

poor records of customer service of banks became a deep-seated comparative disadvantage. In the face of the competitive challenge from new entrants, incumbents could develop in-house their own Fintech-style services or collaborate with FinTech firms to gain access to applications of the new financial technologies through strategic partnerships. For FinTech firms, partnerships with banks constitute an opportunity to secure new and often substantial investment while also providing access to banks' customers. Carbó-Valverde et al. (2021) explain how banks and FinTech might partner: through innovation facilitators, such as regulatory sandboxes; alliances to co-develop products; equity investments; and mergers and acquisitions. Therefore, collaboration is a mutually beneficial solution.

BigTech poses a significant competitive challenge to banks. Measured by market capitalization, the major BigTech companies are larger than the largest banks; BigTech has plentiful financial resources, access to low-cost funds, and brands which are recognized by very large customer bases (FSB, 2019). Furthermore, phantomization and regulatory initiatives, such as open banking (OB) and decentralized finance, will impact the competitive landscape. Arguably, developments concerning the regulatory perimeter will influence the nature of competition and how banks and BigTech firms might interact. FSB (2019) suggests that BigTech could compete directly with incumbents through the establishment of their own online financial services firms. On the other hand, BigTech could partner with banks, for instance, by providing technical services like cloud computing; using their partner, licensed banks to provide funding for loans to customers that BigTech originates or borrowing directly from financial institutions or financial markets; or through interfacing whereby BigTech distributes the financial services of incumbents. The nature of competition between banks and technology firms is evolving and we are now observing co-opetition whereby technology firms and financial firms compete in some market segments while collaborating in other segments.

In addition to the market developments discussed above, the spread of COVID-19 was classified as a pandemic by the World Health Organization in March 2020 with many countries implementing lockdowns or other policies that adversely affected economic activity. The pandemic significantly boosted digitalization. It caused fundamental changes in consumer behavior that typically take many years to manifest under normal conditions as consumers had no alternative other than using digital channels to conduct financial transactions and interact with financial services providers. Therefore, and in a remarkably short space of time, the post-pandemic world is characterized by an increasing use of digital channels and adoption of new digital payments. Carbó-Valverde et al. (2021) report that customers perceive choice to be beneficial and are demanding new, so-called "intelligent relationships" with financial services providers that are based on trust. One can expect a further transformation of banking channels because social distancing has increased the use and popularity of online channels.

Banks and technology firms have responded to the changes induced by the pandemic by developing new financial services to meet the needs of digital customers. Indeed, and prior to the pandemic, banks had been responding to digitalization by raising IT expenditure and allocating significant amounts to implementing new technologies. From a competitive standpoint, banks perceive new technology as an enabler to improve service quality and process efficiency while developing new lines of revenue. Notwithstanding, the prospect of new entrants, many of which (FinTech and BigTech firms) are technology natives, suggests that competition and market structures will continue to evolve. Therefore, to compete effectively, incumbents like banks must continue to embrace the transformative power of digitalization.

The past decade has borne witness to the transformative power of digitalization as new, enabling financial technologies continue to shape competition and existing market structures in financial services. The emergence of innovative and powerful technology firms alongside exogenous shocks like the pandemic has resulted in important structural changes in customer preferences and demand. To compete, to survive, banks and other incumbent financial firms have embraced digitalization and suitably revised their business models. In this sense, digitalization has been facilitating the transformation of whole banking sectors. Indeed, transformation processes have impacted various types of bank activity (like payments, credit assessment) as well as constituent parts of banks' operating structures (front-, middle-, and back-office). While these processes are ongoing, and although still not fully recognized, they are of vital importance for banks and banking sectors and their socio-economic environment.

The starting point for the research contained in this book is to provide a definition of FinTech. The term FinTech derives from the abbreviation of *financial technology*. It is significant that this term can be interpreted in three ways: as functions, technologies, and institutions (subjects) (Gomber et al., 2017; King et al., 2021; Puschmann, 2017). In the first sense, FinTech refers to such economic functions as payments, saving, lending, risk management, and advisory activities. The second meaning concerns the financial technologies themselves; including artificial intelligence (AI), distributed ledger technology (DLT), cloud computing, big data, and others. Of course, this approach can be extended to various solutions using these technologies, for example, crowdfunding or new payment units (bitcoin cryptocurrencies). The third meaning refers to entities whose functions are based on the new technologies. Originally, FinTech firms were startups whose scope of activity was very narrow; they were distinguished by their use of modern technologies, which allowed them to provide a new quality of services. Over time, larger entities, BigTech, became increasingly important while other entities like TechFin, i.e., non-financial entities (e.g., operating on the e-commerce market) attained positions that allowed them to independently offer services previously reserved for financial entities (e.g., payment or lending services).

A universal definition, provided by the Financial Stability Board (FSB), defines FinTech as "technology-enabled innovation in financial services that could result in new business models, applications, processes or products with an associated material effect on the provision of financial services" (FSB, 2017, p. 7). This definition refers to the significant impact of FinTech on financial markets, financial institutions, and the provision of financial services (Locatelli et al., 2021). Indeed, it is significant that the operation of FinTech entities is crucial for the banking sector. They not only affect the services offered but also increasingly transform both bank business models and the banking industry.

The foregoing research on technological transformation in banking is in the early stages of development and has significant research gaps. This book aims to identify, describe, and evaluate the digital transformation of banking along economic, institutional, and social dimensions. A general premise is that the current phase of economic globalization embraces extensive use of financial technologies (FinTech) in banking. Thus, this book contributes by examining many aspects of the transformation process and its impacts on single banks and banking sectors, and in addition, the economic, institutional, and social effects of these transformations.

The growing literature on financial technologies transforming bank services is largely divided into the separate strands of economic and social (Arner et al., 2020; Bhagat & Roderick, 2020; Marszk & Lechman, 2021) vis-à-vis legal considerations (Bani et al., 2020; BIS, 2018; Chiu & Deipenbrock, 2021; Fenwick et al., 2020; Zetzsche et al., 2020). The key areas are strongly interrelated. Many economic processes taking place in banks, between banks and other financial enterprises and their environment, can be observed (the economic dimension), which are strongly regulated by norms and rules (the institutional dimension) and deemed social trust institutions (the social dimension). The major rationale for integrating these strands is that the current ambiguity regarding the ultimate economic and social effects of bank digitalization might stem from the differing institutional setups in markets where they unfold (Babajide et al., 2020; Iman, 2018). Namely, the economic efficiency gains and financial inclusion of disadvantaged groups profoundly differ in various contexts of formal (e.g., legal) and informal (social norms and ways of conduct) institutions of countries and world regions (Acemoglu et al., 2001; Wójcik, 2020, 2021). These idiosyncrasies can be observed among the institutional arrangements in developed countries vis-à-vis emerging markets, Global North vis-à-vis Global South (Bhagat & Roderick, 2020; Coetzee, 2018; Langley & Leyshon, 2021), as well as core vis-à-vis peripheral regions. The institutionally sensitive approach to socio-economic processes and outcomes of banks' digital transformation represents a novel and unique approach and represents a major research gap this book intends to address. Examples of this literature are nascent and scarce (Cassis & Wójcik, 2018; Chen & Hassink, 2021; Chen et al., 2017; Kleibert, 2020).

The development and use of financial technologies is leading to an increasingly far-reaching transformation of banks and banking sectors. This process is increasingly becoming the subject of analysis by researchers in the field of finance; see, for example, studies on the banking sector's digital transformation by Bilan et al. (2019); Nicoletti (2021); Nicoletti et al. (2017); Scardovi (2017); and Tanda and Schena (2019). Other relevant studies include, among others: Anand and Mantrala (2019); Bömer and Maxin (2018); Chen et al. (2017); Jagtiani and Lemieux (2018); Klus et al. (2019); MacDonald et al. (2016); Omarini (2018); and Zhao et al. (2019). Despite much discussion on the impact of FinTech on banking, there remain underexplored aspects in this area. Indeed, attention should focus in particular on (i) the economic dimension of new types of digital banks, the relationship between banks and non-bank entities in the provision of banking services including contractual arrangements and intellectual property ownership, and the role of BigTech; (ii) the institutional dimension on differences in levels of development and structures of banking sectors in countries with different institutional systems (the new industrial organization of the banking sector, such as modularized structures); and (iii) the social dimension, e.g., the inclusion of disadvantaged firms and customers, and the impact of AI on human resources in banking.

The other important consequence of bank and banking sector digitalization is the need for a new institutional context of these processes and the impact of the processes on firms' corporate governance. The extant publications related to the institutional dimension (Bani et al., 2020; BIS, 2018; Lui & Ryder, 2022) strongly focus on specialized legal arrangements. We treat the institutional context in a broader sense comprising not only legal arrangements, as examples of formal institutions, but also a comprehensive institutional framework. This institutional impact can be considered at three levels following O.E. Williamson (2000). The first level of informal institutions comprises, among others, customs, values, path-dependent rules of conduct, and the dominant logic in an industry (Hodgson, 2015; North, 2005; Ostrom, 2010). The level of formal institutions includes legal regulations and political systems that frame how banks adopt financial technologies (sandboxing initiatives, safety, and customer protection; Williamson, 2000). An established and ongoing process of financial deregulation is also facilitating a greater role for FinTechs in the provision of banking services and the transformation of banking sectors toward OB and financial ecosystems. Institutions can either enhance or impede the digital transformation of banking and determine its economic and social outcomes (Helmke & Levitsky, 2004; Zukauskaite et al., 2017). The outcomes of FinTech-driven changes are still underexplored and unequivocal (Arner et al., 2020; Bhagat & Roderick, 2020; Dev, 2006; Lai et al., 2020; Salampasis & Mention, 2018; Tanda & Schena, 2019).

This book intends to identify and compare the impact of FinTech on bank and banking sector transformations in different institutional contexts. Ultimately, it is important to address the institutions of governance, such as contracting rules and collaboration among banks and FinTech businesses. Extant studies mostly focus on identifying the economic efficiency in banking from technology-based products and services (Ayadi, 2019; Holotiuk et al., 2018; MacDonald et al., 2016), but few studies address the issue of governance. The promising and underexploited perspectives to study digital transformation in banking are both the transformations of banks and the conceptual foundations of bank governance transformed through FinTech. Together with an analysis of the social effects of banking sector transformations, it creates an important research area. In this book were undertaken efforts aimed to investigate these abovementioned issues.

1.2 Research Framework and Questions

The unique value of this book stems from addressing the indicated gaps in the extant stock of knowledge and from linking the considerations on many dimensions. This includes a detailed analysis of bank transformation resulting from financial technology, based on a theoretical framework that adopts transaction cost economics (TCE). Moreover, we want to identify and systemize the governance and socio-economic outcomes of the FinTech transformation in the value chains (VCs) of banks and banking sectors. There is still a need to adopt other theoretical approaches, for instance, contract theory, industry economics of the industry (smart specializations based on financial services), and modularity theory (the concept of modularization of VCs). Considering the focus of this book, the promising and underexploited theoretical perspectives to study digital transformation in banking are in particular: (i) the economic dimension on the improvement of the processes within bank organizations and in relation to FinTech as well as the transformation of the banking sector; (ii) in the institutional dimension, the changes in the principles and regulations of banking activity, the security of banking sectors as well as corporate governance in the context of FinTech; (iii) in the social dimension, consequences of the aforementioned processes, for example, financial inclusion, and poverty alleviation. Figure 1.1 shows the research framework setting out the analytical framework of this book.

The three grey-filled rectangles represent the key aspects of this book. FinTech triggers the processes of bank transformation, the institutional conditions are treated as enablers, whereas the socio-economic dimension is the consequence of these processes. The link that transfers the changes occurring in banks to society is banking services. It is worth emphasizing that in the past dozen or so years there has been a change from a supply approach to a demand approach, in which the role of customers has increased.

In the context of Figure 1.1, this book intends to address the most important aspects related to the mechanisms of bank and banking sector transformation, the institutional frames for transformation, and the socio-economic

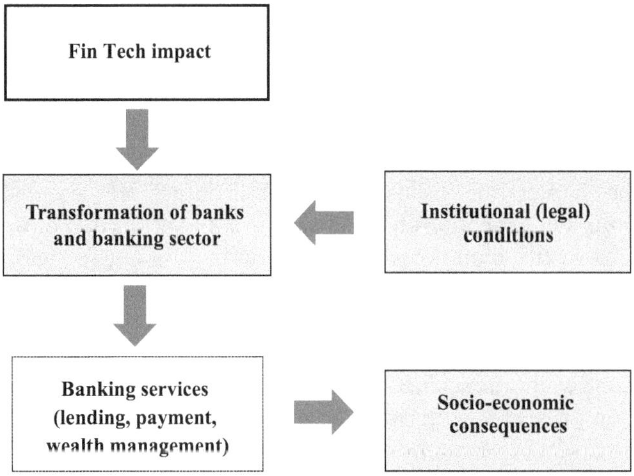

Figure 1.1 The Research Framework of Banks and Banking Sectors' Digital Transformation

Source: Own elaboration.

outcomes of transformations. Our aim is to not focus on financial technologies *per se* as numerous publications already describe AI, blockchain technology, and/or cloud computing. We focus rather on the processes of bank transformation and, in this regard, we formulate the following questions:

1 How do FinTechs affect changes in the delivery model, efficiency, and scope of bank operations?
2 How do FinTechs influence structural changes in the financial sector and what are the economic, legal, and social determinants and effects of these changes?
3 What are the regulatory and legal dimensions related to banking sector digitalization and transformation as well as banking services provision attributable to FinTech?
4 What are the social effects of changes in the structure of banks and banking sectors?

Some of the research questions are universal and answers are available elsewhere. Our aim, however, is to present the joint perspective of banking transformation and banking services provision. Our perspective is that FinTech has been a main trigger for financial digitalization. We consider bank transformation processes at all levels of the business model (micro-level analysis) and the structural dimensions of the banking sector (mezzo-level analysis). Moreover, we do not only focus on the economic dimension of banking transformation but also present institutional (mainly legal) and socio-economic results.

1.3 Organization of the Chapters

The main threads of the book focus on the economic, legal, and social dimensions of the process of digitalization in the banking sector. The various authors show how the digitalization of the financial sector is affecting financial firms like banks and society, as well as what the role of legal conditions is. The chapters that follow can be divided into three groups according to their focus. The first four chapters consider the economic dimension and are dedicated to the economics of banking and banking services. A second group of four chapters follows that relate to social matters including ethics, gender, and sustainability. The final group of four chapters is dedicated to the legal aspects of the digitalization of the banking sector and aspects related to corporate governance. The chapters include theoretical and conceptual considerations, together with case studies, and chapters based on surveys and quantitative analyses of secondary data.

Chapter 2 by **Michał Nowakowski** assesses bank internal governance in the light of the widespread adoption and advancement of AI models and systems. The new governance framework should grasp all the nuances of ethics in AI and link them with more traditional (and less technological) aspects of bank activity. While the existing legal (NIS,[1] CRD/CRR)[2] and regulatory framework (including EBA guidelines and BIS papers) may (and probably have) be a starting point, decision-makers should think about remodeling the rules and the way we regulate the financial sector. The author does not only focus on internal governance itself but also proposes ways in which it should be adopted and implemented (soft versus hard law challenge). The scope of the transition is wide and includes not only technological and operational issues but also cultural challenges that may be much more difficult for the organization than the replacement of IT infrastructure. The chapter also discusses ethical issues that are financial sector specific. The "traditional" approach to models and algorithms that is purely based on human oversight is not enough in the times of "enormous" data that the financial institutions must process. The chapter concludes with a set of relevant recommendations for the new internal governance of financial institutions and an evaluation of challenges associated with the proposals (or at the time of writing adopted versions) of certain legal acts (DORA, NIS2), regulatory guidance, and principles.

Chapter 3 by **Anna Omarini** focuses on the conceptualization of banking business, which has radically changed because of the emergence of processes during the last several years. Deregulation and digitalization have emerged as increasingly important factors that are shaping market structures. Some of their effects include the growing evolution and diffusion of digital platform business models, where networks are increasing entry to the industry for more participants and providing greater business opportunities. The digital vortex is the inevitable movement of industries toward a digital center in which business models, offerings, and VCs are digitized to the maximum extent possible. These developments also create new disruptions and blur the lines of demarcation between industries, which has reduced the importance of banks in their customers' daily lives. Under these circumstances, traditional banking has lost significance *vis-à-vis* other forms of financial intermediation and counterparts (FinTechs and BigTechs). The aims of this chapter are twofold. First, it offers insights on the future organization of the banking industry among the many hype storm words emerging in the market (such as digitalization, FinTech, OB, embedded finance, banking-as-a-service [BaaS], and decentralized finance) that are creating a twisted picture of the digital banking industry. Second, by linking the dots, the chapter outlines the most interesting implications for both the industry and those banks that have decided to undertake a deep changing strategic transformation.

Chapter 4 by **Krzysztof Waliszewski** concentrates on BaaS and embedded banking (EB) issues. The digital transformation of traditional banks accelerated during the COVID-19 pandemic, when due to limitations in physical contact with a bank employee, customers had to use remote solutions. The pandemic strengthened the previously observed trend of the development of non-bank FinTech institutions, using financial technologies to offer financial services, mainly payments (PayTech), loans (LendTech), consulting (robo-advice), or insurance (InsurTech). These services were cheaper and more flexible than those offered by traditional financial institutions (bricks and mortar banks). The dynamic development of e-commerce also made it necessary to develop solutions in the field of financial facilities expected by customers purchasing online, especially during and after the pandemic. Similarly, the introduction of the PSD2 regulation (2015) creating the so-called OB from the legal side has made it possible to make financial services available on sales platforms by third parties (TPP, third-party provider). It has become crucial to integrate both purchase and payment transactions on one platform without needing to log into a bank. The answer to these needs was the creation and development of EB and BaaS as innovative forms of providing financial services. The chapter presents and analyzes these financial innovations as examples of economic platforms from the perspective of traditional banks.

Chapter 5 by **Danilo Abis** and **Patrizia Pia** employs a literature review to examine the relationship between FinTech and financial inclusion. The authors discuss how financial inclusion can be measured and they emphasize the importance of introducing official indicators capable of capturing the effects of new technologies. Their analysis of evidence-based studies suggests that FinTech can boost financial inclusion by providing financial services for all customers, but especially customers either underserved by the traditional financial sector or unbanked. While technologies may be necessary, they are not sufficient. Indeed, the authors show financial inclusion is influenced by several factors, such as investment in the infrastructure that is necessary to take advantage of new technologies. Furthermore, such investment can often also require intervention and action from public institutions. The authors also highlight the impact on financial inclusion of psychological aspects including how human behavior reacts to algorithms. The chapter unambiguously shows the positive impact of FinTech in terms of increasing financial inclusion. However, a carefully considered caveat stresses the need for policymakers both to intervene to create the conditions necessary for the diffusion of new technologies and actively monitor the situation to mitigate risky behaviour from the different actors involved and the risks inherent in new technologies.

Chapter 6 by **Michał Nowakowski** examines an important social dimension, namely, ethics in finance. The application of new financial technologies generates new risks and amplifies those risks, which already exist and are well recognized by financial institutions. As a result, it becomes essential to look at the application of innovative solutions in the banking sector not only from the perspective of common risks, such as operational, security, model, or legal and regulatory risks, but also those that can be attributed to the category of ethics and new technologies. The chapter aims to justify the need to create a new catalogue of ethical principles for the use of new technologies in the financial sector, as well as to present specific solutions that could be further clarified by European Union (EU) regulators in the future. The chapter emphasizes that a lack of an ethical approach in the marketing of financial products and services, as well as in the use of new technologies, can generate several risks for financial institutions, customers, regulators and supervisors, and, in general, the entire financial system and economy. Therefore, the issue of ethics in the use of new technologies from the perspective of the financial sector should be a main subject of interest and involvement not only in the institutions themselves but also for society.

Chapter 7 by **Błażej Prusak** and **Łukasz Wacławek** offers a systematic literature review of research that investigates the case of gender disparity in FinTech activity. The authors emphasize the need to understand whether the development of FinTech reduces the gender gap and use the PRISMA concept for their review of this issue. The chapter shows that the topic of gender disparity in FinTech is relatively little recognized. The authors focus on identifying the main areas of gender disparity in FinTech as well as the negative and positive aspects of the development of the FinTech sector from a gender disparity perspective.

Chapter 8 by **Stefano Cosma** and **Daniela Pennetta** relates to current concerns over sustainability, an important topic in the context of digital finance and FinTech development. Leveraging on new technologies, FinTech firms may contribute to Sustainable Development Goals (SDGs) due to their ability to redirect financial resources toward more sustainable uses and to mitigate financial exclusion. The authors investigate if FinTech firms' SDG orientation has a strategic potential in establishing strategic alliances with banks, which could be crucial for FinTech firms' development and growth path. More specifically, they investigate if FinTech firms' SDG orientation facilitates bank–FinTech relationships and if there are differences among the various types of agreements (equity or non-equity agreements). Using a sample of 124 Italian FinTech firms, their evidence shows that FinTech firms' SDG orientation positively affects the probability of relationships existing between FinTechs and banks. This holds for the social and environmental dimensions introduced by Agenda 2030. FinTech firms that contribute the most to sustainability, and particularly the economic pillar, are more likely to strongly cooperate with banks through equity agreements, which usually imply a stronger commitment by banks to sustaining FinTech firms' activity. Based on these results, the authors highlight important managerial (both for FinTechs and banks) and regulatory implications.

Chapter 9 by **Timothy King** examines the impact of FinTech on climate change and sustainability. Despite global interest in these important issues, very little attention has been paid on the potential of FinTech. Utilizing an Environment, Social, and Governance (ESG) framework, the chapter discusses the huge, untapped potential of FinTech to exert a major impact, *inter alia* through use of sophisticated and large datasets, and the application of cutting-edge statistical techniques, such as AI and innovative uses of blockchain technologies. The chapter explores the extent of current links between ESG and FinTech, and it outlines potential future directions in which FinTech can play a leading role on helping practitioners, firms, policymakers, and wider stakeholders in working to achieve a sustainable, climate friendly, and well-governed future.

Chapter 10 by **Robert Rybski** is the first chapter to consider the legal (institutional) solutions related to the digitalization of banking services. This chapter presents the idea of central bank digital currency (CBDC). Currently, around 100 central banks are researching or developing their own CBDC. A further two projects recently moved into the production phase. The introduction of CBDC by at least one major central bank in the coming years seems unavoidable, which could form a tipping point. CBDC would then enter the mainstream of the banking sector. This trend requires assessing CBDC projects broader than central banks do. This chapter considers concerns regarding introducing the CBDC and its design criteria. Addressing issues at an early stage would allow regulators and decision-makers to mitigate possible problems. The most obvious problem concerns central bank money's public security in an era of growing cyber threats. The other evident concern is privacy. However, one angle of discussion on CBDC does not receive enough attention, and that is sustainability. This chapter assesses whether and how current CBDC projects include sustainability, public security, and privacy. It then addresses areas worth further development to increase the implementation of sustainability by central banks. Finally, the chapter reconstructs a design of CBDC that would be desirable from the perspective of sustainability, public security, and privacy while showing how taking these perspectives into consideration can influence the social acceptance of CBDC.

Chapter 11 by **Grzegorz Kuca** and **Paweł Woroniecki** presents a case study of the legal aspects of electronic money in Poland. This chapter aims to conceptualize the notion of an electronic money institution, the rules on which it is based, its functions in economic activities, and the rights and obligations of the entities involved in the functioning of this institution according to the Payment Services Act of August 19, 2011. All these issues are discussed as elements of FinTech sector regulation, considering the ontic, praxeological, and attribution analysis of electronic money. This chapter presents certain demands aimed at the Polish legislature, which result from the analysis of selected regulations connected with the electronic money institution. In particular, the electronic money institution's growing economic significance in Poland should be emphasized. It is a consequence of the fact that one of the most distinctive features of developed market economies is their "non-cash character". This causes certain problems for the Polish legislature. For example, users of electronic money should be strongly protected from digital fraud. The Polish legislature takes this issue into consideration by inserting (among other things) the requirement to present information about electronic money institution honestly and intelligibly. However, regulations in this area are imperfect and for this reason, this chapter contains proposals to change some of these regulations.

Another legal aspect of electronic payment, but in the EU, is the focus of Chapter 12 by **Jan Byrski** and **Michał Synowiec**. The authors point out that according to EU rules, the account information service (AIS) enables the provision of consolidated information on one or more payment accounts maintained with at least one account servicing payment service provider (ASPSP). This service is commonly referred to as a service based on access to a payment account, and this access is crucial not only for the efficient provision of this payment service but also for the general ability of a TPP to perform the service. The purpose of this chapter is, on the one hand, to present the juridical judicial nature of the AIS service along with *de lege ferenda* proposals and, on the other hand, to identify the legal instruments available to providers of this service (AIS providers – AISPs) for the purpose of accessing users' payment accounts. In the light of ASPSPs' inconsistent practices regarding the rules for granting AISPs access to users' payment account information, it is especially justified to analyze the second of the above issues. This applies where an ASPSP completely prevents an AISP from gaining access to payment accounts or unlawfully seeks to limit such access.

Chapter 13 by **Piotr Łasak** considers the modes of banking governance during the digitalization and extended use of financial technologies in the sector. The digitalization of banking services triggers essential changes in bank business models and ultimately causes the transformation of the whole banking sector. Bank transformation embraces a change from a hierarchical to a heterarchical and market-based structure of banking services. Such processes trigger the changes in banks' governance. The foregoing contractual and relational governance modes are replaced by a new type – blockchain governance. This type of governance suits better when banking sectors are impacted by digitalisation processes and moves towards ecosystem-based banking. A first research question ponders how FinTech is impacting bank governance with a view to increase the role of blockchain governance. A second question concerns the role of the banking ecosystem in the context of blockchain governance. The analysis shows that currently one of the most adequate governance modes during the process of the digitalization of financial markets is blockchain governance. Indeed, the change from a bank-based into an ecosystem-based banking structure enhances the role of blockchain governance.

It should be emphasized that this book presents a narrow approach in the context of the banking sector's digitalization processes. Such processes include the transformation of entire banking sectors and changes to their structures. Ecosystems and banking ecologies are emerging, and in the context of financial technologies, these are often ecosystems based on digital platforms (Gancarczyk & Rodil-Marzábal, 2022; Sironi, 2021). Another example of contemporary processes is the development of bionic banking (Nicoletti, 2022). All these processes should be further investigated in the future.

Notes

1 Network Information Systems Directive adopted by the European Parliament on July 6, 2016. It was replaced by NIS2 Directive on December 14, 2022. It provides legal measures to boost the overall level of cybersecurity in the EU.
2 Capital Requirements Directive/Capital Requirements Regulation. It is the regulatory framework aimed to improve banks' ability to bear risks by strengthening their solvency and liquidity, as well as their risk management.

References

Acemoglu, D., Johnson, S., Robinson, J.A. (2001). Reversal of fortune: Geography and institutions in the making of the modern world income distribution. *NBER Working Papers*, Article 8460. https://ideas.repec.org//p/nbr/nberwo/8460.html

Anand, D., Mantrala, M. (2019). Responding to disruptive business model innovations: The case of traditional banks facing fintech entrants. *Journal of Banking and Financial Technology*, 3, 1, 19–31. https://doi.org/10.1007/s42786-018-00004-4

Arner, D.W., Buckley, R.P., Zetzsche, D.A., & Veidt, R. (2020). Sustainability, FinTech and financial inclusion. *European Business Organization Law Review*, 21, 1, 7–35. https://doi.org/10.1007/s40804-020-00183-y

Ayadi, R. (2019). *Banking Business Models: Definition, Analytical Framework and Financial Stability Assessment*. Springer International Publishing. https://doi.org/10.1007/978-3-030-02248-8

Babajide, A.A., Oluwaseye, E.O., Lawal, A.I., Isibor, A.A. (2020). *Financial Technology, Financial Inclusion and MSMEs Financing in the South: West of Nigeria*. https://www-1proquest-1com-1e7wvbydx02bb.hps.bj.uj.edu.pl/docview/2515190946?accountid=11664

Bani, E., Pachuca-Smulska, B., Rutkowska-Tomaszewska, E. (2020). *Public and Private Law and the Challenges of New Technologies and Digital Markets. Volume II. Legal Aspects of FinTech*. Ksiegarnia.beck.pl. https://www.ksiegarnia.beck.pl/19222-public-and-private-law-and-the-challenges-of-new-technologies-and-digital-markets-volume-ii-beata-pachuca-smulska

BCBS (2018). Sound practices: Implications of fintech development for banks and bank supervisors. *BIS*, February 2018. https://www.bis.org/bcbs/publ/d431.pdf.
Bhagat, A., Roderick, L. (2020). Banking on refugees: Racialized expropriation in the fintech era. *Environment and Planning A: Economy and Space*, 52, 8, 1498–1515.
Bilan, A., Degryse, H., O'Flynn, K., Ongena, S. (2019). *Banking and Financial Markets: How Banks and Financial Technology Are Reshaping Financial Markets* (1st ed.). Palgrave Macmillan.
BIS. (2018). *Sound Practices: Implications of Fintech Developments for Banks and Bank Supervisors*. https://www.bis.org/bcbs/publ/d431.htm
Bömer, M., Maxin, H. (2018). Why fintechs cooperate with banks—Evidence from germany. *Zeitschrift Für Die Gesamte Versicherungswissenschaft*, 107, 4, 359–386. https://doi.org/10.1007/s12297-018-0421-6
Carbó-Valverde, S., Cuadros-Solas, P.J., Rodríguez-Fernández, F. (2021). FinTech and banking: An evolving relationship. In T.P. King, A. Srivastav, S. Stentella Lopes, J. Williams (Eds.), *Disruptive Technology in Banking and Finance: An International Perspective on FinTech* (pp. 161–194). Palgrave Macmillan.
Cassis, Y., Wójcik, D. (2018). *International Financial Centres after the Global Financial Crisis and Brexit*. Oxford University Press.
Chen, Y., Hassink, R. (2021). The geography of the emergence of online peer-to-peer lending platforms in China: An evolutionary economic geography perspective. *International Journal of Urban Sciences*, 26, 2, 1–21.
Chen, Z., Li, Y., Wu, Y., Luo, J. (2017). The transition from traditional banking to mobile internet finance: An organizational innovation perspective - a comparative study of Citibank and ICBC. *Financial Innovation*, 3, 1, 12. https://doi.org/10.1186/s40854-017-0062-0
Chiu, I.H., & Deipenbrock, G. (2021). *Routledge Handbook of Financial Technology and Law*. Routledge.
Coetzee, J. (2018). Strategic implications of Fintech on South African retail banks. *South African Journal of Economic and Management Sciences*, 21, 1, Article 1. https://doi.org/10.4102/sajems.v21i1.2455
Dev, M. (2006). Financial inclusion: Issues and challenges. *Economic and Political Weekly*. https://click.endnote.com/viewer?doi=10.2307%2F4418799&token=WzMzNjUxNTcsIjEwLjIzMDcvNDQxODc5OSJd.ZJCmjqqC1BUMdCFsyQ8iYEhVAyk
Fenwick, M., Van Uytsel, S., Ying, B. (2020). *Regulating Fintech in Asia: Global Context, Local Perspectives* (M. Fenwick, S. Van Uytsel, & B. Ying, Eds.). Springer. https://doi.org/10.1007/978-981-15-5819-1_1
Financial Stability Board (2017). *Financial Stability Implications from FinTech: Supervisory and Regulatory Issues That Merits Authorities' Attention*. 27 June 2017. https://www.fsb.org/wp-content/uploads/R270617.pdf
Financial Stability Board (2019). *BigTech in Finance: Market Developments and Potential Financial Stability Implications*. December.
Gancarczyk, M., Rodil-Marzábal, Ó. (2022). Fintech framing financial ecologies: Conceptual and policy-related implications. *Journal of Entrepreneurship, Management and Innovation*, 18, 4, 7–44.
Gomber, P., Koch, J.-A., Siering, M. (2017). Digital finance and FinTech: Current research and future research directions. *Journal of Business Economics*, *87*(5), 537–580. https://doi.org/10.1007/s11573-017-0852-x
Helmke, G., Levitsky, S. (2004). Informal institutions and comparative politics: A research agenda. *Perspectives on Politics*, 2, 4, 725–740.

Hodgson, G.M. (2015). On defining institutions: Rules versus equilibria. *Journal of Institutional Economics*, 11, 3, 497–505.

Holotiuk, F., Klus, M.F., Lohwasser, T.S., Moormann, J. (2018). Motives to form alliances for digital innovation: The case of banks and fintechs. *Bled EConference*, 22.

Iman, N. (2018). Is mobile payment still relevant in the FinTech era? *Electronic Commerce Research and Applications*, 30, 72–82.

Jagtiani, J., Lemieux, C. (2018). Do fintech lenders penetrate areas that are underserved by traditional banks? *Journal of Economics and Business*, 100, 43–54. https://doi.org/10.1016/j.jeconbus.2018.03.001

King, T., Stentella Lopes, F.S., Srivastav, A., Williams, J. (Eds.). (2021). *Disruptive Technology in Banking and Finance: An International Perspective on FinTech*. Springer International Publishing. https://doi.org/10.1007/978-3-030-81835-7

Kleibert, J.M. (2020). Unbundling value chains in finance: Offshore labor and the geographies of finance. In J. Knox-Hayes, D. Wójcik (Eds.), *The Routledge Handbook of Financial Geography* (pp. 421–439). Routledge.

Klus, M.F., Lohwasser, T.S., Holotiuk, F., Moormann, J. (2019). Strategic alliances between banks and fintechs for digital innovation: Motives to collaborate and types of interaction. *The Journal of Entrepreneurial Finance*, 21, 1, 1.

Lai, J. T., Yan, I. K., Yi, X., Zhang, H. (2020). Digital financial inclusion and consumption smoothing in China. *China & World Economy*, 28, 1, 64–93.

Langley, P., Leyshon, A. (2021). The platform political economy of fintech: Reintermediation, consolidation and capitalisation. *New Political Economy*, 26, 3, 376–3`88.

Locatelli, R., Schena, C., Tanda, A. (2021). A historical perspective on disruptive technologies. In T.P. King, A. Srivastav, S. Stentella Lopes, J. Williams (Eds.), *Disruptive Technology in Banking and Finance* (pp. 9–45). Springer.

Lui, A., Ryder, N. (2022). *FinTech, Artificial Intelligence and the Law: Regulation and Crime Prevention*. Routledge. https://www.routledge.com/FinTech-Artificial-Intelligence-and-the-Law-Regulation-and-Crime-Prevention/Lui-Ryder/p/book/9780367897659

MacDonald, T.J., Allen, D.W., Potts, J. (2016). Blockchains and the boundaries of self-organized economies: Predictions for the future of banking. In P. Tasca, T. Aste, L. Pelizzon, N. Perony (Eds.), *Banking Beyond Banks and Money* (pp. 279–296). Springer.

Marszk, A., Lechman, E. (2021). *The Digitalization of Financial Markets: The Socioeconomic Impact of Financial Technologies*. Routledge.

Nicoletti, B. (2021). *Banking 5.0: How Fintech Will Change Traditional Banks in the 'New Normal' Post Pandemic* (1st ed.). Palgrave Macmillan.

Nicoletti, B. (2022). *Beyond Fintech: Bionic Banking*. Springer International Publishing. https://doi.org/10.1007/978-3-030-96217-3

Nicoletti, B., Nicoletti, W., Weis. (2017). *Future of FinTech*. Springer.

North, D.C. (2005). *Understanding the Process of Institutional Change*. Princeton University Press.

Omarini, A.E. (2018). Fintech and the future of the payment landscape: The mobile wallet ecosystem - A challenge for retail banks? *International Journal of Financial Research*, 9, 4, Article 4. https://doi.org/10.5430/ijfr.v9n4p97

Ostrom, E. (2010). Beyond markets and states: Polycentric governance of complex economic systems. *American Economic Review*, 100, 3, 641–672.

Puschmann, T. (2017). Fintech. *Business & Information Systems Engineering: The International Journal of WIRTSCHAFTSINFORMATIK*, 59, 1, 69–76.

Salampasis, D., Mention, A.-L. (2018). FinTech: Harnessing innovation for financial inclusion. In D. Lee, R.H. Deng (Eds.), *Handbook of Blockchain, Digital Finance, and Inclusion, Volume 2* (pp. 451–461). Elsevier.

Scardovi, C. (2017). *Digital Transformation in Financial Services*. Springer International Publishing. https://doi.org/10.1007/978-3-319-66945-8

Sironi, P. (2021). *Banks and Fintech on Platform Economies: Contextual and Conscious Banking* (1st ed.). Wiley.

Tanda, A., Schena, C.-M. (2019). *FinTech, BigTech and Banks: Digitalisation and Its Impact on Banking Business Models*. Springer International Publishing. https://doi.org/10.1007/978-3-030-22426-4

Williamson, O. E. (2000), The New Institutional Economics: Taking stock, looking ahead, *Journal of Economic Literature, 38*(3), 595–613.

Wójcik, D. (2020). Financial geography II: The impacts of FinTech–Financial sector and centres, regulation and stability, inclusion and governance. *Progress in Human Geography*, https://doi.org/10.1177/0309132520959825.

Wójcik, D. (2021). Financial geography I: Exploring FinTech–Maps and concepts. *Progress in Human Geography*, 45, 3, 566–576.

Zetzsche, D.A., Arner, D.W., Buckley, R.P. (2020). *Decentralized Finance (DeFi)* [SSRN Scholarly Paper]. Social Science Research Network. https://doi.org/10.2139/ssrn.3539194

Zhao, Q., Tsai, P.-H., Wang, J.-L. (2019). Improving financial service innovation strategies for enhancing china's banking industry competitive advantage during the fintech revolution: A Hybrid MCDM model. *Sustainability*, 11, 5, 1419.

Zukauskaite, E., Trippl, M., Plechero, M. (2017). Institutional thickness revisited. *Economic Geography*, 93, 4, 325–345.

2 The Redesign of the Internal Governance of Financial Institutions in Times of Artificial Intelligence

New Challenges, New Approaches, Old Issues

Michał Nowakowski

2.1 Introduction

Data is becoming increasingly important in our digital world (Szpringer, 2022) and an important source of value, including economic value (Giddings et al., 2021). For several years, the European Commission has been taking steps to develop the data area in the territory of the European Union,[1] also in finance, emanating *inter alios* from the concept of open banking[2] or the framework for available finance being developed.[3] The subject of the use of data and advanced data analytics in a broad sense is also addressed within the EU Digital Finance Strategy.[4] Today, it seems that with data, creating more attractive (personalized) products and services will be possible in the coming years, and undoubtedly such products and services are expected by customers (Deloitte, 2020). At the same time, momentum is gaining in so-called decentralized finance (Zetzsche et al., 2020), which relies heavily on distributed ledger technology (DLT) and blockchain, which use significant amounts of data and computing power that can, in turn, be provided by cloud-based solutions (Yan, 2017). It is also not insignificant that more and more regulators and supervisors are starting to use SupTech solutions that allow the collection of data for adequate supervision and its analysis. Such solutions will require data of sufficient quality provided by obliged entities (FSB, 2020).

All this makes financial institutions, not only banks, face a massive challenge in arranging their own organizational and technical solutions, as well as processes, which are related to data acquisition and processing, but also with the use of so-called artificial intelligence systems,[5] that is, solutions using *inter alios* machine and deep learning, natural language processing or less "sophisticated" statistical methods. These solutions undoubtedly represent an opportunity and challenge for many institutions and regulators (Dupont et al., 2020). Some regulators already see the need to provide greater direction to financial institutions (BaFin, 2021). The need for at least more transparency will increase with the development of more sophisticated models, for example for credit risk management. The use of blockchain technology will be a real challenge for institutions to ensure privacy (Ma & Huang, 2022).

DOI: 10.4324/9781003340454-2

Today, financial institutions are among the most (over)regulated, and the increased demand for good quality data makes the legal and regulatory loop ever tighter. As a result, and even despite high standards of corporate governance,[6] many institutions will sooner or later have to consider how to shape their organizational and technical solutions to cope with these challenges while maintaining the viability of their business models and retaining customers who can expect more flexible solutions offered by other – often more agile – institutions with a tech pedigree, such as the BigTech firms (Crisanto et al., 2022). This will force institutions to pay more attention to so-called *AI & Data Governance*, that is, shaping organizational, technical and human solutions in such a way that they consider all aspects of data processing and storage, not only from a legal and regulatory perspective but also from a business perspective.

This chapter will indicate the most significant changes that will await financial institutions in the coming years in connection with the increasing use of artificial intelligence in its broadest sense, that is, *inter alios* building a *data-driven* culture (Davenport & Bean, 2018), which is intended to ensure more efficient and secure use of data that is or will be held by these institutions. At the same time, and very notably in the context of the issue at hand, the "new" challenges related to the so-called ethics of artificial intelligence (Kearns & Roth, 2022), which assumes that institutions will use (personal) data responsibly and for the benefit of society at large, will also be highlighted. The considerations will be complemented by selected issues related to processing personal data for advanced data analytics in the context of obligations under *inter alios* Regulation 2016/679. Specific recommendations for building a structure based on *AI & Data Governance* principles will also be given.

2.2 AI?

Currently, there is a move away from defining artificial intelligence itself, focusing instead on the concept of so-called artificial intelligence systems, which "capture" the spirit of these solutions, that is, their strictly technical rather than anthropomorphic nature (Simpson et al., 2021). One of the manifestations of such shaping of the conceptual grid is the draft regulation on artificial intelligence (AI Act), which is to introduce specific rules for the use of particular solutions using, for example, machine learning or natural language processing, including for credit rating systems (see Gambacorta et al., 2019). The draft of this regulation has had several iterations to date, but for present purposes, we will use the original proposal for the definition of artificial intelligence systems found therein. According to the draft, artificial intelligence systems means software that is developed with one or more of the techniques and approaches listed in Annex I and can, for a given set of human-defined objectives, generate outputs such as content, predictions, recommendations or decisions influencing the environments they interact with.

In a similar vein, the Algorithmic Accountability Act[7] (in the US) defines so-called automated decision systems, which should be understood as a system, software or process (including one derived from machine learning, statistics or other data processing or artificial intelligence techniques and excluding passive computing infrastructure) that uses computation, the result of which serves as a basis for a decision or judgment.

The essential elements found in both definitions are:

1 Technical in nature – some form of software.
2 Human involvement in its development.
3 The use of techniques, such as machine learning.
4 Impact on the external environment.

None of these definitions is perfect, but they capture the essence of artificial intelligence systems, which are also used in the financial sector, including in areas such as risk management (Liebergen, 2017), product personalization (Saniuk et al., 2020) or in countering money laundering and terrorist financing (Chau & van Dijck Nemcsik, 2022) and payment fraud. There are many more applications of artificial intelligence in the financial sector, and developments related to open finance[8] or electronic identification will undoubtedly contribute to an even greater interest in data analytics including behavioral biometrics (Sheng Wang, 2021). At the same time, this will require even more attention and changes to be made by financial institutions in areas, such as organization, infrastructure, culture or competence as well as data-centricity. Among these areas is AI & Data Governance, that is, the entirety of the activities an organization undertakes in using AI and the broader processing of data, not only personal data.

2.3 AI & Data Governance

Estimates in a McKinsey report "Economies that embrace data sharing for finance could see GDP gains of between 1% and 5% by 2030, with benefits flowing to consumers and financial institutions" (Laboure & Deffrennes, 2022) indicates that this will undoubtedly translate into increased interest and demand for data. This data will, in turn, require appropriate protection involving technical and legal measures including having appropriate organizational arrangements in place. This will be – or is – a consequence of the financial sector entering the initial phase of digital r(e)volition (Laboure & Deffrennes, 2022), which forces a specific digital transformation.

Eryurek et al. (2022) define so-called data governance as " (...) data management function to ensure the quality, integrity, security, and usability of the data collected by an organization". On the other hand, AI Governance is far less frequently defined in the literature, although there are such attempts (Dafoe, 2017). It can be assumed that it is nothing more than an organization's actions to maintain an appropriate level of (predefined) effectiveness, efficiency and security of the artificial intelligence systems used. The very fact of the necessity to implement such solutions, according to Plotkin (2021), is the fact that data requires stewardship and accountability, which is, moreover, reflected, among other things, in the principles set out in Regulation 2016/679.

Nowakowski (2022a) defines Data Governance as follows:

> (...) it is a distinct category consisting of:
>
> 1 Organizational arrangements to ensure both appropriate levels of responsibility, decision-making and reporting lines – this is also the area with the most "human" character.
> 2 Policies and procedures for the area of artificial intelligence systems and data management, including in the context of training and validation.
> 3 Internal and external communication.
> 4 Technical solutions to ensure consistency in the activities undertaken within the organization.

These solutions should be based on specific principles, including accountability, transparency, data quality and others as noted Janssen et al. (2020). In turn, Ammanath (2022) points to fairness and impartiality, robust and reliability, transparency, explainability, security, safety, privacy, accountability and responsibility. This catalogue can, in principle, be freely developed. It can be qualified as a broadly understood ethics of artificial intelligence (Stahl, 2022), which implies the attribution of certain assumptions and responsibilities not only to humans but also to technical solutions (insofar as this is technically possible and reasonable). The important caveat here is that the "intensity" of the application of certain principles may depend both on the data and IT architecture used (Soldatos et al., 2022) as well as on the assumptions of the organization itself and – typically – will evolve as a particular institution gains maturity. As will be highlighted later, ethics should be distinguished from laws or regulations, which are (more or less, but) binding.

How the specific solutions comprising AI & Data Governance in a financial institution will be applied – at least to some extent – depend on the time to which (if any) personal data is used. This will be the result of the application of *inter alios* the provisions of Regulation 2016/679[9] (particularly Article 5), but also of sectoral regulations, such as Regulation 2018/389[10] or the CRR Regulation.[11] This may be influenced by relevant guidelines and recommendations of supervisory and regulatory authorities, such as the guidelines of the German supervisory authority BaFin, where we find the following statement:

> Depending on the application and features of the algorithm, data must be used in sufficient quality and quantity. Companies must have

a verifiable process (data strategy) that guarantees the continuous provision of data and defines the data quality and quantity standards to be met. The data strategy must be implemented in a data governance system, and responsibilities must be clearly defined.[12]

Moreover, this excerpt draws attention to an important issue in implementing appropriate AI & Data Governance solutions: applying the principle of proportionality and the risk-based approach.

One should not overlook that the "intensity" with which institutions will implement specific solutions will be determined by aspects, such as the nature and type of activities themselves and, therefore, also by which laws and regulations will apply to a particular institution and what supervisory expectations will be placed upon it.

Financial institutions will undoubtedly need significant changes beyond the "traditional" digital transformation (Vasiljeva & Lukanova, 2016), which will encroach on spheres, such as internal control or corporate governance, risk management or even AML/CFT or anti-fraud policies and procedures. It is worth noting at this point that although the proposed AI regulation in many places allows banks to merely adapt existing solutions (required, for example, under the CRD package[13]/CRR),[14] there is no doubt that more radical changes will be needed in the case of broader use of data and analytics, including changes to the organizational structure, reporting lines or even the introduction of appropriate technical measures to ensure supervision of the operation of AI systems. This is also only a slice of the entire financial sector, including not only credit institutions (banks) but also non-bank payment service providers, insurers, capital market entities or investment funds, all of which have their specificities. Therefore, it will be essential to conduct a proper audit that identifies those "places" where intervention will be necessary.

The scale of these changes will be determined *inter alios* by the business model and level (maturity) of ethics within an organization, which requires the application of specific principles that have their practical translation into areas, such as internal organization or risk management system. These changes will result from changing laws and regulations (Arner et al., 2022), which will undoubtedly influence how financial institutions will revise their business models and, thus, how they will be managed. At the same time, it should not be forgotten that it is not only the use of artificial intelligence alone that will have a bearing on these changes, but also other technologies are beginning to have an increasing impact on both the institutions themselves and their customers. Examples of such technologies are blockchain and distributed ledger technology, and cloud computing. Every financial institution will sooner or later have to understand that to remain competitive, for instance, against so-called BigTech (Crisanto et al, 2022), it will have to evolve into a data-driven organization (Marr, 2022). This means that the people who make up the organization will also be (are) an essential element.

Despite the progressive automation of many processes, humans will still play a key role, which may, on the one hand, be the result of specific experiences of institutions with "artificial intelligence" or maybe a direct result of specific legislation (Article 14 AI Act) or regulations.[15] Institutions must consider this "factor" when changing their structure and organization.

2.4 Ethical AI – Definition, Purpose and Approach to Fintech

In the context of changes in the organization of financial institutions in connection with the increasing development of AI, the issue of so-called AI ethics cannot be overlooked either. AI ethics – alongside hard and soft law – will also determine how financial institutions will approach the implementation of AI & Data Governance demands.

Ethics of artificial intelligence is often confused (or at least equated to) with the concept of moral agents (Martinho et al., 2021) and treated as a protection from harmful actions made by autonomous machines (Brożek & Jakubiec, 2017).[16] The public debate is more about the set of norms and values that, for example, autonomous cars (Kamm, 2020) (or other vehicles) should have implemented to protect passengers, pedestrians and other drivers or how futuristic conscious (Bryson, 2020)[17] robots may eliminate human targets, even though the issue of LAWS (Righetti et al., 2018)[18] is crucial as well. While it is an exciting and vital issue that should not be overlooked, we – humans – should focus on more critical issues that are important right now – the way we gather and process data and what consequences such processing may have for human beings. **Data is not only the fuel for models and algorithms but also our responsibility toward other humans**. Concepts and approaches are evolving, with Stahl (2022) even going further with the ethics of digital ecosystems.

Simpson et al. (2021) – practitioners in the so-called "artificial intelligence" – proposed a term – real-world AI that relates to machine learning and similar techniques and approaches that solve real problems, like predicting cancer or the probability of occurrence of certain events. Such focus on real issues may bring real risks for the developer, operator and (end)users of "AI" systems. A recent (2021) World Health Organization document – Ethics and governance of artificial intelligence for health: WHO Guidance clearly states that

> **[n]ew approaches to software engineering in the past decade move beyond an appeal to abstract moral values,** and improvements in design methods are not merely upgraded programming techniques. **Methods for designing AI technologies that incorporate moral values** in health and other sectors have been proposed to support effective, systematic, transparent integration of ethical values.[19]

This approach is often connected with data protection engineering that emphasizes security and privacy – parts or elements of every software, including based on "AI" must be implemented in line with the "by design and default" principle (ENISA, 2022).

This is especially true regarding real-life applications of the machine and deep learning. As Kearns and Roth (2022, p. 17) indicate, "(...), the scientific and research communities who work on machine learning must be engaged and centrally involved in the ethical debates around algorithmic decision making". We must, however, answer a crucial question – how ethics of machine learning models and algorithms should look like, and what principles should be a background of a (new) framework for truly responsible "AI"? Martens (2022) focuses on data and its role in five stages of data science, namely: (i) data gathering; (ii) data preprocessing; (iii) modeling; (iv) evaluation and (v) deployment. Data (quality, quantity, availability) seems to be the most important element of any algorithm and model, but are efficient and effective data management and governance the only prerequisites for ethical and responsible "AI"? (Kroll, 2018) And maybe an even more important question – what tools should we use to ensure that the "AI" is ethical? (Blackman, 2022)

As indicated above, the lack of definition and scope of ethics of AI is apparent. Still, the question is whether we should seek to define it and at least propose a minimum content (requirements) it should include or let it evolve freely. Martens (2022) rightly points out that "[e]thical data science is all about balancing act: what data can I use, for what purpose, and how should I got about it" and while the ethics of artificial intelligence may be understood as a broader concept that data science, **it underlines that the data should be at the forefront.** Similarly, Coeckelberg (2020, p. 83) states that "(...) many ethical questions about AI concern technologies that are entirely or partly based on machine learning and related data science (...)". A recent report by an internal body of the European Parliament goes even further with the concept of a "data-centric" approach to AI, indicating that "(...) unprecedented amounts of personal data will be collected, and digital technologies will affect the most intimate aspects of our lives more than ever, including in the realms of love and friendship".[20]

But should we try to define what AI ethics is? Blackman (2022) makes an interesting distinction: (i) "AI for Good" and (ii) "AI for not Bad" to make a line between "AI" aimed at the positive impact on the environment and society and the applications of AI that should be at least ethically neutral. According to Wikipedia,

> [t]he ethics of artificial intelligence is the branch of the ethics of technology specific to artificially intelligent systems. It is sometimes divided into a concern with the moral behavior of humans as they design, make, use and treat artificially intelligent systems, and a concern with the behavior of machines, in machine ethics. It also includes the issue of a possible singularity due to superintelligent AI.[21]

While this definition is imperfect, it is a good starting point for further deliberations.

We may need a definition of ethics of AI to ensure that we pay attention to the right components and not confuse ethics with "hard" requirements, that is, law and partially binding, soft law. This distinction is only sometimes clear, as we could see in one of the proposals for amendments to the Artificial Intelligence Act[22] proposed by a group of European Parliament members. In line with the proposed Article 4a(1),

> [t]he developer of an AI system shall, on all stages of development of the AI system, take into account the EU Charter of Fundamental Rights and place on the market or putting into service only **trustworthy AI** that is lawful, **ethical** and robust. (...) (b) 'ethical' means that the AI system was developed to respect the freedom and autonomy of human beings, to protect human dignity as well as mental and physical integrity, and to be fair and explicable.

The above example illustrates that the "standards" included in the paragraph may be called either "legal" or "ethical." The notion of ethics of AI also bears many issues and challenges, as Azoulay (2019) noticed in a United Nations document (Azoulay, 2019).

According to the IEEE standards, 7000-2021 – Standard Model Process for Addressing Ethical Concerns during System Design,[23] "ethical" means "supporting the realization of positive values or the reduction of negative values", while "**ethics**" is defined as a "**branch of knowledge or theory that investigates the correct reasons for thinking that this or that is right**". Dignum (2018) proposed an exciting distinction that shows all the critical and essential parts of the ethics of artificial intelligence and consists of the following:

1 Ethics by Design: the technical/algorithmic integration of ethical reasoning capabilities as part of the behavior of the artificial autonomous system.
2 Ethics in Design: the regulatory and engineering methods that support the analysis and evaluation of the ethical implications of AI systems as these integrate or replace traditional social structures.
3 Ethics for Design: the codes of conduct, standards and certification processes that ensure the integrity of developers and users as they research, design, construct, employ and manage artificial intelligent systems.

The distinction does not create the definition we are looking for but rather indicates all the elements necessary to make autonomous systems – ethical. Muller (2021, p. 14) rightly points out also that there is also a notion of machine ethics that can be understood as "(...) ethics for machines for 'ethical machines', for machines as subjects, rather than for the human use of the machine as objects". The reason is simply that we should overcome "the tendency to anthropomorphize it [artificial intelligence – author]" (Ryan, 2020, pp. 2749–2750) and put focus on the human side of artificial intelligence and its data-driven heart. Therefore, the ethics of artificial intelligence will not – at least in the author's view – be linked to the issue of machines and digital systems as moral agents.

Nowakowski (2022b) has proposed the following approach to the ethics of artificial intelligence: "(…) **the application of certain ethical principles both at the conceptual stage, creation, and application of these** solutions". This also brings us to the notion of "computational ethics", which can be understood as

> scholarly work that aims to formalize descriptive ethics and normative ethics in algorithmic terms, as well as work that uses this formalization to help to both (i) engineer ethical AI systems, and (ii) better understand human moral decisions and judgments.
>
> (Awad et al., 2022)

As a result, applying values and principles will be important both from the perspective of the algorithm or models of artificial intelligence and humans responsible for its development, deployment and monitoring when in motion. This approach will generally align with Bryson (2018) and her strategy for "non-trustable" artificial intelligence systems.

Arguably, the above definition could be better and will evolve further. Heilinger (2022, p. 15) indicates that "[i]n order to make AI ethics more sure-footed and avoid distortions that result from conceptual unclarity, an explicit conceptual specification of the subject of AI ethics will be necessary", and this is where also ethical fintech should start. As the maturity of artificial intelligence is increasing, we should focus on creating standards and requirements for (more) **ethical systems to ensure that they are being run for our good and will not (or the humans responsible for them) harm human beings.**

Nowakowski (2022b) argues that

> in a dynamic and digital world, the creation of ethical standards for the financial sector is essential, although it is no substitute for human integrity and the formation of moral attitudes outside the organizations themselves. However, an important question arises - how these standards should be shaped in the financial sector, that is, whether they should be binding or not, whether they should be based on hard law or soft guidelines and recommendations, and whether they should be linked to appropriate disciplinary instruments. It is also important to identify the (in)possibility of creating a unified catalog of principles which could be applied, for example, at the European Union level.

Fintech Ethics, which Nowakowski (2022b) prefers to call the combination of technology, finance and ethics, will inevitably change how financial institutions provide financial products and services. At the same time, its adoption will require substantial changes in the internal governance of financial institutions and different approaches to supervisory reporting by regulatory bodies. It will also pose new risks (including ethical washing) and call for more data- and ethical-driven culture within organizations. In the short term, it will generate little profit or savings; however, it may be an essential factor for success in a long time. Morley et al. (2021) contend that having ethical AI approaches may increase customer satisfaction and trust and be a source of higher income. At the same time, it will require significant effort to ensure that such an ethical approach is more than a mere slogan.

2.5 Conclusions

The analysis indicates that financial institutions will have to undergo significant changes (transformation) to find their way in innovation and progressive datafication. Concomitantly, it seems neither possible nor reasonable to build a single model (one-size-fits-all) for these changes, particularly in AI & Data Governance, due to the variety of models available. This results from the simple assumption that a specific model should be based, first and foremost, on clearly defined and "personalized" (for the institution in question) principles that will set a particular standard for implementation. In other words, institutions should find their own approach to data (governance).

In addition, these models will change as new legal and regulatory solutions emerge and the role of individual financial institutions changes. Today, it is difficult to assess how these changes will take place and what impact this will also have on the expectations of supervisors, who *nota bene* will have to provide adequate resources to verify the correctness, effectiveness and efficiency of implementations. This will be one of the most critical and challenging topics for future-proof supervision and institutions' internal governance. With more data available, supervisors and institutions will face more risks linked to the digital world and fundamental rights. The balance will therefore have to undertake many – sometimes conflicting – interests.

Notes

1 https://ec.europa.eu/info/strategy/priorities-2019-2024/europe-fit-digital-age/european-data-strategy_en (accessed: 31.10.2022).

2 Commission Delegated Regulation (EU) 2018/389 of 27 November 2017 supplementing Directive (EU) 2015/2366 of the European Parliament and of the Council with regard to regulatory technical standards for strong customer authentication and common and secure open standards of communication, OJ of 2018, L 69/23.

3 https://ec.europa.eu/info/law/better-regulation/have-your-say/initiatives/13241-Open-finance-framework-enabling-data-sharing-and-third-party-access-in-the-financial-sector_en (accessed: 31.10.2022).

4 https://eur-lex.europa.eu/legal-content/EN/TXT/?uri=CELEX:52020DC0591(accessed: 31.10.2022).

5 https://eur-lex.europa.eu/legal-content/EN/TXT/?uri=celex%3A52021PC0206 (accessed: 31.10.2022).

6 www.eba.europa.eu/sites/default/documents/files/documents/10180/1972987/eb859955-614a-4afb-bdcd-aaa664994889/Final%20Guidelines%20on%20Internal%20Governance%20%28EBA-GL-2017-11%29.pdf?retry=1 (accessed: 1.11.2022).

7 https://www.congress.gov/bill/117th-congress/house-bill/6580/text (accessed: 1.11.2022).
8 https://finance.ec.europa.eu/regulation-and-supervision/consultations/finance-2022-open-finance_en (accessed: 3.11.2022).
9 https://eur-lex.europa.eu/legal-content/pl/ALL/?uri=CELEX:32016R0679 (accessed: 6.11.2022).
10 https://eur-lex.europa.eu/legal-content/PL/TXT/?uri=CELEX%3A32018R0389 (accessed: 6.11.2022).
11 For example, Articles 174–177 CRR: https://eur-lex.europa.eu/legal-content/PL/TXT/?uri=celex%3A32013R0575 (accessed: 6.11.2022). See also Nowakowski and Waliszewski (2022).
12 https://www.bafin.de/SharedDocs/Downloads/EN/Aufsichtsrecht/dl_Prinzipienpapier_BDAI_en.pdf?_blob=publicationFile&v=2, p. 8 (accessed: 6.11.2022).
13 https://eur-lex.europa.eu/legal-content/EN/TXT/PDF/?uri=CELEX:32013L0036&from=PL (accessed: 8.11.2022).
14 https://eur-lex.europa.eu/legal-content/PL/TXT/?uri=celex%3A32013R0575 (accessed: 8.11.2022).
15 https://www.eba.europa.eu/sites/default/documents/files/document_library/Publications/Guidelines/2022/EBA-GL-2022-05%20GLs%20on%20AML%20compliance%20officers/1035126/Guidelines%20on%20AMLCFT%20compliance%20officers.pdf (accessed: 9.11.2022).
16 Brożek and Jakubiec (2017, p. 303) rightly point out that "(...) that autonomous machines cannot be granted the status of legal agents" and therefore will not be accountable and liable of any actions made by "themselves".
17 Bryson (2020, p. 3) argues that that "(...) the potential of 'uploading' human intelligence in any meaningful sense is highly dubious". Indeed, we are not able to say how our brain works in practice and therefore 'mimicking' it is highly questionable, at least at the current state of science.
18 LAWS stands for Lethal Autonomous Weapons Systems.
19 A good example of guidance for ethical AI that is based on values is the document prepared by the European Commission's experts - Ethics Guidelines for Trustworthy AI, April 2019; https://ec.europa.eu/newsroom/dae/document.cfm?doc_id=60419 (accessed: 24.07.2022). This document is, however, sometimes unrealistic in its approach to values and principles that should be the ground for trustworthy AI systems.
20 https://www.europarl.europa.eu/RegData/etudes/STUD/2022/729543/EPRS_STU(2022)729543(ANN1)_EN.pdf (accessed: 26.07.2022).
21 https://en.wikipedia.org/wiki/Ethics_of_artificial_intelligence (accessed: 26.07.2022).
22 https://eur-lex.europa.eu/legal-content/EN/TXT/?uri=CELEX%3A52021PC0206 (accessed: 26.07.2022).
23 https://ieeexplore.ieee.org/browse/standards/reading-room/page/viewer?id=9536679 (accessed: 26.07.2022).

References

Ammanath, B. (2022). *Trustworthy AI. A Business Guide for Navigating Trust and Ethics in AI.* Wiley.

Arner, D.W., Castellano, G.G., Selga, E.K. (2022). Financial data governance: The datafication of finance, The rise of open banking and the end of the data centralization paradigm. University of Hong Kong Faculty of Law Research Paper No. 2022/08, European Banking Institute Working Paper Series no. 117.

Awad, E., Levine, S., Anderson, M., Anderson, S.L., Conitzer, V., Crockett, M.J., Everett, J.A.C., Evgeniou, T., Gopnik, A., Jamison, J.C., Kim, T.W., Liao, S.M., Meyer, M.N., Mikhail, J., Opoku-Agyemang, K., Borg, J.S., Schroeder, J., Sinott-Armstrong, W., Slavkovik, M., Tenenbaum, J.B. (2022). Computational ethics. *Trends in Cognitive Science*, 26, 5, 388–405. https://reader.elsevier.com/reader/sd/pii/S1364661322000456?token=48436E819E376881AB57851F965DFFD981E67510BA13A9027EBC1D1164DB1A5AE9C1E480407DD4620F3A9DCAAB906530&originRegion=eu-west-1&originCreation=20220330182910.

Azoulay, A. (2019 January). Towards an ethics of artificial intelligence. *UN Chronicle*, 55, 4.

BaFin (2021). *Big Data and Artificial Intelligence: Principles for the Use of Algorithms in Decision-Making Processes*. June, 1–16.

Blackman, R. (2022). *Ethical Machines. Your Concise Guide to Totally Unbiased, Transparent, and Respectful AI*. Harvard Business Review Press.

Brożek, B., Jakubiec, M. (2017). On the legal responsibility of autonomous machines. *Artificial Intelligence Law*, 25, 3, 293–304. Springer.

Bryson, J. (2018). AI & global governance: No one should trust AI. *United Nations*. https://cpr.unu.edu/publications/articles/ai-global-governance-no-one-should-trust-ai.html

Bryson, J.J. (2020). The ethics of artificial intelligence. An introductory overview for law and regulation. In Dubber, M.D., Pasquale, F., Das, S. (2020). *The Oxford Handbook of Ethics of AI* (pp. 3–25). Oxford University Press.

Chau, D., van Dijck Nemcsik, M. (2022). *Anti-money Laundering. Transaction Monitoring Systems Implementations. Finding Anomalies*. Wiley.

Coeckelbergh, M. (2020). *AI Ethics*. MIT Press.

Crisanto, J.C., Ehrentraud, J., Fabian, M., Monteil A., (2022). Big tech interdependencies - a key policy blind spot. FSI Insights on policy implementation, No 44, July.

Dafoe, A. (2017). *AI Governance: A Research Agenda*. Future of Humanity Institute, The University of Oxford, Oxford University Press.

Davenport, T.H., Bean, R., (2018). Big companies are embracing analytics, but most still don't have a data-driven culture. *Harvard Business Review*, 6, 1–4.

Deloitte (2020 November). *The Future of Retail Banking. The Hyper-personalisation Imperative*. https://www2.deloitte.com/content/dam/Deloitte/uk/Documents/financial-services/deloitte-uk-hp-the-future-of-retail-banking.pdf

Dignum, V. (2018). Ethics of artificial intelligence: introduction to the special issue. *Ethics and Information Technology*, 20, 1, 1–3.

Dupont, L., Fliche, O., Yang, S. (2020 June). *Governance of Artificial Intelligence in Finance*. Banque de France.

ENISA (2022 January). *Data Protection Engineering. From Theory to Practice*. https://www.enisa.europa.eu/publications/data-protection-engineering/@@download/fullReport

Eryurek, E., Gilad, U., Lakshmanan V., Kibunguchy-Grant A., Ashdown J. (2022). *Data Governance. The Definitive Guide. People, Processes, and Tools to Operationalize Data Trustworthiness*. Wiley.

Gambacorta, L., Huang, Y., Qiu, H., Wang, J. (2019). How do machine learning and non-traditional data affect credit scoring? New evidence from a Chinese fintech firm. BIS Working Papers No 834.

Giddings, A., Islam, E., Kao, K., Kopp E., Quiros-Romero G. (2021). *Towards a Global Approach to Data in the Digital Age*. IMF Staff Discussion Note, SDN/2021/005.

Heilinger, J-Ch. (2022). *The Ethics of AI Ethics. A Constructive Critique*. Springer. https://link.springer.com/content/pdf/10.1007/s13347-022-00557-9.pdf

Janssen, M., Brouss, P., Estevez, E., Janowski T., (2020). Data governance: Organising data for trustworthy artificial intelligence. *Government Information Quarterly*, 37, 31–38.

Kamm, F.M. (2020). The use and abuse of the trolley problem: Self-driving cars, medical treatments, and the distribution of harm. In S.M. Liao (Ed.), *Ethics of Artificial Intelligence* (pp. 79–108). Oxford University Press.

Kearns, M., Roth, A., (2022). *The Ethical Algorithm. The Science of Socially Aware Algorithm Design*. Oxford University Press.

Kroll, J.A. (2018). Data science data governance [AI Ethics]. *IEEE Security & Privacy*, 16, 6, 61–62.

Laboure, M., Deffrennes, N. (2022). *Democratizing Finance. The Radical Promise of Fintech*. Harvard University Press.

Liebergen, B.V. (2017). Machine learning: A revolution in risk management and compliance? *Journal of Financial Transformation*, 45, 60–67.

Ma, W., Huang, K., (2022). *Blockchain and Web3. Building the Cryptocurrency, Privacy and Security Foundations of the Metaverse*. Wiley.

Marr, B. (2022). *Data Strategist. How to Profit from a World of Big Data. Analytics and Artificial Intelligence*. Kogan Page Publishers.

Martens, D. (2022). *Data Science Ethics. Concepts, Techniques and Cautionary Tales*. Oxford, University Press.

Martinho, A., Poulsen, A., Kroesen, M. (2021). Perspectives about artificial moral agents. *AI and Ethics*, 1, 4, 477–490.

Morley, J., Kinsey, L., Elhalal, A., Garcia, F., Ziosi, M., Floridi, L. (2021). Operationalising AI ethics: barriers, enablers and next steps. *AI & Society*, 38, 411–423.

Muller, V.C. (2021). Ethics of artificial intelligence. In A. Elliott (Ed.), *The Routledge Social Science Handbook of AI* (pp. 122–137). Routledge.

Nowakowski, M. (2022a). Effective data management and artificial intelligence. Training, transparency and explainability. Legal and regulatory approach. In M. Sakowska-Baryła (Ed.), *Artificial Intelligence. Transfers, Accountability and Other Challenges of Personal Data Protection* (pp. 41–42). Presscom.

Nowakowski, M. (2022b). *Ethical FinTech. The Importance of Ethics in Creating Secure Financial Products and Services*, under review.

Nowakowski, M., Waliszewski, K. (2022). Artificial intelligence in the problem of risk assessment models in financial institutions from a legal and regulatory perspective. *Journal of Finance and Financial Law*, 1, 33, 119–141. https://doi.org/10.18778/2391-6478.1.33.07

Plotkin, P. (2021). *Data Stewardship: An Actionable Guide to Effective Data Management and Data Governance*. Elsevier.

Righetti, L., Pham, Q., Madhavan, R., Chatila, R. (2018 March). Lethal autonomous weapon systems [Ethical, legal, and societal issues]. *IEEE Robotics & Automation Magazine*, 25, 1, 123–126.

Ryan, M. (2020). In AI we trust: Ethics, artificial intelligence, and reliability. *Science and Engineering Ethics*, 26, 5, 2749–2767.

Saniuk, S., Grabowska, S., Gajdzik, B., (2020). Personalization of products in the industry 4.0 concept and its impact on achieving a higher level of sustainable consumption. *Energies*, 13, 5895, 2–3.

Sheng Wang, J., (2021). Exploring biometric identification in FinTech applications based on the modified TAM. *Financial Innovation*, 7, 42, 2–24. https://doi.org/10.1186/s40854-021-00260-2

Simpson, N.P., Mach, K.J., Constable, A., Hess, J., Hogarth, R., Howden, M., Lawrence, J., Lempert, R.J., Muccione, V., Mackey, B., New, M.G., O'Neil, B., Otto, F., Pörtner, H-O., Reisinger, A., Roberts, D., Schmidt, D.N., Seneviratne, S., Strongin, S., van Aalst, M., ..., & Trisos, Ch. H. (2021). A framework for complex climate change risk assessment. *One Earth*, 4, 4, 489–501. https://doi.org/10.1016/j.oneear.2021.03.005

Soldatos, J., Troiano, E., Kranas, P., Mamelli A., (2022). A reference architecture model for big data systems in the finance sector. In J. Soldatos, D. Kyriazis (Eds.), *Big Data and Artificial Intelligence in Digital Finance. Increasing Personalisation and Trust in Digital Finance Using Big Data and AI* (pp. 3–28). Springer.

Stahl, B.C. (2022). From computer ethics and the ethics of AI towards an ethics of digital ecosystems. *AI and Ethics*, 2, 1, 65–77.

Szpringer, W. (2022). *Dataification. The Data-Driven Economy. Competition vs. Regulation.* Poltext. https://virtualo.pl/ebook/datafikacja-gospodarka-oparta-na-danych-konkurencja-a-regulacja-i432792/

Vasiljeva, T., Lukanova, K. (2016). Commercial banks and fintech companies in the digital transformation: Challenges for the future. *Journal of Business Management*, 11, 25–33.

WHO (2021). *Ethics and Governance of Artificial Intelligence for Health: WHO Guidance.* World Health Organization.

Yan, G. (2017). Application of cloud computing in banking: Advantages and challenges. In *2017 2nd International Conference on Politics, Economics and Law (ICPEL 2017)* (pp. 29–32). Atlantis Press.

Zetzsche, D.A., Arner, D.W., Buckley, R.P. (2020). Decentralised finance. *Journal of Financial Regulation*, 6, 2, 172–203.

3 From Digital Technologies to New Economics in Banking

How to Drive the Future of Digital Money and Data Information Knowledge

Anna Omarini

3.1 Introduction

During the last decade, banks have been subjected to several severe shocks: these include the new regulatory paradigm resulting from the Global Financial Crisis (GFC), European payments directives (PSD1 and PSD2) and similar trends in other geographies that have caused markets to evolve toward a data-driven economy. Among the many factors affecting the industry (for example, the fight against climate change initiatives, a low interest rate environment and two external shocks, namely, COVID-19 lockdowns and the Russian invasion of Ukraine), the digital revolution on its own is posing an existential threat to banks and the future of the banking industry.

Although technology has been at the core of the banking industry since the 1950s, and banks have been considered to be special (Bossone, 1999), at present they are adept at incorporating it in their businesses and processes, the present and future framework of the financial services system is changing with the entry of new competitors, products and business models. Consequently, the financial services industry has started undertaking a deep transformation where the most successful disruptors have employed "combinatorial disruption", in which multiple sources of value – cost, experience and platform – are fused to create disruptive new business models and exponential gains (Varian, 2001). All the above reveals a set of nascent ecosystems of independent actors, where the traditional supply-centered oligopoly is coupled with FinTechs, BigTechs, retailers, etc. This is a key milestone in the unbundling, modularization and re-bundling of banking services that are challenging the financial services landscape.

While the core objectives of financial intermediation may remain the same, the methods and functionaries relating to those objectives change with new technology and market developments, namely, platforms and ecosystems (Blakstad & Allen, 2018). The digital dimension is also facilitating inter-industry collaborations and partnerships industries implying that other factors in addition to competition are shaping the industry (OECD, 2011). We are observing so-called coopetition, which Bouncken et al. (2015) explain is a paradoxical strategic process in which economic agents create value through cooperative relationships, while simultaneously competing to capture part of

DOI: 10.4324/9781003340454-3

the value created. The adoption of coopetition strategies, therefore, allows companies to enhance their competitive advantages (Ritala & Hurmelinna-Laukkanen, 2009) because of the development of products or services, which without the participation of the coopetition partner would be almost impossible to produce (Dvorsky et al., 2019; Walley, 2007). The key factor underpinning all this is the realization by some banks that, with the right approach, the opportunities can be interesting for them in comparison with FinTech companies and other entrants in the many and different value chains.

Over time, these developments are potentially game changing, and the big challenge becomes how to balance the "old" to maintain (what?) and the "new", here already and/or on coming. In doing so, the next generation of banking ecosystems is searching to find both financial and economic equilibria.

The aim of this chapter is to understand to what extent the above factors are going to influence institutional changes and lead to economic and social consequences in the industry. This chapter is organized as follows: on the one hand, it offers insights on some of the hype storm words, such as digitalization, FinTechs, open banking, embedded finance, banking-as-a-service, decentralized finance, that are creating a twisted picture of the digital banking industry (Section 3.2). On the other hand, by linking the dots, this chapter will outline the most interesting implications for the industry, incumbents, FinTech firms and those banks that have undertaken a deep strategic transformation (Sections 3.3 and 3.4). Finally, Section 3.5 presents the main conclusions.

3.2 Drivers of Change in Banking Business

The banking industry is changing at a rapid pace. Many trends are supported by the increasing demands of consumers for more online channels and greater personalization. Others are driven by the breakthrough of both regulation and digital technologies. Meanwhile, COVID-19 has been transforming the sector with banks emerging from the pandemic with new priorities and strategies. Amid this changing landscape, we examine the three biggest drivers of change in banking.

3.2.1 Digital Technologies

Technology in banking has always had the power to affect business fundamentals, such as information and risk analysis, distribution, monitoring and processing (Llewellyn 1999, 2003). However, it is useful to distinguish between technologies of the past and the digital technologies of the present. New digital technologies not only have the power to improve efficiency and the effectiveness in services, but they have also started exerting influence on banks' products and delivery methods (European Central Bank, 1999). Through the application of digital technologies innovation has started to lead to further improvements, which in turn is impacting banks' profitability.

Today, the way a company can adapt to technology and exploit its potential depends on its capacity to translate those benefits into products and services, processes and overall new business models to secure and improve its competitiveness. Banking is changing as value chains become fragmented, products are componentized and new adaptive players emerge. Therefore, if we take a broader industry perspective, on the one hand, we see technology can enhance economies of scale thereby changing the proportion of fixed *versus* variable costs and lowering entry barriers. On the other hand, some business models require reaching a certain number of transactions to be resilient. Hence, we are witnessing an increase in market contestability in banking as a business useful to boost others' value chains, which invites more agile companies to populate the banking landscape.

Digital-only players with non-linear business models are attacking the foundations of the vertically integrated banking model with new value propositions that disrupt the value chain and break products into discrete components. This process – which has already played out in payments via innovators like Currencycloud and Wise – is now unfolding in commercial banking, personal credit, deposits, investments and more. The offerings and roles new actors are going to take to the market are thus modular and dependent on other complements along different value chains. As products and services are increasingly embedded in digital technologies, it is becoming more difficult to disentangle business processes from their underlying IT infrastructures. This trend is likely to continue, which means that banks will become even more dependent on technology both at an operational and strategic level. A critical point may arise because changes have their own source from outside the banking industry, and this may introduce an exogenous culture when the new has to be incorporated inside a single bank.

The factors listed above are made possible because digital technologies are highly malleable. They open larger domains to new potential functionality (Yoo, 2010; Yoo et al., 2010), disrupting every industry to various degrees. This is because their impacts are spreading also at the societal level (Alijani & Wintjes, 2017), where the borderless extension of financial innovation is experiencing great change. In addition, the new FinTech phenomenon has started developing and reshaping the industry's value propositions and related business models (IMF & World Bank, 2019). Application Programming Interfaces (APIs), cloud computing, artificial intelligence (AI), machine learning, blockchain and Decentralized Finance (DeFi), are technologies considered able to shape the future of banking.

3.2.2 *Regulation: From Challenging to Boosting Competition in Financial Services*

The new technologies as applied in the financial sector have attracted regulatory attention. The most significant action has been the introduction of a regulatory framework for Financial Technology in the European Union via the Payment Services Directive (PSD1 and overall PSD2). The latest piece of regulation, adopted in 2015 and effective from 13 January 2018, drastically aims to revolutionize the EU payments landscape and, as a result, the banking industry. PSD2 is a key contributing factor in shaping and changing the banking industry and its value chain in Europe. The new directive encompasses several goals at different levels, applying common standards; enhancing transparency; incentivizing new players to introduce innovative services to enter the market; increase competition, improve and enlarge choice to benefit consumers. Furthermore, the centerpiece of the regulation is the obligation to provide third parties, conditional upon the customer authorization, with access to data and information of the payment account the customer holds at their bank. In this way, consumers could freely choose among a wide array of services from different providers, as banks are mandated to open information and interact with all other players (Omarini, 2022a, p.251).

The Competition Policy Commissioner, Margrethe Vestager, has stressed that PSD2 approval provides (European Commission, 2015):

> A legislative framework to facilitate the entry of (such) new players [...] and enabling new services to enter the market [...] All these premises substantiate the argument of interdependence between firms and modularity of services within the banking industry and outside, leading to the peculiar definition of business ecosystem.

Under these circumstances and the ones from the PSD2 evolutionary framework, the new paradigm of banking sees banking becoming a modular and flexible enabler of different activities aiming at satisfying more diverse customers' needs, habits and demographic requirements. In fact, open banking relates to open innovation (Chesbrough, 2003, 2011) to the extent that not only banks but also anyone interested in using banking may rely on the flow of ideas from inside and outside its industry to develop products and services and innovative processes. In some countries, such as the UK and Australia, the industry is verging on a further step, namely, an open finance framework where data sharing goes beyond transactions (Figure 3.1) and moves toward an open data economy.

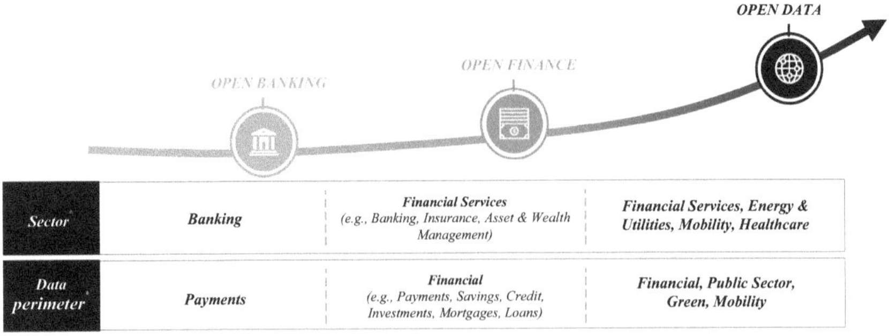

Figure 3.1 Open Banking to Open Finance versus Open Data Economy

Source: Own elaboration.

Cortet et al. (2016) maintain that PSD2 goes a step beyond the regulatory scope. The directive is indeed an impressive accelerator of the digitization process that is already affecting banking.

While the initial focus for PSD2 at most banks has been on retail banking, strong competitors are already implementing open APIs in transaction banking and investor services to offer superior customer experience, insight and value to corporate customers as well as retail customers, while extracting bank wide efficiencies as a result. Thus, we note that this regulation could severely influence revenue streams from the medium to long-time horizon that were considered sticky by banks.

3.2.3 Consumer Habits and Behavior

Several important social and economic trends have occurred in the market and influenced (and continue to influence) the market for personal financial services. However, once more digital technologies, focused on improving the client experience, have harnessed the vast amounts of data available, and in doing so technology promises to simplify everything people do by understanding their needs and preferences, and offering insightful recommendations or reducing mundane tasks. For instance, digital technologies focus on improving the client experience through harvesting vast amounts of available data to provide tailored products and services at more affordable prices and via more convenient and easy-to-use delivery channels. This simplicity of use and greater understanding of customer needs and preferences to offer insightful recommendations would appear to be highly valued by customers.

In countries like the US, FinTech firms play a central role in the financial services ecosystem. According to a recent report (Pymnts and Ingo Money, 2022) at least 68 million US consumers used a FinTech as a bank for some type of financial service in 2022, and that number is growing. The ever-expanding group of consumers using FinTechs fall into two major camps: consumer who use FinTechs as their primary financial institutions (FIs); and consumers who use FinTechs as secondary FIs or supplementary financial service providers. FinTechs are most popular among bridge millennials, low-income consumers and paycheck-to-paycheck consumers who struggle to pay their bills. Consumers are twice as likely to cite cost as the main reason for using a FinTech as their primary FI, adding credence to the hypothesis that some consumers perceive FinTechs – like Chime[1] – as a cost-effective alternative to traditional banks. The services financial customers obtain through FinTechs are for payments (peer-to-peer payments for both sending and receiving, debit card and savings).

Arguably, new players in the banking industry have a different understanding of what customers' value and are more committed to customers than traditional financial service providers. They provide solutions to customers as they experience important life changes (employment, unemployment, marriage, divorce, child rearing, retirement, etc.). Under these circumstances, customers require help with a wide range of problems, which are frequently highly influenced by emotions. Managing this kind of banking entails the use of unfamiliar methods, such as information processing, social responsibility, customer education, self-organization and even gossip. Awareness of social responsibility and customer education are included in the new players' value propositions. Moreover, their commitment is also about caring. Thus, a holistic perspective may be more effective when selling solutions to customers; as such, an approach is indeed what customers are looking for. The essence of an integrated consumer banking approach is the notion that in place of traditional savings and loans, customers should be provided with integrated instruments and integrated pricing supported by integrated information (Omarini, 2019). Such a way of serving customers gives rise to the following phenomena: embedded finance and contextual banking experiences. Embedded finance is the integration of financial services like lending, payment processing or insurance into non-financial businesses' infrastructures and value chains without the need to redirect to traditional financial institutions. If this is also happening in given situations when a customer undertakes a white-label digital transaction banking platform to manage' personal cash and trade. This can be addresses as contextual banking, which may also leverage from machine learning and predictive analytics delivered through APIs and an omni-channel user experience.

The transformation in financial services is ongoing and increasing attention is being paid to customization and the personalization of services. These trends in the service perspective find their roots in the increasing trend of modularity, which rests on the ability of companies to move toward product componentization (Tuunanen et al., 2012; Accenture, 2020, 2021, Deloitte, 2020). At this point, when digital technologies enter an industry, the real core business is the value delivered to customers rather than the business of controlling a single value chain related to that product/service with the consequence that new emerging business frameworks emerge in the economy rather than in the financial services industry only.

3.3 Trends and Emerging Business Frameworks in the Banking Industry

Times have changed, and not even one of banking's main products has remained exclusively in the hands of either banks or other conventional financial intermediaries. Many new and emerging trends have started entering and reshaping the industry, for instance:

- Unbundling and re-bundling,
- Modularization,
- Embedded banking/finance,
- Contextual banking,
- Banking-as-a-service and
- Banking platforms and ecosystems.

In the new game, a big challenge is seeking a balance between what to keep from the "old" banking system and what to obtain from the "new" one to meet customers' demand.

When FinTech first entered the market, it facilitated an unbundling of fully integrated banking services that were provided by incumbent banks into component services. FinTech firms have served the market for each of these separate services in innovative, more convenient and efficient ways. The unbundling phenomenon reflects the deconstruction of value chains into different modules of products or services and combining them together. To illustrate, a consumer may want to manage his/her loan via SoFi, while using PayPal to manage payments, Rocket Mortgage for his/her mortgage, and Robinhood to manage and trade with stocks (see Box 3.1).

FinTechs have seized the initiative – defining the direction, shape and pace of innovation across almost every subsector of the financial services industry – and have succeeded as both stand-alone businesses and as crucial parts of others' financial value chains. FinTechs have helped to reshape customer expectations setting new and higher bars for user experience.

The above factors explain the introduction into the industry of the framework of modularization that often changes the service design experienced by the customer. While services differ in their experiential intensity, in transactional services customer satisfaction focuses on the efficiency and

Box 3.1 A set of players involved on an everyday customer journey

- SoFi (established 2012) is an online personal finance company and online bank. At present, SoFi provides financial products including student and auto loan refinancing, mortgages, personal loans, credit card, investing and banking through both mobile app and desktop interfaces. SoFi Technologies serves customers in the United States.
- PayPal (established 2002) is a technology platform that enables digital payments and commerce experiences on behalf of merchants and consumers across the world. It operates a global, two-sided network at scale that connects merchants and consumers with millions of active accounts across more than 200 markets.
- Rocket Mortgage (established 1985) is a leading online mortgage lender in the US Rocket parent Quicken Loans (established 1985) pioneered the first all-online mortgage application.
- Robinhood (established 2013) is a stock brokerage that allows customers to buy and sell stocks, options, ETFs and cryptocurrencies with zero commission. People can also store money and trading stocks using its application.

convenience of the service delivery, whereas in experience-centric services evoking emotional processes in customers is at the core of the service (Voss et al., 2008; Zomerdijk and Voss, 2010). Today, most traditional banking products are componentized into new micro-products and services that may be sold separately or in their re-bundled versions (see Figure 3.2).

This situation enables any other player – a retailer, BigTech or neobank – to use these components to create banking experiences or embed financial solutions into their core customer experience. Consider, for instance, how consumer credit is becoming embedded in the shopping experience via *buy-now-pay-later* services (BNPL), which impacts customers' habits and behavior

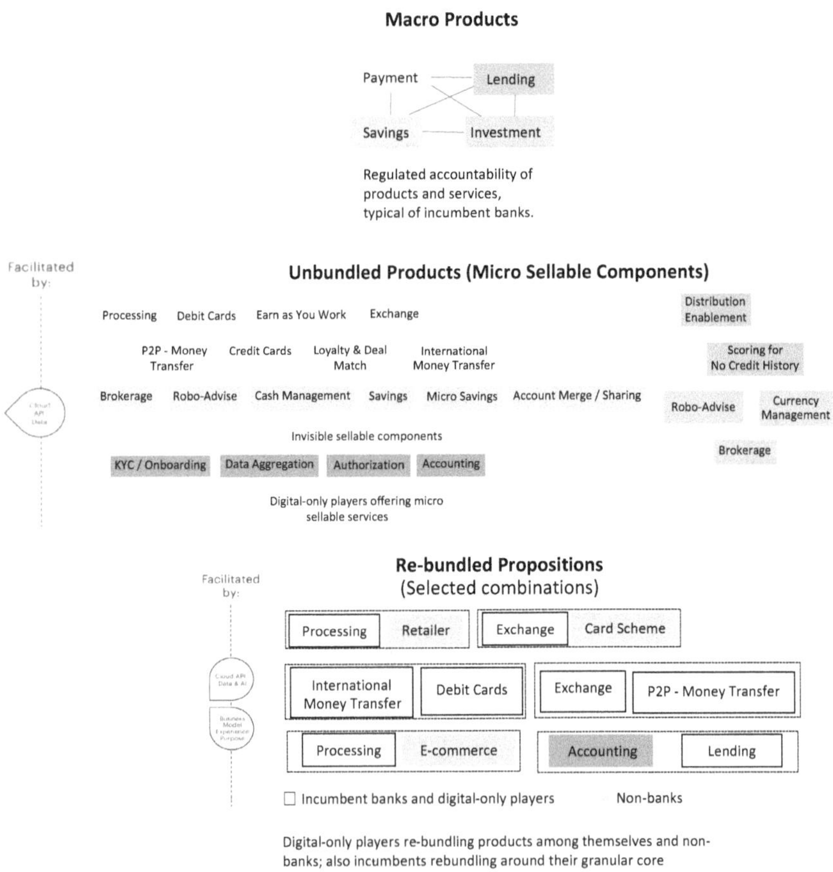

Figure 3.2 FinTechs and Banks Can Create Further Value by Re-bundling Unbundled Product Propositions

Source: Accenture (2021, p. 19).

and implies that the banking experience becomes contextualized into another one experience. FinTech firms, such as Klarna and Affirm, are leading proponents of BNPL. Such companies, therefore, enter the business arena of the banking-as-a-service (BaaS), that is, the provision of banking products to non-bank third parties through APIs (Monetary Authority Singapore, 2016). This new business is becoming interesting to both FinTechs and incumbents who might consider it a new, interesting source of revenues originating from a non-linear business model.

These trends are also developing along the structure of platforms and business ecosystems. Platforms create values by eliminating frictions from transactions and exchanges – for example, a marketplace – whereas (platform-based) ecosystems do so by orchestrating the contributions of multiple companies, which collaborate to create a unique value proposition within a thematic customer journey. Ecosystems, platform-based, are more complex to develop, operate and manage than mere platform business models because they have more constituent parts. To understand the two models' business focus and critical factors, it is necessary to appreciate their differences: while platforms need scale to dominate their intended market, platform-based ecosystems require a combination of scale and scope.

The successful development of both businesses requires the ability to sustain large-scale investments, often over a period of time.

These trends are also consistent with the oncoming diffusion of Open Banking (BIS, 2019; EBA, 2017, McKinsey, 2018) and Open Finance that may work on a multitude of use cases. This implies that financial service providers can help consumers turn their financial behavior into habits (see Figure 3.1). To exemplify, Revolut offers users a categorized view of all consumer spending. While these insights alone do not necessarily contribute to forming better habits, they are useful tools nonetheless to give purpose for consumers.

The new banking will emerge with richer ecosystems where the deep de-integration of financial solutions will find its way throughout the embedded and contextual banking user experiences. These developments will constitute major transformative trends although not completely new to the market. In fact, we can go back to older times when to buy a car one could have asked for a loan from that merchant. However, the "new" comes from the digitalization process that has developed an array of different use cases boosted by API technology. The success comes from new value propositions that can leverage on rich business ecosystems. The next step for embedded banking is a phase of tech-enabled mass adoption of banking-as-a-service, which infers that more big brands will enter the market and take market share away from incumbent banks and neobanks. Big brands will combine data through Artificial Intelligence (AI) and Machine Learning (ML) and extend their reach by developing additional customized services and products (Omarini, 2022a, p.200, 2022b, 2022c).

As banking moves onto digital platforms, cross-industry interconnections will increase and result in new competitive threats. Providers of banking services will come to see themselves more and more in the role of "enablers" of transactions occurring on platforms and within business ecosystems. Retail banks, in the role of being enablers, will shift from being "content" gatekeepers to becoming "customer" gatekeepers. In this new role, trust will remain a core business asset.

3.3.1 *From Business Model Transformation to New Trends and Related Risks in the Market: A Brief Overview*

As the industry undertakes a deep transformation in business model frameworks in the next years, we note that the nature of economic competition will also change. New players view "value for customers" differently and their organizations are more customer-committed compared to traditional service providers. This is because the core business for new players is the value transferred to customers through ease-of-access to services and a more caring system, rather than the business of controlling the entire value chain of a given product or service. To make sense of these developments, two observations are worth considering. First, new financial service providers aspire to develop the core purposes of financial intermediation with new methods and tools, such as robo-advisory services that offer financial advice to a wider market. Parallel to this are the crowdfunding platforms that are increasing financial inclusion while also offering new investment and lending opportunities. Second, more often than not, there is still a banking organization – centralized infrastructure now – somewhere in the FinTech stack. This is because, so far, circumstances have shown the transformational potential of FinTechs (and BigTechs) in a way that they have introduced more incremental innovations rather than radical ones. Thus, the innovations may be considered more "architectural" in nature for the following reasons:

- On the one hand, FinTechs create a reconfiguration of the institutional linkages and systemic components with other providers including incumbents who are able to rapidly appropriate the same or similar core technologies to refine products, services or processes. For example, revisit the case of Nordea Bank which has provided its mobile banking customers with account aggregation and personal financial management tools from the Swedish vendor Tink. The new features allow Nordea's app users to obtain a comprehensive overview of their finances in one place, including mortgage, savings, loans and current accounts from multiple banks. Founded in 2012, today Tink connects to over 2,500 banks, reaching over 250 million bank customers across Europe. (Customers outside the Nordic region include NatWest in the UK and BNP Paribas.) Recently (March 2022) Tink has been bought by VISA (a leader card network provider).
- On the other hand, many FinTech firms have struggled to create new infrastructures and establish new financial services ecosystems, such as

alternative payment rails or alternative capital markets. Yet, they have been much more successful in making improvements within traditional ecosystems and infrastructures. FinTechs have materially changed the basis of competition in financial services, but not yet materially changed the competitive landscape (World Economic Forum, 2017, p. 12).

The evidence shows FinTechs are good at combining value chains among themselves and other service providers and reconfiguring new ones. Under these circumstances, we note the emergence of two new trends and related risks:

1 Banks and other financial service providers are increasingly relying on third-party providers, which increases their mutual interconnection and raises concerns about the potential risks related to this. Particularly, systemic risks could arise from firms being "too-connected-to-fail" rather than "too-big-to-fail".
2 As banking becomes more embedded in customers' everyday lives and boosted by an ever-improving user experience, the more banking will be invisible to customers. That change will not occur overnight, but seeds are already sprouting in several different areas. For example, banks might offer short-term loans through a given merchant that may encourage customers to buy a given product or service. Customers may believe the loan comes from the retailer, not the bank itself and the bank may be comfortable about being invisible in that transaction providing the customer receives a good loan. The worst-case scenario would occur if a loan is not suitable for the customer or that he/she is unable to provide the appropriate cash flow to repay it (debt affordability). This risk may require a higher degree of transparency when financial services are becoming more and more embedded in different value chains.

Further changes will come from decentralized finance (DeFi), which is expected to facilitate the development of parallel infrastructures in the areas of payments, loans, and investments.

One possible scenario associated with DeFi is the provision of financial services without intermediaries, using automated protocols on blockchains and stable coins to facilitate fund transfers (BIS, 2021). DeFi allows developers to create new types of financial products and services, expanding the possibilities of financial technology. While DeFi is said to eliminate counterparty risk, cutting out middlemen and allowing financial assets to be exchanged in a trustless way, as with any innovative technology, its related innovations will introduce a new set of risks. To provide users and institutions with a robust and fault-tolerant system capable of handling new financial applications at scale, we should acknowledge some of these risks (see Box 3.2). In the absence of proper risk mitigation, DeFi will remain an exploratory technology, restricting its use, adoption and appeal.

Box 3.2 Some Blockchain-Related Risks

- DeFi's foundation is public computer code known as a smart contract. Therefore, smart contract risk can take the form of a logic error in the code or an economic exploit in which an attacker can withdraw funds from the platform beyond the intended functionality. Protocol governance refers to the representative or liquid democratic mechanisms that enable changes in the protocol. To participate in the governance process, users and investors must acquire a token that has been explicitly assigned protocol governance rights on a liquid marketplace. Once acquired, holders use these tokens to vote on protocol changes and guide future direction. Governance tokens usually have a fixed supply that assists in resisting attempts by anyone to acquire a majority (51%); nevertheless, they expose the protocol to the risk of control by a malicious actor. While we have yet to witness a true governance attack in practice, new projects like Automata18 allow users to buy governance votes directly and will likely accelerate the threat of malicious/hostile governance. The founders often control traditional FinTech companies, which reduces the risk of an external party influencing or changing the company's direction or product. DeFi protocols, however, are vulnerable to attack as soon as the governance system launches. Any financially equipped adversary can simply acquire a majority of liquid governance tokens to gain control of the protocol and steal funds.
- Oracles are one of the last unsolved problems in DeFi and are required by most DeFi protocols to function correctly. Fundamentally, oracles aim to answer the simple question: How can off-chain data be securely reported on chain. Without oracles, blockchains are completely self-encapsulated and have no knowledge of the outside world other than the transactions added to the native blockchain. Many DeFi protocols require access to secure, tamper-resistant asset prices to ensure that routine actions, such as liquidations and prediction market resolutions, function correctly. Protocol reliance on these data feeds introduces oracle risks.
- The scalability of a system refers to how big it can grow without encountering performance degradation. In blockchain architectures, this is often referred to as throughput. DeFi's scalability is essential since the network undergoes a dramatic increase in transactions. Consequently, in case the network will not be able to manage all transactions, it cannot expand.
- "Regulatory risk" may come the more DeFi market increases in size and influence; it will face greater regulatory scrutiny on the medium to long-term horizon.

Source: Author's elaboration adapted from Campbell et al. (2022).

3.4 "New" Paths to Profitability for Banks, Incumbents and FinTech Platform-Based Companies

New trends could influence both banks and FinTechs in different ways and with different intensities. On the one hand, FinTech companies have de-integrated the way financial services can be conceived, produced and delivered. On the other hand, new platform-based business models and platform-based ecosystems may offer new opportunities to regain profitability. Before delving into these two effects, which are emerging from the trends described above, it is worth outlining that most of the companies are low-margin firms meaning they require a given number of clients to generate enough revenue to cover fixed costs. Typically, these companies do not work on margins, but on volumes. This might represent a difficulty as they must scale up their market share. Yet, FinTechs face difficulties both in scaling up and becoming profitable. This is because firms must spend heavily to sustain customer acquisition rates; often firms report an above-average cost to serve while their marketing expenses are about half of their operating expenses.

3.4.1 BNPL Business: De-integration, Low Margins and Need High Volumes

To explain the above, we consider the example of the BNPL service that can be compared to consumer credit. Much of this exposure is related to auto loans and personal loans, which are typically of larger amounts.

In the immediate future, credit cards and revolving exposures have a higher chance of being disrupted by BNPL. According to UK Finance, since the start of lockdown in 2020, spending on credit cards has fallen by about 50% and an increasing number of shoppers have considered alternative payment options like BNPL. Younger generation consumers perceive this payment method as a budgeting tool though many other consumers view credit cards as an easy way to get into debt. Furthermore, BNPL may be more intuitive compared to traditional credit cards. A recent report from Money.co.uk has focused on how, in the end, BNPL does not seem to offer much more than traditional credit cards, with the standard UK Pay in three options being like a credit card without interest for a given period. Additionally, from a business model perspective, loyalty schemes that are typical of credit card offerings, are often subsidized by merchants rather than being cross-subsidized by consumers rolling their balances. Moreover, credit cards allow holders to build a credit score, which is positively influenced if due amounts are repaid on time and holders are encouraged to take on a more sustainable plan if consumers are late in clearing their credit. This does not happen yet with BNPL providers, many of which will directly pass on unpaid debt-to-debt collectors.

Yet, evidence from Australia suggests that BNPL providers have caused some disruption in the credit card market for traditional offers. This is mainly due to overall aversion to revolving credit, rapid repayment of existing debt, greater adoption of alternative payment methods and reduced generosity of credit card rewards programs.

Estimates suggest that BNPL diffusion will result in slower growth for credit cards rather than a decline in their usage. Moreover, regulation is moving toward a level playing field for BNPL and credit cards due to the imposition of credit checks on consumers that could potentially slow BNPL growth compared to credit cards' growth. At the current state of the market, it seems unlikely that BNPL will overtake credit cards, especially given the different benefits offered and the innovations in the pipeline within the card industry. In August 2020, American Express launched its Pay It Plan to US card members. Barclays is promoting online POS products through their successful partnerships with Apple in the UK and Amazon in both Germany and the UK. Santander and Credit Agricole are launching BNPL products while BNP is establishing a presence in the BNPL market through the acquisition of Floa. These examples indicate how fast credit card companies are adapting to changes in the market and are responding to the challenge of BNPL.

The market is moving fast and not only incumbents are taking action to stay up to date with a variety of dynamic changes. BNPL providers have also started offering additional products to scale up and enhance profitability. In fact, considering how the top BNPL players are developing, one could determine what the key trends in the BNPL industry are and what the future might look like for its key players. If the COVID-19 pandemic has pushed online e-commerce to the highest levels ever seen, the easing of restrictions worldwide has led shoppers to return to purchase in-store. BNPL providers have started leveraging the opportunity represented by physical retailers and have devised ad hoc strategies. Players, such as Zilch in the UK, have based their key value proposition on a close partnership with Mastercard to provide a virtual credit card and deliver retailer agnostic BNPL solutions to consumers; this allows for greater flexibility and no need for integration with merchants' checkout processes. Leading global players, such as Klarna or Clearpay (the UK branch of Afterpay) have been offering similar solutions based on physical or mobile payments cards similar to credit cards.

Another key trend in the BNPL sector is the increasing number of services offered by BNPL providers. BNPL players have started to combine BNPL with POS financing, allowing consumers to choose their plan in terms of the number of installments and the duration of credit depending on the purchase size, type and/or consumer preferences. For instance, Klarna offers longer or higher-ticket financing, that is, features that are more common to POS financing options. Additionally, to increase their share of wallets and drive more customers to merchants, BNPL providers are providing "Buy Now, Pay Now" solutions to offer merchants wider payments processing capabilities. Often, consumers are rewarded with discounts, loyalty points or cashback solutions for paying immediately. To be competitive, continue growing, and increase customer numbers and wallets, BNPL companies will likely need to offer more products and services. Analysts from Morgan Stanley (2021) potentially see BNPL business models evolve into marketplace platforms as BNPL Apps are already pushing through more functionalities, including price drop notifications, daily tailored deals and suggestions, CO_2 tracking, a number of post-purchase tools or even new income streams from sponsored listings, such as Afterpay Ads, recently launched by Afterpay.

On the other hand, with BNPL leading apps, consumers might start seeing BNPL as only the "entry point" with the intention to cross-sell many more products including a broader suite of financial services, and potentially become a "super-app" following the framework of a platform-based ecosystem. In this regard, BNPL providers could apply for a banking license and start cross-selling additional financial services, such as deposits and SME lending amongst others. Klarna already has a banking license and Afterpay has recently launched Afterpay money in Australia with the stated aim to increase potential revenues from transactions and accounts, cashback, retail stockbroking and mortgage referrals. Thus, BNPL-focused providers may start offering more traditional lending products like personal loans while leveraging their already consolidated user base.

Until now, most of BNPL providers have reverted to partnerships with retailers to scale up and increase their business. More recently, payments' facilitators have also started collaborating with BNPL providers to develop streamlined, hassle-free and innovative solutions. In the past few years, numerous partnerships between legacy financial institutions, large tech players and BNPL providers have been consolidated.

3.4.2 *Platform-Based Business Models and Platform-Based Ecosystems*

On the second point concerning challenges to profitability, platforms and ecosystems may benefit from higher price-to-earnings ratios because of their superior performance, compared to the so-called linear business models if they become good at retaining customers within their business model. In the payments sector, the case of Square is an excellent example of a complementary platform and ecosystem. Square began as a linear business with a simple plastic dongle that enabled small merchants to accept card payments in the US. Square's payment value proposition evolved into a platform before becoming a platform-based ecosystem in less than nine years. The Square value proposition now encompasses a whole range of tasks linked to running and growing a small business. Simple platforms or linear business models, over time, may become wide-ranging platform-based ecosystems with a strong vision toward this goal. If a company cannot provide a useful addition to the customer journey on its own, it can develop an ecosystem partnership to create added value for the customer.

3.5 Conclusions

Banking will continue to become more modular, flexible and contextual. Customers will expect to be able to integrate e-commerce, social media and retail payments increasingly with other services. Consequently, many financial services will become less visible to customers as they become embedded in and combined with non-financial offers and activities. The competitive game is constantly spiraling into new forms. New innovative concepts of products and services enhance customer engagement. The spread of mobile devices enables the onboarding of customers to platforms where their activities generate data. Data collection and analysis span all areas of business, such as advertising, financial advice, credit scoring, pricing, claims management and customer retention. Locking customers into a given platform while granting them seamless switching across platform services generates further data. Supported by artificial intelligence and machine learning, the analysis of the wide array of data streams will allow companies to offer products and services better fitting customers' purposes on a recurring basis. Just how much additional value could be generated by knowing customers better seems to be limited only by the ingenuity of the platform company and the actors in the related business ecosystem (Omarini, 2018).

In addition, open banking and open finance are ongoing to improve competition in the market. The future will comprise different frameworks of banking (from conventional banking delivered throughout incumbents and their related digital transformation, to new players both FinTechs and BigTechs). The situation will be partially a kind of a learning curve experience. For instance, the recent example of the Australian Prudential Regulatory Authority's action to impose stricter conditions on applicants for deposit-taking licenses follows the recent (December 2020) collapse of digital challenger, Xinja. A review of Australia's licensing regime found the approach needed greater focus on longer-term sustainability rather than the short-term ambition of receiving a license. Under the new guidelines, restricted Authorized Deposit-Taking institutions (ADIs) must achieve a limited launch of both an income-generating asset product and a deposit product before being granted a full license. There is also increased clarity around capital requirements at different stages for new entrants, who will be expected to have more advanced planning for a potential exit, including a focus on the return of deposits as an option. This approach seeks to ensure that newly licensed banks are better equipped to succeed.

Our analysis introduces an important discussion, which is going to be a big challenge, on how to communicate and educate customers in becoming more aware of the changes the market is undertaking. Just think of how embedded finance may revolutionize the way people buy goods and services, so that this can also reset how they bank – and even redefine what they think of as a bank. This is because a customer might find himself/herself in a one-stop financial hub. On this same issue, the European Commission (DG FISMA) and the OECD International Network on Financial Education (INFE) will jointly develop a financial competence scheme for the European Union. The project will be developed in the framework of the EU Capital Markets Union (CMU) Action Plan, which mandates the European Commission to work toward the development of a dedicated EU financial competence framework.

It will reflect recent and emerging issues, including financial digitalization and sustainable finance. The new EU scheme aims to provide a common terminology and framework at EU level for informing the development of financial literacy policies and programs, identifying gaps in provision and creating assessment, measurement and evaluation tools.

Note

1 Chime – www.chime.com – is a financial technology company founded on the premise that basic banking services should be helpful, easy and free. Chime declares it wants to profit with its members and not from them. Thus, their model does not rely on overdraft fees, monthly service fees, service fees and minimum balance requirements etcetera. Chime collaborates with regional banks to design member first financial products. This creates a more competitive market with better, lower-cost options for everyday citizens who the company claims are not being served well enough or deeply enough by traditional banks. As a result, Chime claims it is helping to drive innovation, inclusion and access across the industry.

References

Accenture. (2020). *Banking in 2020. 10 New Trends to Watch.* https://www.accenture.com/in-en/insights/banking/10-key-trends-banking-2020

Accenture. (2021). *The Future of Banking. It's Time for a Change of Perspective.* https://www.accenture.com/sg-en/insights/banking/future-banking-business-models

Alijani, S., Wintjes, R. (2017). *Interplay Between Technological and Social Innovation* (Simpact Working Paper Vol. 2017 No.3). SIMPACT Project.

Bank for International Settlements (BIS). (2019). *Open Banking and Application Programming Interfaces.* https://www.bis.org/bcbs/publ/d486.htm

Banking for International Settlements (BIS). (2021). *DeFi Risks and the Decentralisation Illusion.* https://www.bis.org/publ/qtrpdf/r_qt2112b.htm

Blakstad, S., Allen, R. (2018). *FinTech Revolution. Universal Inclusion in the New Financial Ecosystem.* London: Palgrave Macmillan.

Bossone, B. (1999). What makes banks special? A study on banking, finance, and economic development. World Bank Policy Research Paper, No. 2408.

Bouncken, R., Gast, J., Kraus, S., Bogers, M. (2015). Coopetition: A systematic review, synthesis, and future research directions. *Review of Managerial Science*, 9, 3, 577–601.

Campbell, R., Harvey, D., Santoro, J. (2021). *DeFi and the Future of Finance.* London: Wiley.

Chesbrough, H.W. (2003). *Open Innovation: The New Imperative for Creating and Benefiting from Technology.* New York: Harvard Business School Press.

Chesbrough, H.W. (2011). *Open Services Innovation: Rethinking Your Business to Grow and Compete in a New Era.* London: John Wiley & Sons.

Cortet, M., Rijks, T., Nijland, S. (2016). PSD2: The digital transformation accelerator for banks. *Journal of Payments Strategy & Systems*, 10, 1, 13–27.

Deloitte. (2020). *Banking on the Future: Vision 2020.* https://www2.deloitte.com/content/dam/Deloitte/in/Documents/financial-services/in-fs-deloitte-banking-colloquium-thoughtpaper-cii.pdf

Dvorsky, J., Petrakova, Z., Polach, J. (2019). Assessing the market, financial, and economic risk sources by Czech and Slovak SMEs. *International Journal of Entrepreneurial Knowledge*, 7, 2, 30–40.
European Banking Association (EBA) (2017). Open banking: Advancing customer-centricity. Analysis and overview. Open Banking Working Group. https://www.abe-eba.eu/thought-leadership-innovation/open-banking-working-group/
European Central Bank (1999). *The Effects of Technology on the EU Banking Systems*. European Central Bank. https://www.ecb.europa.eu/pub/pdf/other/techbnken.pdf
European Commission, 2015, European Parliament adopts European Commission proposal to create safer and more innovative European payments, https://ec.europa.eu/commission/presscorner/detail/en/IP_15_5792
International Monetary Fund & World Bank (2019). *Fintech: The Experience So Far.* https://www.imf.org/en/Publications/Policy-Papers/Issues/2019/06/27/Fintech-The-Experience-So-Far-47056
Llewellyn, D.T. (1999). *The New Economics of Banking. The New Economics of Banking*. Société Universitaire Européenne de Recherches Financières, SUERF Studies: 5.
Llewellyn, D.T. (2003). Technology and the new economics of banking. In M. Balling, F. Lierman, A. Mullineux (Eds.), *Technology and Finance. Challenges for Financial Markets, Business Strategies and Policymakers* (pp. 51–67). London: Routledge.
McKinsey (2018). *PSD2: Taking Advantage of Open-Banking Disruption*. https://www.mckinsey.com/industries/financial-services/our-insights/psd2-taking-advantage-of-open-banking-disruption
Monetary Authority Singapore (2016). *Finance-as-a-Service: API Playbook*. https://abs.org.sg/docs/library/abs-api-playbook.pdf
Morgan Stanley (2021). *Buy Now Pay Later: Banking on Global Financial Innovation*. https://www.morganstanley.com/ideas/buy-now-pay-later-apps-credit-card-alternative
OECD (2011). *Competition Issues in the Financial Sector. Key Findings*. https://www.oecd.org/regreform/sectors/47836843.pdf
Omarini, A. (2018). Banks and Fintechs. How to develop a digital open banking approach for the bank's future? *International Business Research*, 11, 9, 23–26.
Omarini, A. (2019). *Banks and Banking: Digital Transformation and the Hype of Fintech: Business Impacts, New Frameworks and Managerial Implications*. Milano: McGraw-Hill Education.
Omarini, A. (2022a). A new framework in the financial services industry. Where is the market going? Too early to say. In T. King, F.S. Stentella Lopes, A. Srivastav, J. Williams (Eds.), *Disruptive Technology in Banking and Finance. An International Perspective on FinTech* (pp. 241–262). Switzerland: Palgrave MacMillan.
Omarini, A. (2022b). Fintechs: From unbundling to re-bundling the industry of banking. In T.K. Liaw (Ed.), *The Routledge Handbook of FinTech* (pp. 193–215). London & New York: Routledge.
Omarini, A. (2022c). The changing landscape of retail banking and the future of digital banking. In M. Heckel and F. Waldenberger (Eds.), *The Future of Financial Systems in the Digital Age. Perspectives from Europe and Japan* (pp. 133–158). Singapore: Springer.
Pymnts and Ingo Money. (2022). *The Role of FinTechs*. https://www.pymnts.com/wp-content/uploads/2022/10/PYMNTS-The-Role-Of-FinTechs-October-2022.pdf

Ritala, P., Hurmelinna-Laukkanen, P. (2009) What's in it for me? Creating and appropriating value in innovation-related coopetition. *Technovation,* 29, 12, 819–828.

Tuunanen, T., Bask, A., Merisalo-Rantanen, H. (2012). Typology for modular service design: Review of literature. *International Journal of Service Science, Management, Engineering, and Technology (IJSSMET),* 3, 3, 99–112.

Varian, H.R. (2001). *The Economics of Information Technology.* http://people.ischool.berkeley.edu/~hal/Papers/mattioli/mattioli.pdf

Voss, C.A., Roth, A.V., Chase, R.B. (2008). Experience, service operations strategy, and services as destinations: Foundations and exploratory investigation. *Production and Operations Management*, 17, 3, 724–735.

Walley, K. (2007). Coopetition: An introduction to the subject and an agenda for research. *International Studies of Management & Organization*, 37, 11–31.

World Economic Forum (2017). *The Global Competitiveness Report 2017–2018.* https://www3.weforum.org/docs/GCR2017-018/05FullReport/TheGlobalCompetitivenessReport2017%E2%80%932018.pdf

Yoo, Y. (2010). Computing in everyday life: A call for research on experiential computing. *MIS Quar*terly *Review*, 34, 2, 213–231.

Yoo, Y., Henfridsson, O., Lyytinen, K. (2010). Research commentary: The new organizing logic of digital innovation: An agenda for information systems research. *Information Systems Research*, 21, 4, 724–735.

Zomerdijk, L.G., Voss, C.A. (2010). Service design for experience-centric services. *Journal of Service Research*, 13, 1, 67–82.

4 Banking-as-a-Service and Embedded Banking as Innovative Methods of Providing Banking Services

Krzysztof Waliszewski

4.1 Introduction

Banking and other financial services are undergoing unprecedented change. Digital technologies have now reached a level of sophistication and ubiquity where they drive major disruptions in fundamental market definitions, operations and business models (Diamond et al., 2019). The COVID-19 pandemic significantly accelerated the integration of financial solutions with the offer of entities in many industries, mainly e-commerce, which began to gain greater and greater importance. Singapore, India and the United Kingdom witnessed the highest interest in EmFi (embedded finance) compared to other countries (Ozili, 2022a). Further research reveals that global interest in internet information about EmFi was more popular in Asian and European countries (Ozili, 2022b) as a new and prospective source of revenue. Finance will become the background and experience in the future for the user; they will be an integral part of the entire purchasing process, and not a separate application or separate system, as has been the case so far. The new area of FinTech operations, which is embedded banking (EB)/invisible banking and banking-as-a-service (BaaS), fits perfectly into these trends. BaaS is the provision of a financial service to an entity that, while not being a bank, can provide banking services to its clients (then it is embedded finance, i.e., banking services embedded in the ecosystem of other services of a given provider and tailored to its needs). EmFi (or contextual finance) follows the logic that, in many cases, financial services are part of the settlement phase of an economic transaction and serve to support a primary transaction (e-commerce). It allows automotive, retailing or gaming companies to keep the link to their customers and is believed to contribute to customer experience. The concept is enabled by BaaS offerings from FinTech companies and increasingly also from incumbents (Alt & Huch, 2022). These services can be provided by traditional banks as well as challenger banks (neobanks), which marks a new area of competition. FinTech, including EB and BaaS, allows financial exclusion to be reduced, as it enables consumers to use financial services who so far have not used banking services due to financial self-exclusion or forced exclusion (Honecker & Chalmers, 2022). The interest in EmFi is growing

DOI: 10.4324/9781003340454-4

across all industries. E-commerce companies, retailers, travel companies and companies of all kinds are actively incorporating financial products into their customers' experience (Grigorieva, 2022). The aim of this chapter is to present innovations in banking, namely, EB and BaaS in the context of opportunities and threats for traditional banking and for consumers based on the example of Buy-Now-Pay-Later (BNPL) services offered in e-commerce and recently also in stationary commerce.

4.2 Banking-as-a-Service

In FinTech typology, BaaS is defined as end-to-end process ensuring the overall execution of a financial service provided over the web (Moro-Visconti, 2021). BaaS is background banking, where a bank provides financial products to another company, for example, accounts or cards with the help of API (Application Programming Interface). As a result, this trading company can most often offer its own customers banking services without producing these solutions on its own. The BaaS concept is derived from the SaaS concept (Software-as-a-Service), which means a software use model, where the provider is responsible for maintaining this software (most often operating in the cloud) and fully controls it, making it available to the user, while the user uses it over the Internet. SaaS is a software distribution model, in which a third-party provider hosts applications and makes them available to customers over the internet – along with APIs are helping banks to offer customers a wider array of options, constantly upgrading without having to invest in the requisite research, design and development of new technologies. On the other hand, online banks are relying on transparency, service quality and unlimited global access for millennials, accessing multiple service channels.

In the BaaS model, the banking service is available at the user's request and allows for easy fulfillment of needs, which most often include:

- Cash storage (bank account service).
- Making payments (transfer of funds between market participants), e.g., payments in online stores or auction websites.
- Financing of purchase transactions (loan and credit services), e.g., through BNPL, which is a combination of a payment and loan service offered, for example, by Klarna.

BaaS is the provision of banking products and services through third-party distributors. By integrating non-banking businesses with regulated financial infrastructure, BaaS offerings are enabling new, specialized propositions and bringing them to market faster. These new propositions, built on specificity and agility, are displacing existing offerings, disaggregating many profitable elements of the traditional banking value chain in the process. While smaller banks and FinTechs initially dominated the market, incumbent banks are now beginning to wake up its potential with recent entrants including BBVA and Goldman Sachs (Cowley & Malani 2021). In the coming years, the driving force in the development of BaaS services will be the popularization of the open banking (OB) model in many markets. An increasing number of technologically strong banks will stop seeing this solution as a threat coming from external entities. For FinTech companies, BaaS will be an alternative solution to the process of obtaining a banking license and a payment service provider license. It will also enable them to scale their businesses more quickly, including on the international markets (Ciesielski, 2020).

OB is a step toward BaaS, additionally supported by cloud computing. OB, new services and payment institutions, an electronic money institution and the infrastructure provided by the FinTech sector allow the implementation of BaaS largely bypassing banks, in a simpler and more flexible form. At the same time, breaking the banks' monopoly on access to banking secrecy means the democratization of access to financial services for people who have not used or used the banks' offer to a limited extent. However, one should bear in mind the issue of securing the interests of the client and the funds deposited by him or her, as well as the specificity of the sector, which is subject to numerous regulations and financial supervision. In addition, OB and BaaS can be reduced to functions with an open application programming interface, which are available for creating applications and services in the vicinity of financial institutions (FinTechs – BigTechs) that contain their data and/or infrastructure. Services with these programs represent a new data and finance feature that changes the way products are offered, and the way customers use traditional financial services (Szpringer, 2020). According to estimates by Allied Market Research, the global BaaS market in 2030 will be worth US$11.34 billion (Pramod et al., 2021). An example of an entity that wants to be a European BaaS leader is the licensed Aion Bank and technology company Vodeno. Thanks to the cooperation with Aion Bank and Vodeno, companies can offer banking under their own brand. The point is for financial products to meet the needs of customers in the here and now, and for the end-user experience to be as good as possible.

4.3 Embedded Banking

Undoubtedly, a key turning point in BaaS over the past few years has been the sharp increase in the use of financial tools by companies in the non-financial sector – embedded finance (EmFi). With BaaS, EmFi enables any company to integrate banking or FinTech software directly into their products, mobile applications or online resources without redirecting users to third-party portals. The first obvious result of the proliferation of EmFi was the rapid spread of BNPL schemes that provide consumer credit directly at the point of sale. EmFi is still gaining momentum as it allows the provision of additional services to clients without significant investment in the development of FinTech. At the same time, every company on the market can effectively integrate payment, transfer, insurance and loan services in its own products in an accelerated manner.

EB refers to the offering of additional services or products (banking, payment, insurance) by companies that have not been involved in financial activities so far, such as Starbucks and Uber. Such companies very often closely cooperate with FinTech companies that help them to provide these additional services desired by customers (for instance, related to making or splitting payments). The introduction of financial services allows traders to create a new source of income. Collecting multiple services in one application or on one website improves customer experience and increases customer loyalty to a specific brand. EmFi is based on the phenomenon of unbundling, that is, defragmentation of a standard financial service into prime factors and offering it via API by specialized entities in new user interfaces and business contexts. Providers of payments, bank accounts and currency conversion services are created, which "supply" other entities; for example, Revolut uses this model of operation. They are called neobanks or challenger banks. In this model the finance is embedded in another context – a checkout line, a mobile app, etcetera. From the consumer perspective, it could be summarized as "invisible payments" or "invisible finance", because the key message is that the financial transaction becomes naturally integrated into what you are doing to the point it feels invisible. EmFi is different because it enables companies across industries, with existing audiences, to cater to their customers' financial needs at the point of context. It is an enabler of new revenue streams, stronger customer engagement and better visibility and access to key pieces of data. Most importantly, it equips technology companies, brands and retailers with the ability to provide a banking and payments experience to their customers in a seamless, convenient and authentic way, by providing financial services when they need it most, naturally integrated into the experience (Sieber & Guibaud, 2022).

This trend will allow financial services to be provided in new contexts. It will enable new entities (like technology companies) to enter the financial industry. It will also enable new startups offering niche solutions to quickly enter the market (through rebundling – submitting new broad financial services from multiple API providers; see Figure 4.1). The four dominant areas of embedded finance are: payments, lending, banking and insurance.

The expansion of financial services beyond their traditional providers will certainly not only make it easier to reach diverse target groups but will also translate into better meeting their specific needs "here and now". Over time, the importance of direct access channels to banking services, such as online banking, will decrease in favor of services embedded in common processes carried out by clients. Examples of EB are online payments (embedded payments), consumer lending (embedded lending), insurance (embedded insurance) and wealth management (embedded investments). The largest usage of EmFi today is for payments, such as making it possible for e-commerce companies to perform payments on their sites without entering bank details.

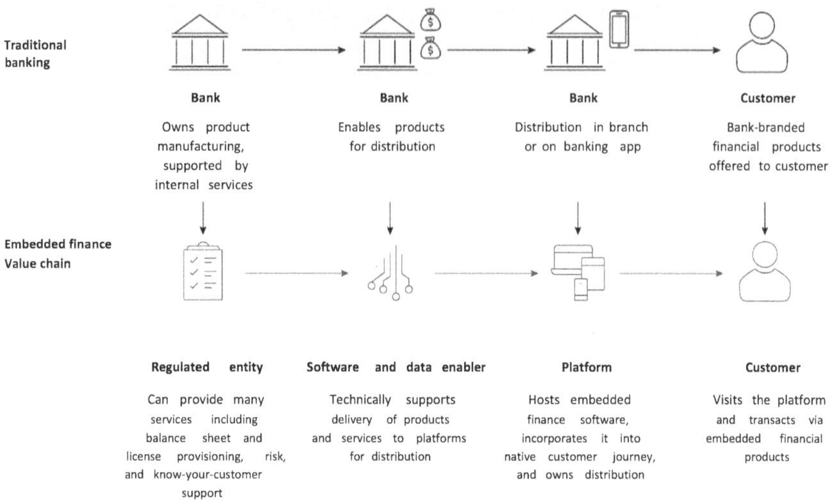

Figure 4.1 Embedded Finance Is Unbundling the Traditional Banking Value Chain

Source: Harris et al. (2022).

The EmFi finance ecosystem consists of:

1 **Providers:** a financial service-providing suite will plug products, tools and services into the platforms. These providers offer exquisite FinTech development and management services through various products, tools and services.
2 **Enablers:** use technologies and platforms to make an existing system easier to use or improve. BaaS companies rent out their core banking platform to ensure multiple FinTech services and apps. Enablers, based on the API interfaces used in OB, enable the integration of the distributor's systems, that is, entities offering its clients dedicated financial products and the bank providing the BaaS service. This creates a unique experience for the end customer, who purchases in one application without being aware that other entities are behind the financial solutions.
3 **Consumers:** end user of the financial product delivered through the BaaS ecosystem. They like access to financial services through a variety of channels. The channels include web, mobile and point-of-sale. Containers establish a link between the financial institution and customer data, thereby creating a platform for users to access end-to-end financial services.
4 **Distributors** (also referred to as **Embedders**): organizations that embed banking services directly into their existing customer journeys for retail or corporate customers. Examples include retailers and e-commerce businesses, which, by promoting their own brand, increase customer loyalty and conversion rate, as well as reduce costs, because building an appropriate value chain on their own would be much more expensive.

The technology benefits the financial institution and the non-bank partner. Financial institutions can extend their reach into new markets while realizing a lower cost of customer or member acquisition. Deposits may also increase, as new consumers and businesses access your brand. Additionally, financial institutions gain new opportunities to cross-sell and engage with existing customers. The non-bank partner wins by offering invaluable convenience to those using its software. When the partner creates a seamless transition to financial services, its users can complete financial transactions at the point of need and, as a result, retain better control of their finances (American Banker, 2022).

Many statistics prove that the market for EmFi is a skyscraping market. A strong indicator for this is the prognosis of the market value of EmFi companies in the segments of payments, lending and insurance for the year 2030, which is estimated to be higher than the current valuation of all FinTech and global top 30 bank and insurance companies combined. Additionally, the estimation of the market size is also seen large and fast-growing with US$65 billion in 2022 and an expectation of US$183 billion in 2027, which means a 182% market growth within five years (Tetnowski, 2022). A reason for this is seen in the increasing availability of APIs from financial service providers as key enablers of EmFi (Figure 4.2).

The market size of the new FinTech trend EmFi has grown rapidly in recent years, despite it being such a young concept. Its widespread adoption has disrupted the role of traditional banks and many non-financial businesses are planning to offer EmFi services within the near future. The worldwide value of venture capital investments in EmFi reached almost US$4.2 billion as of September 2021, which is more than double the investment value during the whole previous year. The EmFi market is expected to grow heavily, especially for payments where the market value in the United States is expected to experience a nearly ninefold increase by 2025 compared to the value in 2020. The most offered EmFi service among European non-financial companies as

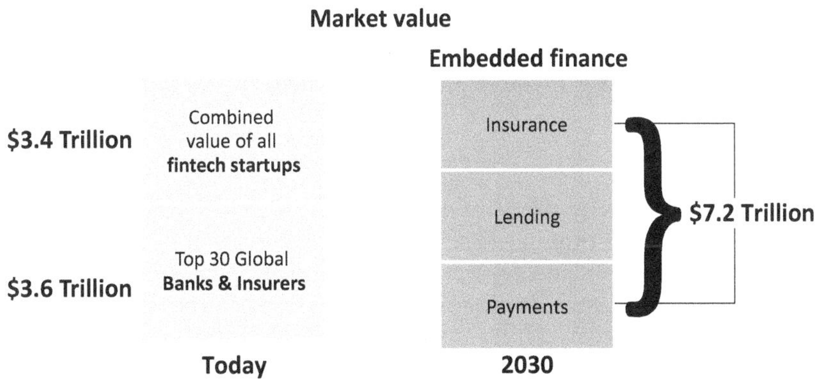

Figure 4.2 Valuation of Embedded Finance Companies

Source: Own elaboration based on Chiavarini (2022).

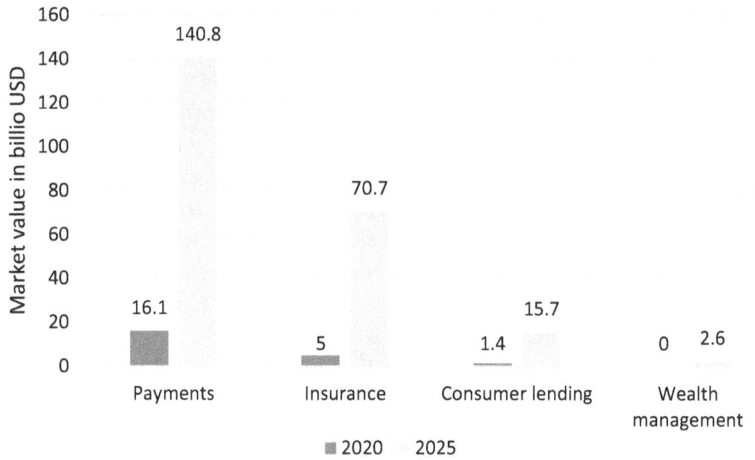

Figure 4.3 Market Value of the EmFi in the United States in 2020, Forecast for 2025 (US$ Billion)

Source: Statista (2022a).

of 2021 was EB. Many European firms also plan to offer EB and embedded payments within the next five years. In the United States, the revenue generated by EmFi in 2020 was estimated at US$22.5 billion and was forecast to reach over US$230 billion by 2025 (Statista, 2022a). The largest share is, and according to forecasts, payments (approximately 60–70%), followed by insurance (approximately 6–7%; Figure 4.3).

Growing interest in EmFi is translating into predictions of rapid adoption. Although forecasts vary, annual growth of more than 40%, in flows of EmFi over the next few years, is around the middle of the range we see. The early leaders in EmFi tend to be digital-native challengers – FinTechs, many of which have historically faced less regulatory scrutiny than banks. The areas in which they have achieved the greatest scale – payments and BNPL – provide a map of where EmFi has advanced furthest to date.

4.4 Relations Between Embedded Banking and BaaS

EmFi is simply the integration of financial services into the service or product of a non-financial institution. EmFi is about enabling non-financial services companies to provide financial services to customers. EmFi involves embedding financial services as an add-on service into the business processes of non-financial institutions. It allows customers to access financial services in a non-financial service shop, such as in a grocery store, a car dealership, a hospital or within a non-financial app. In banking, EmFi enables non-financial services companies to provide banking services. This is possible by using BaaS and API-driven banking and payments services to integrate banking services within a non-financial environment and ecosystem (Peterson & Ozilli, 2023).

To meet the rising demand for EmFi, financial institutions are increasingly offering BaaS – bundled offerings, often white-labeled or cobranded services, that nonbanks can use to serve their customers. Making it work will require new technologies and capabilities, because BaaS is usually distributed to clients via APIs and requires strong risk and compliance management of the EmFi partner. FinTechs offering to intermediate BaaS relationships also have emerged. Banks will also need new business models, such as pay-for-use monetization, B2B2C and B2B2B distribution capabilities, and a careful consideration of branding. EmFi is the incorporation of financial solutions into the offer of various entities that have contact with the final customer, who is their recipient. In this approach, financial products appear under the white label of the seller–distributor, who operates as a commercial network or digital platform with a diverse range of products and services. Offering these services, however, requires a market regulator's license, which enables the customer to be verified as required by law (including KYC, AML, compliance). Therefore, it can be carried out by banks by lending their operational facilities, that is, providing a service BaaS. They can also be suppliers of financial products, but this requires technological advancement, for example, in the form of cloud banking. Therefore, banks in fully digital and FinTech usually have only a payment license or use a license from another operator. If the software platform as a SaaS service wants its customers to be able to take stock credits in the admin panel, it selects the BaaS provider. When it implements BaaS in the administration panel, this will result in EmFi.

The rapid growth in demand for EmFi is reflected in the dynamics of venture capital funds' investments in startups that develop appropriate solutions in this area for various market sectors. According to Dealroom (2022), they exceeded US$11 billion in 2021 and were several times higher than the year before. Investors spent US$6.1 billion on the integration of banking (BaaS) solutions, US$1.5 billion in payments, and US$0.8 billion in insurance. The largest pool of funds, almost half, went to startups offering integrated financial solutions for the retail and e-commerce sector – 17% out of a total of US$11.4 billion received technology companies cooperating with the health and fitness insurance industry (financial solutions integrated with the applications of the respective companies; Figure 4.4).

The share of venture capital funding for FinTechs that is flowing into EmFi is also growing. In 2018, the share was 0.8%, but by 2021, that had quadrupled to 3.2%, thanks in part to the boost e-commerce received during the pandemic. And although FinTechs currently dominate the conversation about embedded finance, banks are starting to engage, particularly in retail BNPL, while in the commercial space, payments, cash management and working capital propositions are also emerging. This trend will gather pace as banks build out their embedded finance capabilities and broaden the range of services they can integrate into other companies' propositions. 2030 embedded insurance, lending and payment is expected to grow to US$7.2 trillion (Chiavarini, 2022).

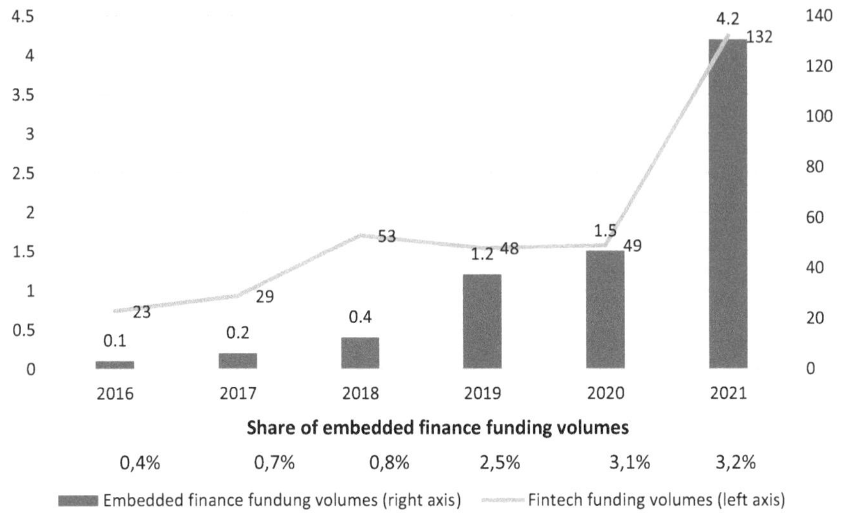

Figure 4.4 Venture Capital Investment Volumes in EmFi and FinTech (2016–2021, US$ bn)

Source: Venture capital investments in embedded finance 2016–2021 (2022).

4.5 EB and BaaS: Opportunity and Risk for Traditional Banks

With EmFi, the financial business model has shifted to a platform-based model. The power of customer connect is shifting from banks to the brands offering embedded services. This presents a challenge for traditional banks. How can they adapt to survive the ever-evolving financial landscape? Banks will now have to shift their focus and rethink BaaS. They will need to be ready to take on new roles and expand into non-banking abilities. Goldman Sachs, for instance, is embracing the BaaS explosion, having recently launched Transaction Banking-as-a-Service. New offerings and partnerships will take the financial ecosystem by storm, a key partnership being one with FinTechs (Netscribes, 2022).

Each financial institution needs to decide on the exact role it will play in the EmFi model. Generally, financial institutions have a role to play in API integration. An API is a code used to share information between two systems (Ozili, 2022a). The next step for EB adoption is a phase of tech-enabled mass adoption of BaaS, which means that more big brands will enter the market and take market share away from incumbent banks and neobanks. They will combine data through AI and machine learning (ML) and will extend their reach by developing very customized services and products (Omarini, 2021). EB is a part of Banking 5.0 (Nicoletti, 2021). The risk for banks and insurers connected with EB is losing control of the customer relationship and becoming more of a supplier of commoditized services. But there is also a huge opportunity to improve the distribution of the services and expand the addressable market (Figure 4.5).

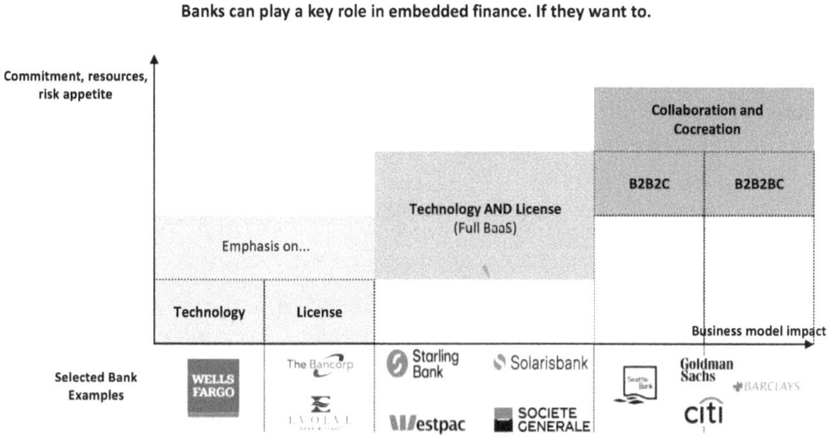

Figure 4.5 The Influence of Embedded Finance on Banking Business Models

Source: Chiavarini (2022). Dealroom The rise of embedded finance.

For traditional banks, involvement in EmFi solutions, and, in their case, BaaS, is both an opportunity and a threat (Bareisis & Greer, 2021). The opportunity is access to new customer segments, generating commission income thanks to concluded partnership agreements, and a significant reduction in customer acquisition costs, which for e-commerce channels are even four times lower than in the case of a bank. These conditions may have a positive impact on stock market valuations. Risks, on the other hand, arise from the risks associated with entering new unrecognized market segments. Therefore, it may be difficult to predict their profitability, as well as the loss of direct contact with the client and the lack of access to some of the data about him or her, which are obtained by the beneficiaries of BaaS solutions, that is, e-commerce platforms. The possibility of innovative activities may also be limited. The risk for traditional banking players is also not taking any action in the field of EmFi, because when they start operating with the customer experience in the background, acquiring new ones will become more difficult, and losing the existing ones may gain momentum. At the same time, banks encounter technological difficulties related to connecting their APIs with cloud-based platforms, and these investments only start to pay off after 2–3 years. 27% of the banks surveyed in The Economist Impact Survey (2022) only claimed that they had the right tools to implement new digital products and services, and an additional barrier was the proper understanding of the needs of customers in new market segments.

There are four ways through which EmFi can change how financial and non-financial companies do business in an era of embedded financial services (Ozili, 2022b):

- Rearranging relationships between financial providers and businesses.
- Creating new revenue streams for financial and non-financial companies.

- Creating new forms of competition in financial services and other industries.
- Launching new partnerships among financial providers on behalf of businesses and providing them with the know-how to benefit from EmFi without hiring teams of software developers and compliance experts.

In the future, EmFi will continue to pivot customer centricity around three vectors (Chandra, 2022):

1. Higher customer lifetime-value – embedment of derived structured financial products into elevated customer journeys, increasing customer value-add and lifetime value, while lowering churn.
2. Lower acquisition cost – with growing addressable market combined with context-aware offerings, firms will lower customer acquisition costs, thus boosting profits.
3. Richer consumer interlinkage spearheaded by emerging technologies – hybrid cloud-based platforms for managing Premium APIs and integrated with third-party partners and service providers.

Financial technology has evolved to a level where online banks and BaaS are challenging incumbents and the nature of banking mediation. Banking is rapidly transforming because of changes in such technology (Broby 2021).

4.6 Embedded Banking: Chance or Dangerous for Consumers; the Example of BNPL

The pandemic period fastened the development of e-commerce and buying services on-line. In order to streamline the purchasing process and increase the value of a single customer basket, as well as reduce the scale of the so-called abandoned carts, online merchants began to offer the BNPL payment service associated with a free payment deferral for a specified period, after which the customer could use a paid consumer loan. The consumer credit provider can be the merchant himself, bank/neobank cooperating with him e.g., Allegro Pay and Aion Bank in Poland, or PayTechs such as Klarna, Twisto, and Paypal.

BNPL is a type of short-term financing that allows consumers to make purchases and pay for them at a future date, often interest free. Also referred to as "point of sale installment loans," BNPL arrangements are becoming an increasingly popular payment option, especially when shopping online. Using BNPL financing can be convenient for consumers, but there are some potential downsides to consider (Lake, 2022; Table 4.1).

In BNPL payment and credit services are embedded in the purchase process and the customer does not have to switch to other pages – purchase and payment are integrated on the merchant's platform. It should be noted that

Table 4.1 The Pros and Cons of BNPL for Consumers

Pros (Advantages)	*Cons (Disadvantages)*
Convenient, disciplined way to pay for purchases over time.	Payments can be hard to track.
Frequently zero-interest or lower interest than credit cards.	Missing or late payments result in late fees/damage credit score.
Good credit/high credit score not necessary to qualify. Fast approval.	No rewards or cash back earned on purchases.
	Payments may continue even if item is returned

Source: Lake (2022).

currently the BNPL service is starting to be offered by traditional banks, and in the post-pandemic period it is starting to be offered in stationary sales. It is a convenient, safe, and cheap solution for the customer, who can thus defer payment for goods or services for up to several months. In fact, when using BNPL, the average basket value increases compared to traditional payment methods, which is beneficial for merchants because it increases their turnover. However, especially for young people, the use of several BNPLs at the same time may lead to excessive indebtedness and, consequently, failure to pay for goods/services within the prescribed period. In this way, young people worsen their credit history and credit scoring for many years, excluding themselves from access to bank loans. As empirical research shows emerging point-of-sale lending firms, and particularly those in the rapidly growing "Buy Now, Pay Later" space, are driving students toward risky loan products (Center 2022). BNPL arrangements have rapidly emerged as a short-term debt option, and like other innovative and disruptive FinTech, challenge existing regulation. BNPL arrangements avoided prescribed "responsible lending" legislative obligations, which applied to similar short-term credit products. So, attention should also be paid to the regulation gap – lack of regulation or insufficient regulation of BNPL, which may mean a violation of consumer interests. Therefore, it is important to include them in the new regulations under the new Consumer Credit Directive (CCD2). Instead, BNPL relies on "responsible spending" in providing a potentially cheaper option than alternatives such as credit cards (Gerrans et al., 2022). The average amount of this first BNPL service is many times smaller than a traditional loan obligation. Therefore, BNPL provided by loan companies is a product that meets completely different needs than an ordinary non-bank loan. BNPL is mainly used to finance e-commerce: clothing and footwear, small household appliances, health and beauty, entertainment, and household goods. There are also differences in the use of BNPL by generations – it is most popular among Gen Z and Millennials and the least popular among Baby Boomers (see Figure 4.6).

The sewn credit service is not treated by them as a typical credit obligation, such as in a bank, which means that consumers may make ill-considered or

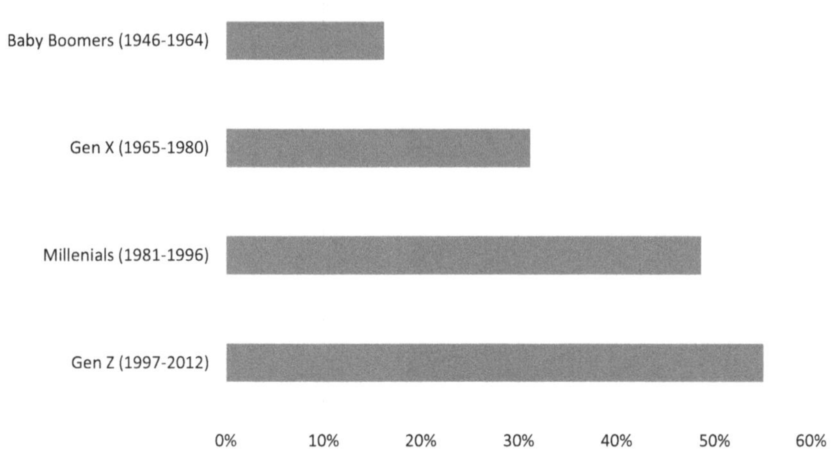

Figure 4.6 US BNPL Use Penetration by Generations as % of Digital Buyers* (July 2022)

Source: Lebow (2022).

Note: * ages 14+; internet users who has accessed a BNPL account digitally and have made a payment toward a purchase at least once in the past year; includes purchases of goods and services.

impulsive purchasing decisions. It is equally important to report customers' BNPL debts to credit reference agencies so that banks, lending institutions and other consumer credit providers can see all customer debt and monitor timely repayment.

According to GlobalData global buy now, pay later (BNPL) transactions are predicted to increase by over 450 billion US$ between 2021 and 2026 from 120 million US$ to 576 billion US$. This would mean a further acceleration of what was seen between 2019 and 2021 – when the alternative payment method increased by almost 400%.

There is geographical variation in the use of BNPL services in e-commerce (Figure 4.7).

In 2021, eight out of the ten leading global BNPL markets worldwide were in northwestern Europe as consumers sought new e-commerce payment methods. The market share of BNPL services in domestic e-commerce payments in both Sweden and Germany, for instance, was around ten times higher than the same market share in global e-commerce payments. This is likely due to the popularity of Sweden's BNPL provider Klarna, one of the most used online payment methods among German consumers in 2020. Klarna has implemented the topic "Embedded Finance" excellently and is constantly developing into an e-commerce platform with payment options (Locher & Mesch, 2022).

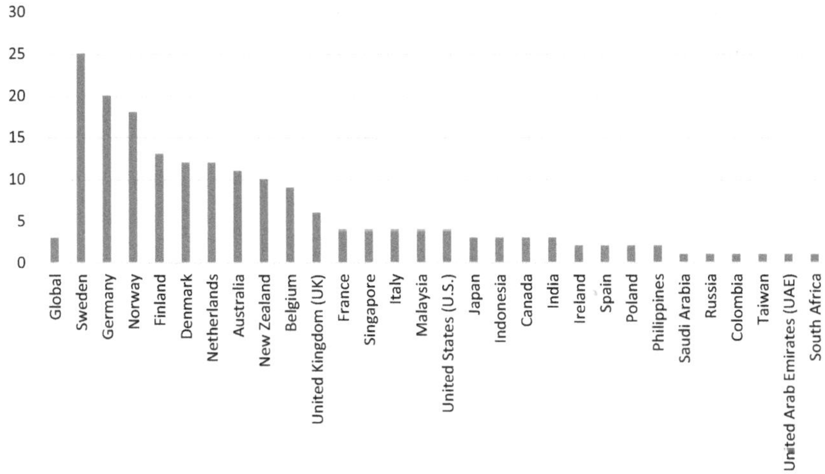

Figure 4.7 Market Share of Buy-Now-Pay-Later (BNPL) in Domestic E-commerce Payments in % (2021)

Source: Statista (2022b).

4.7 Conclusion

This chapter sought to identify the opportunities and threats of EB and BaaS for traditional banks and consumers. Traditional banks need to adapt these modern solutions to compete with non-bank players, such as FinTech and BigTech firms. For consumers, EB and BaaS services mean convenience, time savings, security, and financial benefits, but also risks related to insufficient consumer protection, insufficient regulation, and the risk of falling into a debt spiral at a young age. Therefore, regulations should consider various stakeholders – financial institutions, consumers, financial supervision and the regulator. The EB model allows financial institutions, banks, insurance companies, to distribute their products more cost-effectively and broadly, but also requires them to surrender control over customer relations to non-financial companies. EmFi permits the integration of loans, insurance, debit cards, savings and investment instruments in the platform or process of a non-finance company, organization, or institution (Ozili, 2022a). The essence of built-in finance is that it improves financial processes. Before the development of EmFi, there was usually a gap between the consumer and the company they were using. The consumer often needed a traditional financial service provider such as a bank to fill this gap. Thanks to the built-in financing, this external bank or insurance company has disappeared from the customer's perspective. Built-in financial firms have found a way to act as a bridge between themselves and the consumer. Built-in finance is the introduction of financial services to non-financial platforms – technologies, software, operating mechanisms – with the intention of offering customers financial products directly at the source. Customers are looking for holistic experiences, facilitated by an integrated ecosystem of people, products, and financial offerings on a single platform. Along with the development of the FinTech sector, there was an exponential increase in technology adaptation. However, several factors, including regulators, restrict banks from offering innovative, customer-friendly payment and loan services. Therefore, BaaS has become the most profitable solution. Directives, such as PSD2 and OB, popularized the development and use of API interfaces. Companies have modernized IT and BaaS to up-sell and cross-sell their product range. Companies are looking for ways to exceed traditional revenue streams and increase profits based on targeted offerings and payment experiences. The digital experience has now become paramount, and non-financial players want to offer EmFi as part of their product module. Working with exclusive brands that can boast brand loyalty has become the ideal platform for banks to reach Generation X.

References

Alt, R., Huch, S. (2022). *FinTech Dictionary. Terminology for the Digitalized Financial World*. Springer, Cham, Switzerland.

American Banker (2022). *Embedded Banking: An Opportunity for Financial Institutions of All Sizes*, September 1.

Bareisis, Z., Greer S. (2021). *Demystifying Embedded Finance: Promise and Peril for Banks*. Celent. https://www.celent.com/insights/320916338

Broby, D. (2021). Financial technology and the future of banking. *Financial Innovations*, 7, 47. https://doi.org/10.1186/s40854-021-00264

Center (2022). Student Borrower Protection, Point of Fail: How a Flood of "Buy Now, Pay Later" Student Debt Is Putting Millions at Risk (November 2, 2022). Student Borrower Protection Center Research Paper. Available at SSRN: https://ssrn.com/abstract=4265276 (accessed 5.01.2023).

Chandra, A. (2022), Embedded finance: Amplifying consumer experience via banking-as-a-service. *Financial Express*, October 11.

Chiavarini, L. (2022), Dealroom talks: The rise of embedded finance. Dealroom The rise of embedded finance. https://dealroom.co/uploaded/2022/03/Dealroom-embedded-finance-v2-.pdf?x15144

Ciesielski, M. (2020), BaaS — Banking without a license. *Obserwator Finansowy*. https://www.obserwatorfinansowy.pl/in-english/financial-markets/baas-banking-without-a-license/ (accessed 3.01.2023).

Cowley, A., Malani, N. (2021) Banking as a service explained: What is it, Why it's important and how to play. *Deloitte Digital*. https://www2.deloitte.com/content/dam/Deloitte/cn/Documents/financial-services/deloitte-cn-fsi-importance-of-banking-as-a-service-en-211019.pdf (accessed 2.01.2023).

Diamond, S., Drury, S., Lipp S., Marshall, A., Ramamurthy, S., Wagle, L. (2019). The future of banking in the platform economy. *Strategy & Leadership*, 47, 6, 34–42. https://doi.org/10.1108/SL-09-2019-0139

Gerrans, P., Baur, D.G., Lavagna-Slater, S. (2022). Fintech and responsibility: Buy-now-pay-later arrangements. *Australian Journal of Management*, 47, 3, 474–502. https://doi.org/10.1177/03128962211032448.

Grigorieva, E.M. (2022). The impact of digitalization on the introduction of innovations into BFSI activities. In D.B. Vukovic, M. Maiti, E.M. Grigorieva (Eds.), *Digitalization and the Future of Financial Services. Contributions to Finance and Accounting* (pp. 121–140). Springer, Cham, Switzerland.

Harris, M., Davis, A., Adams, B., Tijssen, T. (2022). Embedded finance: What it takes to prosper in the new value chain, September 12. https://www.bain.com/insights/embedded-finance (accessed 15.11.2022).

Honecker, F., Chalmers, D. (2022). Fintech for financial inclusion. In H.Y. Chen, P. Jenweeranon, N. Alam (Eds.), *Global Perspectives in FinTech*. Palgrave Macmillan, Cham. https://doi.org/10.1007/978-3-031-11954-5_8

Lake, R. (2022). *Buy Now, Pay Later (BNPL): What It Is, How It Works, Pros & Cons.* https://www.investopedia.com/buy-now-pay-later-5182291 (accessed 4.01.2023).

Lebow, S. (2022). *Gen Z Buys into Buy Now, Pay Later*. Insider Intelligence. https://www.insiderintelligence.com/content/gen-z-buy-now-pay-later

Locher, C., Mesch, S. (2022). Digitale Transformation im Consumer Banking durch FinTech. In J. Hoffman (Ed.), *Digitalisierung in Industrie-, Handels- und Dienstleistungsunternehmen*. Springer. https://doi.org/10.1007/978-3-658-35950-8_25

Moro-Visconti, R. (2021). *Startup Valuation, From Strategic Business Planning to Digital Networking*. Palgrave Macmillan Cham. https://doi.org/10.1007/978-3-030-71608-0

Netscribes (2022). *Embedded Finance and Its Impact on the Financial Services Industry*, July 11. https://www.netscribes.com/embedded-finance/

Nicoletti, B. (2021). *Banking 5.0. How FinTech Will Change Traditional Banks in the 'New Normal' Post Pandemic. Palgrave Studies in Financial Services Technology*. Palgrave Macmillan, Cham, Switzerland. https://doi.org/10.1007/978-3-030-75871-4_7

Omarini, A. (2021). *FinTech and Regulation: From Start to Boost — A New Framework in the Financial Services Industry. Where Is the Market Going? Too Early to Say*. In T. King, F.S. Stentella Lopes, A. Srivastav, J. Williams (Eds.), *Disruptive Technology in Banking and Finance: An International Perspective on FinTech.* Palgrave Studies in Financial Services Technology. Palgrave Macmillan. https://doi.org/10.1007/978-3-030-81835-7_9

Ozili, P.K. (2022a). Embedded finance: Assessing the benefits, use case, challenges and interest over time. *Journal of Internet and Digital Economics*, 2, 2, 108–123. https://doi.org/10.1108/JIDE-05-2022-0014

Ozili, P.K. (2022b). Assessing global interest in decentralized finance, embedded finance, open finance, ocean finance and sustainable finance. *Asian Journal of Economics and Banking*. https://doi.org/10.1108/AJEB-03-2022-0029

Peterson, K., Ozili, P.K. (2023). Digital finance research and developments around the world: A literature review. *International Journal of Business Forecasting and Marketing Intelligence*, 8, 1, 35–51. https://doi.org/10.1504/IJBFMI.2022.10049390

Pramod, B., Shadaab, K., Vineet, K. (2021). *Banking-as-a-Service Market*. https://www.alliedmarketresearch.com/request-sample/14627 (accessed 12.11.2022).

PSD2 (2015). Directive (EU) 2015/2366 of the European Parliament and of the Council of 25 November 2015 on payment services in the internal market, amending Directives 2002/65/EC, 2009/110/EC and 2013/36/EU and Regulation (EU) No 1093/2010, and repealing Directive 2007/64/EC, Official Journal of the European Union L 337/35.

Sieber, S., Guibaud, S. (2022). *Embedded Finance: When Payments Become An Experience*. Wiley.
Statista (2022a). *Embedded Finance – Statistics & Facts*.
Statista (2022b). *Buy Now, Pay Later (BNPL) - Statistics & Facts*.
Szpringer, W. (2020). *Digital Platforms and the Sharing Economy*. Poltext.
Tetnowski, D. (2021). *Embedded Finance: Key Trends, Segment Analysis & Market Forecasts 2022–2027*, Juniper Research.
The Economist Impact Survey Group (2022). *Threat Assessment 2022: Digital Competition in Global Finance*. https://impact.economist.com/projects/digital-competition-in-global-finance/digital-competition-in-finance/
Venture Capital Investments in Embedded Finance 2016–2021 (2022). Statista Research Department, May 31, 2022.

5 Financial Inclusion

Is Financial Technology the Solution?

Danilo Abis and Patrizia Pia

5.1 Introduction

Whereas the relationship between technology and finance began a long time ago, it is in the last fifteen years that Financial Technology, or FinTech, has initiated and rapidly accelerated its development thereby starting a new FinTech phase (Arner et al., 2015). After the 2008 global financial crisis (GFC), an increasing number of new digital firms[1] started to use technology to provide financial services directly to customers, bypassing the traditional intermediation channels and changing the market structure for financial services. Not only has technology reduced the cost of financial intermediation and increased competition (Philippon, 2019). The presence of FinTech and BigTech firms in financial services is growing rapidly, especially in emerging markets and developing economies (Croxson et al., 2022).

Financial innovation aims to reduce search costs associated with matching transacting parties, achieve economies of scale, acquire cheaper and more secure information and reduce verification costs (Thakor, 2020). We are witnessing a potentially disruptive phenomenon involving new players (i.e., FinTech firms and BigTech firms), incumbent firms like banks, and regulators. For the banking system, financial technology is a major challenge to which banks have responded by starting their own innovation process whereby they develop in-house financial technologies services and/or acquire FinTech firms (Williams, 2021). Technology is not only changing people's perception and behaviour towards financial services but also ensuring access for those excluded from traditional channels of finance (Tok and Heng, 2022) by becoming a key enabler of financial inclusion and reducer of income inequalities (Demir et al., 2020).

The COVID-19 pandemic has accelerated the spread of digital financial services, changing the way people access the world of finance. Appaya (2021) states:

> FinTech can democratize access to finance and the world can move closer to achieving financial inclusion.

DOI: 10.4324/9781003340454-5

Sahay et al. (2020, p. 1) provide two anecdotes, which are useful to understand FinTech's contribution to individuals' daily lives and its effect in increasing participation in the financial system:

> Somewhere remote in a low-income country, in the early hours of the morning, a woman wakes up and dials her cell phone. She is borrowing a very small amount of money digitally to buy vegetables in the local market. During the day, she will sell her inventory in her shop located in the outskirts of the town. Some customers will pay her using their mobile wallet, others with cash. She will transfer the cash onto her phone at the shop next door, where the merchant is also a mobile money agent. At the end of the day, she will be able to pay back her loan and keep her profit in her mobile wallet. She can use this mobile money to pay for the gas she uses to cook dinner, as the utility company has recently connected its payment system to the mobile money infrastructure.
>
> Somewhere central in a rich country, just a few weeks before the winter holiday season, a machine in a chocolate factory breaks down. Without a new device, the profits during the busiest part of the year will vanish. The owner tries frantically to obtain credit from his bank to replace his machine. Even though the factory has operated for several years and has a profitable track record, the bank is just too busy for this small client and schedules an appointment in the new year—way too late. A few years ago, this could have been the end of the business. But a friend told him about an online lender. Within a week, the online lender had assessed the creditworthiness, approved the loan, and disbursed the money. The machine was delivered just in time—two weeks before Christmas.[2]

The Word Bank claims that financial inclusion means that individuals and businesses have access to useful and affordable financial products and services that meet their needs – transactions, payments, savings, credit and insurance – delivered in a responsible and sustainable way.[3] According to The Global Findex Database 2021, 71% of adults in developing economies have a formal financial account compared to 42% in 2011. Moreover, the gap in access to finance between men and women in developing economies has fallen from 9 percentage points to 6 percentage points.

Financial inclusion plays a crucial role in achieving Sustainable Development Goals (SDG) and is considered by the World Bank as a *key enabler to reducing poverty and boosting prosperity*.[4] Despite the progress made over the past decade, in developing economies the number of unbanked remains high in and access to credit access too low (Demirgüç-Kunt et al., 2022).[5]

How FinTech can increase financial inclusion is very topical and involves academia, governments and institutions. Financial inclusion become a key policy goal also for Central Banks and, in some cases, it is one of the explicit aims of their mandate (Auer et al., 2022). For these reasons, it is crucial to develop a financial inclusion measure and a monitoring system.

5.2 How to Measure Financial Inclusion: The Challenge of the FinTech Era

Measuring financial inclusion is very challenging. The rapid technological evolution makes it complex to establish a measurement methodology capable of representing reality and being able to adapt to continuous changes. Whilst some studies have sought to build financial inclusion indices (e.g., Chakravarty and Pal 2010; Sarma 2012) there is not an official methodology to measure financial inclusion. Some studies focus mainly on supply-side aggregate data yet this approach could generate biased results.

Camàra and Tuesta (2017) have developed a composite index that measures the extent of financial inclusion at country level, which accounts for both demand and supply side. To better understand what we are referring to when we talk about financial inclusion and the potential contribution of financial technologies, it may be useful to better specify what are the determinants that have been identified to build the index. The Financial Inclusion Index (FII) is determined by three dimensions: usage, barriers and access.[6] Inclusive financial systems maximise usage and access while minimise the barriers that cause involuntary exclusion.

1 The *usage* dimension refers to the use of different financial products. The FII considers the owners of accounts in financial institutions, and the individuals who save money or have a loan in the formal financial system.
2 The *barriers* to financial inclusion are all the obstacles that prevent unbanked individuals from using formal financial services. Barriers can be analysed from a demand perspective or a supply perspective. In the first case, a voluntary financial exclusion could be related to cultural reasons, a lack of money or the lack of perceived benefits. The supply perspective considers involuntary exclusion, which may be determined by physical barriers, such as distance from bank branches, a lack of necessary documents and an inadequacy of supplied products.[7]
3 *Access* refers to the possibility that individuals use formal financial services. In the FII, this dimension is measured by looking at access points, say, the numbers of bank branches, agents and automated teller machines (ATMs) per 100,000 adults.

Usage, barriers and access have been measured mainly looking at traditional financial systems. It can be expected that financial technologies services may contribute to improve all three dimensions.

Càmara and Tuesta (2017) show that access is the most important dimension. However, they focused on physical access points and did not consider the new technologies. Nowadays, both FinTech firms and incumbents can provide platform-based services, which could potentially improve the use of financial products. Furthermore, Càmara and Tuesta (2017) show that, according to the Global Findex dataset, the distance from access points is one of the biggest obstacles to owning a bank account especially in less-developed countries.[8] Proponents claim that FinTech firms can break down this type of barrier to become the first point of contact for financial services (Boot et al., 2021). Notwithstanding, it is a challenge to find ways to include new technologies in the indicators. Thus, we consider the definition of financial inclusion parameters that are capable of capturing the complex and constantly evolving financial services market is a fundamental task for policymakers.

Despite its global importance, the relationship between FinTech and financial inclusion has not deeply analysed. This is despite plentiful evidence that shows FinTech's positive impact in enhancing financial inclusion. As a caveat, it could be risky to not consider the *dark side* of FinTech. The *dark side* refers to algorithm bias and predatory lending or the risk of exclusion of specific categories, such as youngsters, women and minority groups (Tok and Heng, 2022). Although to date the dimension of the phenomenon is not such as to envisage a systemic crisis, there are potential risks like dominant market positions that regulators must monitor and adapt regulations in accord with the market's evolution (Williams, 2021).

The next sections provide a review of the main studies published in academic journals,[9] to identify the state of the art and most important evidence. We shall consider the potential contributions towards enhancing the three dimensions of the FII by analysing evidence from three sectors: lending, payments and investment.

5.3 FinTech and Financial Inclusion: Evidence from the Financial Services Sector

FinTech firms have penetrated credit markets mainly through innovative delivery channels. For instance, crowdfunding and peer-to-peer (P2P) platforms are widespread across many countries and further growth is expected. The size of the P2P global market is expected to increase from $67.93 billion in 2019 to $558.91 billion by 2027 (Valuates Reports, 2020).

Maskara et al. (2021) investigate the role of P2P platforms in enhancing financial inclusion. They focus on rural areas in the US, known as *"bank deserts"* because of the lack of access to traditional banks. Hence, the population must turn to *Alternative Financial Services (AFS)*, which some call the *"bank for poor"* due to the relationship between banking deserts and poverty. P2P platforms provide a huge opportunity for these populations with P2P lending increasing credit market access and improving financial inclusion for rural communities. The results also confirm that P2P lending enhances financial inclusion in ways different from urban communities by offering an alternative to those less proximate to banks.

Tang (2019) analyses whether P2P lending platforms are substitutes for banks or complements. Using data from Lending Club, the largest online P2P lending platform in the US, Tang has developed a conceptual framework in which the P2P platform can operate both as a substitute for or a complement to banks to predict the impact of negative events on the quantity and quality of P2P loans. Results show that negative shocks in bank credit supply lead to a migration of low-quality bank borrowers to P2P platforms. This result demonstrates that P2P platforms operate as bank substitutes. Nevertheless, the expansion involves mainly *infra-marginal bank borrowers* and consequently the quality P2P borrower pool becomes worse. Tang also shows that P2P platforms can operate as complements by providing small loans. In this scenario, the credit expansion resulting from P2P lending likely occurs only among borrowers who already enjoy access bank credit.

The benefits from adopting digital platforms can be extended to traditional channels. Balyuk (2022) finds that banks increase credit access for consumers who obtain P2P loans with the effect stronger for consumers who face greater credit constraints. One possible explanation is related to the information available. Balyuk shows that behind this mechanism, there is the banks' propensity to update their beliefs about P2P borrowers' credit quality. Furthermore, higher-quality borrowers reduce their bank debt more significantly after P2P loan take-up, which suggests how FinTech firms might generate pricing benefits. Liberti et al. (2022) analyse the crucial rule of information in the lending market. They study the implications of adopting voluntary information-sharing technology for competition and credit access. Their results demonstrate that a borrower's credit increases by 3.2% more than peers after its file has been shared with other lenders. However, access to credit improves only for high-quality borrowers in markets with greater lender adoption. However, asymmetric information is a significant problem that regulators and P2P platforms owners face (Caglayan et al., 2020). Although P2P platforms can improve access to financial resources for the most credit-constrained, the provision of valuable and verifiable information is central for transaction success. This is a big challenge especially for countries where the informal economy prevails.

Netzer et al. (2019) examine over 120,000 loan requests from the online crowdfunding platform Prosper. They show how participants can better assess the risk of default by interpreting and incorporating soft unverifiable data into their analysis. It is thus possible to extract borrowers' future financial behaviour using technology as an alternative to human perception and sensibility. Using data collected from Facebook and Kickstarter, Jin et al. (2020) empirically measure the relationship between crowdfunding projects and social media. The results demonstrate the positive impact of social media activities, for instance, a "like" on Facebook, in terms of project visibility and investment attraction. The impact is more significant during the first period of a crowdfunding campaign when there is an evident quality-signalling effect; a herding effect occurs in the closing period. The impact of social media follows a J-curve over time suggesting that it is beneficial to implement different strategies for each crowdfunding period. Social media may embed information that can be used to predict borrowers' default in P2P lending. Using the loan data of the largest Chinese P2P platform and borrowers' information and activities in their Weibo account (the mirror of Twitter), Ge et al. (2017) show that borrowers who disclose their account information have a significantly lower default probability compared to those who do not. Furthermore, analysis of borrowers' social media account information shows an inverse relation between social media presence (number of friends or number of posts) and the probability of default.

It is interesting to notice how FinTech lenders and borrowers' features may change over time. Di Maggio and Yao (2021) study personal credit markets in the US and show that in the first stage new entrant FinTech firms lend money to *less creditworthy* borrowers and, over time, increase loans to borrowers with higher credit scores. Although the probability of default on FinTech loans is higher than incumbent banks, FinTech possesses superior credit evaluation capabilities, which allows it to better predict default probabilities and extend loans to borrowers denied elsewhere but are good customers. The evidence of the positive correlation between default probability and interest rate suggests an efficient pricing strategy.

In contrast, the results of Fuster et al. (2019) are inconsistent with those already described. They analyse mortgage lending in the US and identify several frictions that characterise this market, including slowness in processing loans, capacity constraints, inefficient refinancing and limited access to finance for borrowers. Next, they study the impact of FinTech to verify if it can reduce these frictions. In terms of financial inclusion, there is no evidence that FinTech lenders target low income and credit history borrowers. FinTech loans, compared with mortgages insured by the Federal Housing Administration (FHA) – the riskier segment of the market which primarily serves lower income borrowers – register a lower default rate which implies that riskier borrowers are not the main target. Despite being seemingly counterintuitive, given their familiarity with technologies, young people prefer face-to-face interaction for first-time mortgages due to their lack of experience and uncertainty surrounding the entire process. In this case, a lower level both of financial experience and literacy significantly impacts borrowers' decisions. The authors also consider the future of the mortgage loans market. They argue that the FinTech model, characterised by online and automatic processes, could be replicated by traditional lenders able to invest in the appropriate technology. However, incumbents may be negatively affected by complex legacy processes and information systems even if the low cost of deposit funding and spread of branches represent a considerable competitive advantage to satisfy consumers with different needs.

Online digital payments are one of the widespread financial technologies solutions. Mobile money services allow individuals to pay, transfer or receive money using a mobile phone. This is a great opportunity for unserved people and low-income countries. Kanga et al. (2021) analyse factors shaping the diffusion of FinTech innovations, in particular ATMs, mobile phones and payments systems and the interaction of diffusion with financial inclusion and living standards. Their empirical analysis shows that the extent of FinTech diffusion increases financial inclusion and living standards. The world's most successful mobile banking innovation is the M-Pesa, in Kenya (see Lashitew et al., 2019). These authors show that successful models need a leading partner who guides the process, such as M-Pesa, but also the presence of a conducive environment like a regulatory system, which facilitates and supports the entire process. Yang and Zhang (2022), using Chinese regional-level data, provide evidence on how Alipay's digital payment technology allows households to fulfil their consumption needs. This is a relevant aspect in terms of *usage* especially for consumers in emerging markets and a country like China where there has been rapid growth in household incomes. However, Yang and Zhang (2022) highlight the potential dark side of digital payment adoption, such as overconsumption, especially in younger segment, which may be too optimistic about their future incomes.

Kabengele and Hahn (2021) investigate which combinations of factors at the level of providers and their interaction with target market institutions are associated with the widespread adoption of mobile money services. They construct a unique dataset of 110 mobile money services in 46 emerging countries that combines publicly available firm and country data. They draw on institutional theory to derive seven conditions that may affect adoption rates of mobile money services. They classify the conditions with reference to the theoretical literature into three broad categories, namely (1) institutional environment, (2) firm-level decisions and (3) firm characteristics. The findings suggest that the adoption of mobile money is determined by various combinations of firm characteristics, decisions and institutional factors.

When we discuss financial inclusion, an individual's investment in the financial market might be considered a secondary aspect. Nevertheless, considering the usage dimension, individuals could need help to manage savings; for instance, tools that hedge against inflation can be very useful for people with limited amounts of money, especially in countries with a high level of average inflation. FinTech represents an opportunity to increase market participation and providing alternatives with lower fees than traditional services. Tan et al. (2021) conducted a case study on Yu'E Bao, a very large Chinese money market fund to study how FinTech may involve the *Grassroots Investment Consumers* and how to empower the *grassroots consumer*. Starting from this case study, Tan et al. (2021) implemented a two-stage theoretical model, shedding light on IT-enabled empowerment strategies for achieving firm success and promoting financial inclusion by removing psychological and physical barriers.

Bertsch et al. (2020) suggest that bank misconduct may have played an economically significant role in facilitating the expansion of FinTech products, services and instruments. They find that the positive association between bank misconduct and the expansion of online lending is robust to the inclusion of county-level bank credit supply shocks. Banks' misconduct may also be a factor that led to the birth and diffusion of robo-advisors, considered one of the most valuable innovations.[10] (Chen et al., 2019). Relatedly, D'Acunto et al. (2019) study a robo-advising tool and show how automatic advice can increase portfolio diversification and market-adjusted volatility. Similarly, Baulkaran and Jain (2022) analyse users of robo-advisors. They find that the majority clients of robo-advisory are small retail investors who invest using both systematic investment plans (SIPs) and one-time lump sum investments. Robo-advisors facilitate market access to mass consumers who seek personalised financial advice at a lower price than traditional financial advice. In addition, the study highlights robo-advisors' positive impact for saving and retirement. Small retail investors, through systematic investment plans (SIPs), can save and invest for retirement also in the absence of employer-sponsored plans. A key factor for the demand for robo advisory is financial literacy. Isaia and Oggero (2022) study the potential demand of robo-advisory among millennials and Generation Z; they show that only individuals with an advanced level of financial literacy are more likely to be potential users of robo-advisors.

5.4 FinTech and Financial Inclusion: The Role of Institutions

As noted, discussion about financial inclusion involves several players. This group of actors includes institutions which play a central role because they can target and promote financial inclusion polices.

Bernards (2019) analyses the application of psychometric credit scoring[11] in retail credit in Zimbabwe and in urban microfinance in India. Results show that stand-alone technology is not able to improve financial inclusion, which is related to several complex factors, such as government decisions or social and economic situations.

Palladino (2019) argues that democratising investment requires public engagement. Given the difficulties experienced by *private crowdfunding platforms* to reach an adequate size to attend to unserved consumers, Palladino proposes the creation of a *public investment platform* to enable small local businesses to access an alternative fundraising channel and permit households to invest through public investment accounts, the amount of which could be related to household worth. The role of state institutions and their interaction with other players is discussed by Gabor and Brooks (2017) who focus on behavioural finance and follow the *"know your irrational client"* vision. Technology enables lenders to map, know and manage riskier populations, which allows technology to "nudge" individual behaviour in desired direction.

Monitoring the evolution of the FinTech ecosystem is necessary also to identify behaviour that can compromise market efficiency. Bollinger and Yao (2018) analyse online microfinance platforms in emerging markets. Platforms utilise local field partners (FPs) to disburse and administer the loans. FPs are lending agencies in the borrowers' country that operate as intermediaries between lenders and borrowers.[12] Using an analytic model, the authors demonstrate that FPs are profit-maximising, and they have an incentive to increase interest rates because much of the default risk is transferred to lenders. Bollinger and Yao (2018) suggest an alternative loan payback method, maintaining the presence of intermediaries, which can minimise moral hazard by removing incentives to increase interest rates.

A controversial phenomenon relates to blockchain and crypto, which have become very popular among investors. The number of firms with the terms blockchain and crypto have increased significantly in the last five years. However, Akyildirim et al. (2020) argue that many firms are trying to take advantage of the popularity of these technologies even though they are not going to adopt cryptocurrency. Despite this practice producing a substantial and persistent stock market premium, the results highlight that the name change directly harmed firms' short-term profitability along with decreasing financial leverage in the following quarter after announcement. The decision to introduce terms like blockchain and crypto seems to be related to the perception by stakeholders rather than fundamental reasons, triggering a *crypto-exuberance* that presents similarities with the Dotcom bubble. A sort of perceived quality may hence be created, which does not necessarily correspond to the real one and might in fact reflect behavioural bias.

Lin and Pursiainen (2021) highlight an interesting bias in the crowdfunding platform Kickstarter. They show that borrowers exhibit a strong round number heuristic[13] when they decide the target amount for the crowdfunding campaign. Nevertheless, results show a negative relation between round number heuristics and crowdfunding performance. Entrepreneurs affected by this heuristic in their crowdfunding campaigns are systematically more likely to fail. The tendency to use cognitive shortcuts suggests the importance of initiatives designed to change individual behaviour.

The role of institutions is important also to build and maintain trust in the financial system. Trust is an important barrier to financial inclusion. The Cambridge Dictionary defines the verb trust as follows: *to believe that someone is good and honest and will not harm you, or something is safe and reliable*. New technology can cause anxiety and when interacting with human-like machine interfaces, such as chatbots or robots, consumers have reported experiencing some form of creepiness.[14] Rajaobelina et al. (2021) examine the antecedents of creepiness and its impact on loyalty when interacting with a chatbot. Their findings show that creepiness directly impacts loyalty in a chatbot context. Luo et al. (2019) also investigate AI chatbots in partnership with a large financial service company. They conduct a randomised experiment on chatbot disclosure in which customers randomly received sales calls from chatbots or human workers. The results show that in response to varying the disclosure of chatbots[15] and humans (proficient or inexperienced), consumers' behaviour changes. More specifically, findings reveal that undisclosed chatbots are as effective as proficient workers and four times more effective than inexperienced workers in engendering customer purchases. However, the disclosure of chatbot machine identity before a conversation reduces purchase rates by over 79.7%. When consumers are conscious of interacting with a machine, they feel uncomfortable, perceiving chatbots less knowledgeable and empathic. Consequently, consumers are brusque and conversations shorter than with human or undisclosed chatbot conversations; furthermore, customers purchase less when they know the conversational partner is not human. These results conform with algorithm aversion (Dietvorst et al., 2015).

Gupta et al. (2021) analyse an aspect of FinTech adoption, namely, the perception and rate of adoption of India's Millennials (Gen Y, Gen Y1 and Gen Y2). The results revealed positive and significant relationships between awareness, adaptability, perceived ease of use and intention towards adoption of FinTech. As awareness about services provided by technology-based financial services organisations increases and if providers can ensure ease of use, then customers will use more of the services. Adaptability is a key factor; it also has been found to have a significant direct association with use. Providing customers with these features ensures they become more comfortable in using alternative financing services. Therefore, the results of this study support the idea that the features offered by technology are another key attraction and shape consumer decisions about FinTech adoption among Indian Millennials. Security concerns also positively influence the intention to adopt FinTech; the trustworthiness of new technologies is important to ensure secured personal information and it is the most important fundamental in designing the financial technology to create consumer assurance on personal data protection.

5.5 Conclusion

This chapter has reviewed the impact of FinTech on financial inclusion. FinTech is constantly growing and providing new solutions for consumers either unserved or underserved by incumbents. A sizeable body of evidence indicates that FinTech improves financial inclusion. Notwithstanding, it might be illusory to consider technology the panacea for financial inclusion. New actors may not target unbanked consumers thereby reducing potential benefits for this segment (Feyen et al., 2021). Huge investments are needed in many areas to create the infrastructure capable of exploiting the potential of the new technology. Technology is rapidly breaking down physical barriers. Furthermore, access to financial markets can be affected by psychological barriers. How people interact with algorithms is a controversial issue and depends on people's perceptions. The are several determinants of financial inclusion in the FinTech era and no official methodology is available to measure it. Indicators capable of capturing the complexity of the phenomenon would be a decisive result for policymakers.

The current FinTech area constitutes a challenge for institutions. Technologies are continuously and rapidly evolving, and it is necessary to monitor and promptly intervene to mitigate potential risks from arising. The dark side of FinTech is an open field that requires further investigation. In sum, FinTech and the new financial technologies already have made a significant contribution to the enhancement of financial inclusion. While it is reasonable to expect further inclusivity in the future, we strongly advise that the realisation of the full benefits of financial inclusion requires also appropriate ecosystem and policy measures.

Notes

1 The number of FinTech start-ups worldwide increased from 12,131 in 2018 to 26,393 in May 2023. (Statista, 2023)
2 A true story played out in the City of London.
3 The World Bank (2022). Financial Inclusion Overview.
4 See endnote 3.
5 24% of adults remain unbanked and about only half of all adults in developing economies can access funds within 30 days to cover an unexpected expense.
6 Dimensions are the results of different indicators. They include demand-side individual indicators for usage and barriers, measured using the World Bank's Global Findex 2011 and 2014, and supply-side country-level indicators for access, using the International Monetary Fund's Financial Access Survey 2015.
7 To measure the barriers' dimension, Càmara and Tuesta consider the supply perspective using the Global Findex questionnaire that measures the perceived barriers by unbanked individuals. Distance is one of the most important reasons.
8 Other reasons include *trust* (% of unbanked not owning a bank account for lack of trust in formal financial systems); *affordability* (% of unbanked not owning a bank account because they perceive them as too expensive); *documents* (% of unbanked not owning a bank account because they perceive they are not able to provide the necessary documentation).
9 We mainly focus on studies published in peer-reviewed journals ranked 3, 4 and 4* by ABS Academic Journal Guide.
10 US Security and Exchange Commission (SEC) describes "robo-adviser" as an automated digital investment advisory program. In most cases, the robo-adviser collects information regarding your financial goals, investment horizon, income and other assets and risk tolerance by asking you to complete an online questionnaire. Based on that information, it creates and manages an investment portfolio for you. Robo-advisers often seek to offer investment advice for lower costs and fees than traditional advisory programs, and in some cases require lower account minimums than traditional investment advisers".
11 See Arráiz et al. (2015) for further details about psychometric credit scoring.
12 Bollinger and Yao (2018) describe seven phases. (1) A borrower requests a loan from FP; (2) The FP provides the terms of the loan (if eligible); (3) The borrower decides whether to accept the terms of the loan; (4) If the loan is granted and accepted, the FP posts the loan on the microfinance platform.; (5) Lenders may choose to lend to the borrower; (6) If the amount of lent money is sufficient to cover the loan amount, the loan is funded through microfinance, which means the lenders pay the FP the principal of the loan; and (7) Borrowers submit monthly payments, which are split between the lenders and FP to pay off the principal and interest, respectively.

13 Lin and Pursiainen (2021) define round numbers heuristic as the general tendency to adopt round numbers as cognitive shortcuts when facing complicated and uncertain situations.
14 Creepiness can be defined as "a potentially negative and uncomfortable emotional response paired with perceptions of ambiguity toward a person, technology or even during a situation".
15 The experiment has the following options: no disclosure, disclosure before conversation, disclosure after conversation or disclosure after decision.

References

Akyildirim, E., Corbet, S., Sensoy, A., Yarovaya, L. (2020). The impact of blockchain related name changes on corporate performance. *Journal of Corporate Finance*, 65 (December), 101759.

Appaya, S. (2021). On fintech and financial inclusion. *World Bank Blogs*. https://blogs.worldbank.org/psd/fintech-and-financial-inclusion

Arner, D.W., Barberis, J., Buckley, R.P. (2015). The evolution of Fintech: A new post-crisis paradigm. University of Hong Kong, faculty of Law Research, *Paper No. 2015/047*.

Arráiz, I., Bruhn, M., Stucchi, R. (2015). Psychometrics as a tool to improve screening and access to credit. World Bank Policy Research Working Paper No. 7506.

Auer, R.A., Banka, H., Boakye-Adjei, N.Y., Faragallah, A., Frost, J., Natarajan, H., Razali, M., Oppong, K., Poddierohin, A. (2022). Central bank digital currencies: A new tool in the financial inclusion toolkit? FSI Insights on policy implementation No 41 (BIS).

Balyuk, T. (2023). FinTech lending and bank credit access for consumers. *Management Science*, 69, 1, 555–575. https://doi.org/10.1287/mnsc.2022.4319.

Baulkaran, V., Jain, P. (2023). Who uses robo-advising and How? *Financial Review*, 58, 1, 65–89. https://doi.org/10.1111/fire.12324

Statista (2023). Number of fintech startups worldwide from 2018 to 2023, by region (Graph). Accessed July 19, 2023. https://www.statista.com/statistics/893954/number-fintech-startups-by-region/

Bernards, N. (2019). The poverty of Fintech? Psychometrics, credit infrastructures, and the limits of financialization. *Review of International Political Economy*, 26, 5, 815–838.

Bertsch, C., Hull, I., Qi, Y., Zhang, X. (2020). Bank misconduct and online lending. *Journal of Banking and Finance*, 116 (July), 105822. https://doi.org/10.1016/j.jbankfin.2020.105822

Bollinger, B., Yao, S. (2018). Risk transfer versus cost reduction on two-sided microfinance platforms. *Quantitative Marketing and Economics*, 16, 3, 251–287.

Boot, A., Hoffmann, P., Laeven, L., Ratnovski, L. (2021). Fintech: What's old, what's new? *Journal of Financial Stability*, 53, 100836.

Caglayan, M., Talavera, O., Xiong, L., Zhang, J. (2020). What does not kill us makes us stronger: The story of repetitive consumer loan applications. *TheEuropean Journal of Finance*, 28 (1), 46–65.

Càmara, N., Tuesta, D. (2017). Measuring financial inclusion: a multidimensional index. IFC Bulletin No 47. https://www.bis.org/ifc/publ/ifcb47p.pdf

Chakravarty, S., Pal, R. (2010). Measuring financial inclusion: An axiomatic approach. *Indira Gandhi Institute of Development Research*, Working Paper no. WP 2010/003.

Chen, M.A., Wu, Q., Yang, B. (2019). How valuable is fintech innovation? *The Review of Financial Studies*, 32, 5, 2062–2106. https://doi.org/10.1093/rfs/hhy130
Croxson, K., Frost, J, Gambacorta, L., Valletti, T. (2022). Platform-based business models and financial inclusion. *BIS* Working Papers No 986.
D'Acunto, F., Prabhala, N., Rossi, A., (2019). The promises and pitfalls of Robo-advising. *The Review of Financial Studies*, 32, 5, 1983–2020.
Demir, A., Pesqué-Cela, V., Altunbas, Y., Murinde, V. (2020). Fintech, financial inclusion and income inequality: A quantile regression approach. *The European Journal of Finance*, 28 (1), 86–107.
Demirgüç-Kunt, A., Klapper, L., Singer, D., Ansar, S., (2022). *The Global Findex Database 2021: Financial Inclusion, Digital Payments and Resilience in the Age of COVID-19*. World Bank: Washington, DC.
Di Maggio, M., Yao, V. (2021). Fintech borrowers: Lax screening or cream-skimming? *The Review of Financial Studies*, 34, 10, 4565–4618.
Dietvorst, B.J., Simmons, J.P., Massey, C. (2015). Algorithm aversion: People erroneously avoid algorithms after seeing them err. *Journal of Experimental Psychology: General*, 144(1), 114–126.
Feyen, E., Frost, J., Gambacorta, L., Natarajan, H., Saal, M. (2021). Fintech and the digital transformation of financial services: implications for market structure and public policy. *BIS Papers* No. 117. https://www.bis.org/publ/bppdf/bispap117.htm
Fuster, A., Plosser, M., Schnabl, P., James Vickery, J. (2019). The role of technology in mortgage lending. *The Review of Financial Studies* 32, 5, 1854–1899. https://doi.org/10.1093/rfs/hhz018
Gabor, D., Brooks, S., (2017). The digital revolution in financial inclusion: international development in the Fintech era. *New Political Economy*, 22, 4, 423–436. https://doi.org/10.1080/13563467.2017.1259298
Ge, R., Feng, J., Gu, B. & Zhang, P. (2017) Predicting and deterring default with social media information in peer-to-peer lending. *Journal of Management Information Systems*, 34, 2, 401–424. https://doi.org/10.1080/07421222.2017.1334472
Gupta, M., Verma, S., Pachare, S. (2021). An analysis of conventional and alternative financing—Customers' perspective. *International Journal of Finance & Economics*, 28,3, 2404–2414.
Isaia, E., Oggero, N. (2022). The potential use of robo-advisors among the young generation: Evidence from Italy. *Finance Research Letters*, 48, 103046. https://doi.org/10.1016/j.frl.2022.103046
Jin, Y., Ding, C., Duan, Y., Cheng, H.K. (2020). Click to success? The temporal effects of Facebook likes on crowdfunding. *Journal of the Association for Information Systems*, 21, 5, 1191–1213.
Kabengele, C., Hahn, R. (2021). Institutional and firm-level factors for mobile money adoption in emerging markets–a configurational analysis. *Technological Forecasting and Social Change* 171 (October): 120934. https://doi.org/10.1016/j.techfore.2021.120934
Kanga, D., Oughton, C., Harris, L., Murinde, V. (2021). The diffusion of fintech, financial inclusion and Income per Capita. *European Journal of Finance*, 28, 1, 108–136.
Lashitew, A., van Tulder, R., Liasse, Y. (2019). Mobile phones for financial inclusion: What explains the diffusion of mobile money innovations? *Research Policy*, 48, 5, 1201–1215. https://doi.org/10.1016/j.respol.2018.12.010

Liberti, J., Sturgess, J., Sutherland, A. (2022). How voluntary information sharing systems form: Evidence from a U.S. commercial credit Bureau. *Journal of Financial Economics*, 145, 3, 827–849. https://doi.org/10.1016/j.jfineco.2021.08.023

Lin, T.C., Pursiainen, V. (2021). The round number heuristic and entrepreneur crowdfunding performance. *Journal of Corporate Finance*, 68, 101894.

Luo, X., Tong, S., Fang, Z., Qu, Z. (2019). Frontiers: Machines vs. humans: The impact of artificial intelligence chatbot disclosure on customer purchases. *Marketing Science*, 38, 6, 937–947.

Maskara, P.K., Kuvvet, E., Chen, G. (2021). The role of P2P platforms in enhancing financial inclusion in the United States: An analysis of peer-to-peer lending across the rural–urban divide. *Financial Management*, 50, 3, 747–774.

Netzer, O., Lemaire, A., Herzenstein, M., (2019). When words sweat: Identifying signals for loan default in the text of loan applications. *Journal of Marketing Research*, 56, 6, 960–980.

Palladino, L. (2019). Democratizing Investment. *Politics & Society*, 47, 4, 573–591.

Philippon, T. (2020). On fintech and financial inclusion. *BIS Working Papers No 841*. https://www.bis.org/publ/work841.pdf

Rajaobelina, L., Prom Tep, S., Arcand, M., Ricard, L. (2021). Creepiness: Its antecedents and impact on loyalty when interacting with a chatbot. *Psychology & Marketing*, 38, 12, 2339–2356.

Sahay, R., von Allmen, U.E., Lahreche, A., Khera, P., Ogawa, S., Bazarbash, M., Beaton, K. (2020). The promise of Fintech: Financial inclusion in the post COVID-10 era. *International Monetary Fund (IMF)* Monetary and Capital Markets Department No. 20/09.

Sarma, M.S. (2012). Index of financial inclusion A measure of financial sector inclusiveness. *Berlin Working Papers on Money, Finance, Trade and Development*, Working Paper no. 07/2012.

Tan, T., Zhang, Y., Heng, C. S., Ge, C. (2021). Empowerment of Grassroots Consumers: A Revelatory Case of a Chinese Fintech Innovation. *Journal of the Association for Information Systems*, 22(1).

Tang, H. (2019). Peer-to-peer lenders versus banks: Substitutes or complements? *The Review of Financial Studies*, 32, 5, 1900–1938.

Thakor, A.V. (2020). Fintech and banking: What do we know? *Journal of Financial Intermediation*, 41 (January), 100833. https://doi.org/10.1016/j.jfi.2019.100833

Tok, Y.W., Heng, D. (2022). Fintech: Financial inclusion or exclusion? *International Monetary Fund (IMF) Working Paper* No. 2022/080.

Valuates Reports. (2020). *Peer to Peer Lending Market by Business Model: Global Opportunity Analysis and Industry Forecast, 2020--2027*. https://reports.valuates.com/market-reports/ALLI-Manu-3B23/peer-to-peer-lending

Williams, J. (2021). Fintech—A perfect day or walk on the wild side? In T.P. King, T.P. S. Stentella Lopes, S., A. Srivastav, A., J. Williams, J. (Eds.), *Disruptive Technology in Banking and Finance: An International Perspective on FinTech*. Palgrave Macmillan, 283–313.

World Bank (2022). Financial inclusion overview. https://www.worldbank.org/en/topic/financialinclusion/overview

Yang, T., Zhang, X. (2022). FinTech adoption and financial inclusion: Evidence from household consumption in China. *Journal of Banking & Finance*, 145 (December), 106668. https://doi.org/10.1016/j.jbankfin.2022.106668

6 Ethical FinTech

The Importance of Ethics in Creating Secure Financial Products and Services

Michał Nowakowski

6.1 Introduction

The development of new technologies, understood primarily as the so-called artificial intelligence (AI) (Ozili, 2021), distributed ledger and blockchain technology (Varma, 2019) and biometric data processing (Wang, 2021), has a significant potential for the development of many areas of the economy, including the financial sector.[1] At the same time, the application of new technologies can generate new risks (Matsuda et al., 2021), as well as amplifying those already existing and well recognized by financial institutions. Financial products and services may, on the one hand, be more efficient, both from the perspective of financial institutions and customers, better adapted to the expectations of their recipients, and – at least potentially – more affordable, but at the same time, they may influence decisions and behavior in a way that may raise doubts. How and for what purpose customers' personal data is used may also be questionable. This is a point in time when many raise legitimate questions from an ethical, legal and regulatory perspective, as evidenced, for example, in the growing number of studies by international[2] and national (BaFin, 2021) organizations and institutions.

New technologies pose numerous challenges to the institutions using them, users and supervisory and regulatory authorities, which are not only of the nature of "classic" risks related, for example, to potential cyber-security threats but also to ethical aspects related to finance (Boatright, 2010). This is mainly due to the fact that innovative solutions using, among other things, machine and deep learning, but also based on distributed ledger technology, use significant amounts of data, including personal data, which may raise – legitimate – privacy concerns. Not even Central Bank Digital Currencies are an exception (Bossu et al., 2020), which arouse emotions in connection with the de-anonymization of the flow of funds. At the same time, this is not only the domain of private institutions because the increasing interest in new solutions in SupTech (Supervision Technology) by supervisory and regulatory bodies may also involve specific challenges of an ethical nature (Financial Stability Board, 2020) also in the context of a type of outsourcing of public authority.

DOI: 10.4324/9781003340454-6

As a result, it becomes essential to look at the application of innovative solutions in the financial sector (Bernards & Campbell-Verduyn, 2019) not only from the perspective of the most common risks, such as operational, security, model or legal and regulatory risks, but also those that can be attributed to the category of ethics and new technologies. The existing approach seems to be insufficient and the need to build requirements based also on moral standards (Mele et al., 2017), including that characteristic for new technologies, is beginning to crystallize. This requires a change in the approach not only to building codes of ethics based on self-governance, which often turn out to be ineffective, but also to creating hard legal requirements (although ethics itself is rather soft in nature) if such self-governance does not fit.

This chapter is devoted to the issue of ethics in the financial sector from the perspective of the application of new technologies, including AI. This chapter aims to justify the need to create a new catalogue of ethical principles for the use of new technologies in the financial sector – *Ethical FinTech*, as well as to present specific solutions that could be further clarified by EU regulators (and potentially policymakers) in the future. The challenges of using these solutions will be offered both from the perspective of financial institutions and their clients, as well as regulatory and supervisory authorities. The chapter will also point to specific solutions that can contribute to the safe and efficient development of the modern financial services market from an ethical perspective, also in the context of the use of RegTech (*Regulatory Technology*) solutions, even though these threads are often omitted in studies devoted to this issue (European Banking Authority, 2021), or at least are not indicated directly.

It should be stressed that the lack of an ethical approach in the marketing of financial products and services, as well as in the use of new technologies, can generate several risks (indirect[3] and direct) both on the part of institutions, customers, regulators and supervisors and – probably – the entire financial system and economy. Therefore, the issue of ethics in the world of new technologies from the perspective of the financial sector should be the subject of interest and involvement not only the institutions themselves.

6.2 New Technologies in Finance – An Overview

Before analyzing the issue of ethics in the financial sector based on new technologies, it is necessary to distinguish "what" these new technologies applicable in finance are. In principle, the following types are mentioned here:

1 AI, advanced data analytics and the use of big data.
2 Distributed ledger technology and blockchain, particularly in decentralized finance (DeFi) (Chen & Bellavitis, 2020).
3 Use biometrics (also behavioral, see Shanmuganathan, 2020), including remote user identification (EBA, 2021b).

4 Cloud computing (Hajizadeh & Hajizadeh, 2020) and application of SaaS models.
5 Web3[4] and digital worlds – including metaverse (Gilbert, 2022).

The above are examples of technologies that have gained the attention of financial institutions, but also of the customers of these institutions, in recent years, particularly in DeFi. Each of these solutions, individually and together, may contribute to the creation of innovative [internal] solutions and products and services previously unavailable to customers. At the same time, their application may entail differentiated risks for both the institutions and clients. Rarely discussed issues in the context of progressing digitization of finance are ethical problems, which do not necessarily have to coincide with the ethics of finance applied for the last dozen or so years, while the approach based on the *ethics by design* principle should constitute one of the bases for designing new solutions using new technologies (Albrechtslund, 2007).

Technological solutions in the financial sector using, for instance, data analytics, biometrics or even distributed ledger technology, are associated with significant acquisition and processing of data, including personal data, and therefore may generate risks to privacy, data protection, but also to the users themselves, for example, given the possibility of manipulation by more advanced solutions. Maintaining high standards in terms of, for example, privacy is simultaneously one of the biggest challenges institutions face. At the same time, there is a temptation to use this data to increase institutions' profits, for example, through recommendation or decision-making systems, which do not always respect the users and their rights.

For this reason, in the context of digital finance, which is mentioned among others by the European Commission in its strategy[5] (with the caveat that the very concept of ethics in this document appears in only three cases), attention should be paid to the need to set the direction of creating solutions considering certain ethical assumptions, which must be specific to the financial sector and not necessarily [globally] universal.

In the following sections, referring to new technologies, we should bear in mind the so-called breakthrough technologies and those solutions that have been functioning for many years, although they have gained popularity only recently. Undoubtedly, however, the greatest most significant emphasis will be put on the issue of ethics in the context of AI, which on the one hand can be a source of many benefits for society, but when used inappropriately can also pose a considerable threat, also in the financial sector.

6.3 Ethics of New Technologies

Further considerations should begin with an attempt to define the concept of ethics of new technologies, with theoretical considerations being limited to the necessary minimum, as the idea of ethics raises many doubts and controversies and is out of the content of this chapter. Awad et al. (2022)

propose (referring to AI itself) that such ethics should be understood as a combination of philosophy, computer science, law and economics to solve new ethical problems that new technologies may generate. In practice, it is not entirely clear how the ethics of new technologies and AI should be understood (Ocone, 2020). This is a consequence of essentially two issues: linking ethical and legal issues (Raab, 2020), and a different understanding of ethics based on new technologies, that is, subjecting it either to humans alone or to technological solutions with human participation.

In practice, a complete resolution of this issue seems – at least for today – optional and possible. The level of development of AI systems does not allow – and probably will not change for many years – to grant these solutions an autonomous status that would justify "requiring" these solutions to be accountable also on ethical grounds (leaving aside entirely the question of legal personality and accountability).

For this reason, let us assume that the ethics of new technologies, and AI, refer to the application of certain ethical principles both at the conceptual stage, creation and application of these solutions. I therefore propose to apply at each of these stages the following principle:

"Ethics by design and default"

This is not, however, an easy task. The challenges to be confronted are the following:

1 Selecting an underlying set of values and ethical standards – including whether a universal catalogue is possible.
2 Indicating the responsible and accountable entity and addressing standards in this domain.
3 Choosing the proper model, that is, self-regulation, legislation, soft regulation or mixed model.
4 Identifying specific requirements for organizations implementing new technologies, including those of a technical nature.

These issues are typical for discussions on the ethics of new technologies – in general – and, in the case of a regulated sector such as the financial sector. In the regulated sector, the matter seems even more complicated since it requires an exceptionally individualized and proportionate approach. We should also remember about the existence of numerous interconnectedness and internal and external link that may arise between the various legal and regulatory requirements and possible ethical standards.

The approach and direction (the choice of particular elements of the model) should be vague because the area of application of new technologies is subject to dynamic changes, as well as risks and challenges. Therefore, it is worth remembering these dynamics and considering them when developing appropriate solutions.

However, before attempting to create such a model of universal principles, it is also necessary to consider how ethics should be understood in the financial sector and whether already existing standards and approaches can also be used in the context of new technology ethics in the financial sector, that is, to create a concept of *ethical FinTech.*

6.4 Ethics in the Financial Sector

Ethical norms and expectations [of institutions] are often anchored in the financial sector in the form of codes of ethics. As Ragatz and Duska (2010) point out, "[t]he codes of ethics in financial services are unique insofar as they deal specifically with the obligations that financial services practitioners have in virtue of their status as professionals" (Ragatz & Duska, 2010, p. 297), and this is done as part of regular ethics management at every stage of the institution's activities (de Bruin, 2014). It is worth noting that also, in the context of the digitalization of financial services in the early 2000s, concepts of "modified" ethical standards for this area of banks' activities were emerging (Harris & Spence, 2002), although this topic seems to have been sidelined for the last two decades. It is worth noting here, as pointed out by, among others, Marcinowska (2013a), that ethics are, along with such elements as greater responsibility and risk control, a more robust regulatory framework, new supervisory authorities, as well as strengthened macroprudential supervision, a necessary component for creating and maintaining a robust financial system.

The development of ethics in the financial sector is likely to experience a renaissance soon, thanks to new ESG obligations (European Commission, 2022), which, especially in the European Union, have taken on a real – complex – character, turning "soft" ethics into binding standards. However, this raises the question of to what extent ethics in the financial sector – beyond ESG – should remain a non-binding area that appeals more to our beliefs and feelings, and to what extent it should become a binding set of obligations and duties.

Arbizu (2018) has suggested four dimensions of ethics in finance:

1 Ethics as part of the function [profession] performed.
2 Ethics as so-called CSR, or social responsibility of institutions.
3 Ethical banking.
4 Ethics as part of the microfinance business.

The boundaries between CSR and financial ethics can sometimes become blurred (Lentner et al., 2015), as it is not easy to separate these issues, at least in some areas clearly. A similar remark can be made about the dynamically developing region of ESG. This makes it difficult to define unambiguously what ethics are in the financial sector, how to understand and shape such norms as part of the organization's culture, and what the consequences will be if an institution does not apply an ethical approach (Liu, 2018).

Arguably, ethics in the financial sector should be understood as a set of norms and values, which [should be] applied by financial institutions and their employees [and persons related to them] to ensure the highest standards of conduct toward customers, supervisory and regulatory authorities, other financial institutions and entities with which the institutions interact. The application of such solutions is to guarantee that the institution behaves correctly – although defining "what"[6] is not an easy task, while Marcinkowska (2013b) is right to point out that the critical "capital" of banks is their reputation and trust. Although other financial institutions perform slightly different functions, this statement seems equally accurate. At the same time, ethical standards do not necessarily have to be anchored in specific provisions of internal codes, norms or good practices, because – by their very nature – they are instead a certain "postulate" of how one should, and not how one MUST act. Of course, this does not exclude that unethical behavior cannot expose an institution to real sanctions or penalties. Still, it is one thing to be (un)compliant with laws and another to be (un)ethical. Regardless, the line is a thin one.

In this context, the challenge is how to influence the addressees of ethical behavior to comply with the organization's values and standards and enforce these standards (Stix, 2021) [including those created, for example, at the regional level]. This is relevant internally and externally (also in the context of so-called self-governance) and can fundamentally affect the functioning of the whole organization, primarily if new technology-based solutions are used to make or support decisions (Brendel et al., 2021).

There are some requirements for ethical behavior in the EU legal and regulatory framework, emanating from both Article 91(8) of the CRD[7] and the EBA's Guidance on Internal Governance (EBA, 2021a), including Guideline 99 et seq. Still, these provide what should be the necessary organizational framework rather than indicating *what* standards should apply. This is therefore left to the discretion of institutions [with some exceptions, for instance, on diversity or non-discrimination. Of course, they still need to keep in mind constraints of a legal and regulatory nature.

6.5 The Ethics of New Technologies in the Financial Sector

Having defined – albeit quite generally – the notion of ethics of new technologies as well as ethics in finance, one may wonder whether, in connection with the dynamic development of new solutions and digitization of finance, it is necessary to rebuild or re-establish the foundations for innovative finance from an ethical perspective. This is important because a lack of solutions in this area can have negative consequences for both institutions and their clients and the financial system.[8]

The ethics of new technologies in the financial sector, which we have defined as *Ethical FinTech*, should form the basis of activity for all financial institutions that develop new solutions based on diverse future technologies (and present). At the same time, it is a demand addressed not only to institutions already regulated and supervised by the financial sector but also to technology solution providers – Technical Service Providers and the developing area of DeFi (Michalikova & Polyakova, 2021). The specificity of financial technology – FinTech – requires that specific ethical standards apply here. It is worth mentioning at this point that within EIOPA, a special Expert Group on Insurance Digital Ethics (EIOPA, 2019) was established in 2019, one of whose tasks is to create principles for ethical insurance which, as the group itself indicates, "*digital responsibility principles will address the use of new business models, technologies and data sources in insurance from the perspective of fairness and taking into account ethical considerations*".

To create such an ethical compass, existing guidelines and recommendations, which are already applicable, for example to AI systems,[9] can be used and extended to include aspects specific to the financial sector. However, it should be borne in mind that while it is possible to create some general principles that should be universally applicable, it will still be up to the institutions to decide how these principles are "laid out" within their organizations, in particular how they are enforced. The focus of universality will, therefore, not stand in opposition to the direction of individualization for the needs of a specific entity.

The Digital Ethics in Insurance Group (2021) produced an interesting report in 2021, "Artificial Intelligence Governance Principles: Towards Ethical and Trustworthy Artificial Intelligence in the European Insurance Sector". A report from EIOPA's Consultative Expert Group on Digital Ethics in insurance (EIOPA, 2021) provides a set of principles and practices for applying AI in the insurance sector. While this is not a binding compilation, it will undoubtedly significantly impact the practice of institutions under the supervision of EIOPA and perhaps more widely.

Arguably, in a dynamic and digital world, creating ethical standards for the financial sector is essential. However, it is no substitute for human integrity and the formation of moral attitudes outside the organizations themselves. However, an important question arises – how these standards should be shaped in the financial sector, that is, whether they should be binding or not, whether they should be based on complex law or soft guidelines and recommendations and whether they should be linked to appropriate disciplinary instruments. It is also essential to identify the possibility of creating a unified catalog of principles what should be applied, for example, at the European Union level. This is an easier task than creating such a universal global catalog, where different patterns, including cultural ones, clash.

At the same time, it is worth considering whether the financial sector needs "new" ethical rules that could limit the effects of negative actions, for example, in the field of manipulation or money laundering and terrorist financing, which are a significant source of risk for the financial sector and entire economies.[10] At the end of the 1970s, Carroll (1979) pointed to the importance of ethics in creating socially responsible organizations whose role is not only to increase profits but also to positive impact on the environment. In today's difficult and complicated times, the importance of ethics will be even more important, and the increasing use of new high-risk technologies [for humans] should undoubtedly be an incentive to intensify actions. Thus, we note how many benefits new technologies can bring, but also how many less noticeable risks they can also generate, e.g., discrimination in the credit process (Brookings, 2020), algorithmic trading (BBC, 2012), product mismatch and others.

It is unnecessary to enter a discussion about the very definition of ethical standards, which can be understood in many ways (Amigoni & Schiaffonati, 2005), just as AI can be understood in many ways. It is not the author's goal to elaborate on the necessity to create more requirements if it is not absolutely necessary.

The financial sector, and in particular the banking sector, has a vital – social – role, which means that expectations of ethical behavior can be much higher than in sectors of lesser importance to society (Goyal & Joshi, 2011). At the same time, some sources report that "more ethical" entities that realistically implement principles of this nature may be less profitable (Climent, 2018) due to their more significant impact on the environment and support for initiatives in the broader ESG area, which is also a challenge for supervisors and regulators. However, there is undoubtedly a need to build public trust in financial institutions so that all stakeholders can benefit from good and effective cooperation in the long term. More so as clients' awareness and expectations in this respect are also growing (Callejas-Albinana et al., 2017).

At the same time, the use of new technologies, which may themselves be sources of specific risks and challenges of an ethical nature, makes the combination of these two "difficult" fields seem extremely important from an ethical point of view. The already mentioned cases of violating citizens' fundamental rights by solutions based on "artificial intelligence", for example, are proof of this. This is more important because those responsible for the use or supervision of such solutions may not be aware of such risks, and the introduction of a new standard will, "force", the construction of expected attitudes. For this reason and considering the growing use of new technologies in the financial sector, it should be assumed that regulatory and supervisory bodies should create new standards in this area, and perhaps – leaving this subject for a separate study – legislators.

6.6 The Foundations of Ethical FinTech

The catalogue of moral (ethical) norms does not have to coincide with principles of a legal nature (Federwisch, 2015), so that is legal may still be ethically reprehensible. An example might be the behavior of a financial adviser who uses practices which are approved by law, but which remain questionable in the context of a moral assessment. However, the boundary here is thin and not always possible to draw as the ambiguity is quite high. The fact that ethical behavior is based on, among other things, norms, incentives, principles and behaviors makes it difficult to quantify what is good and what is not. In practice, unethical behavior is also – even indirectly – subject to prohibitions under complex law.

Therefore, the creation of foundations for ethical finance within the new technologies will be based on a combination of law, regulation and ethics *sensu stricto*. At the same time, it should be noted that such a catalogue of principles does not have to be permanent and "stable" but rather dynamic and open, because although certain principles and patterns may remain valid regardless of time, the world is subject to dynamic changes, including cultural and technological ones, which may – although not necessarily – force us to amend the area accordingly (and sometimes significantly). Therefore, let us try to build a specific catalogue of fundamental principles for Ethical FinTech to determine whether and how to make them concrete for the needs of the financial sector.

Let us look at the European Commission's experts proposed principles for so-called trustworthy AI. According to the proposed direction, four fundamental principles must be applied when creating this type of solution, that is:

1 Respect for human autonomy.
2 Prevention of harm.
3 Fairness.
4 Explicability.

These principles then evolve into the following requirements:

1 Human Agency and Oversight.
2 Technical robustness and safety.
3 Privacy and Data Governance.
4 Transparency.
5 Diversity, non-discrimination and fairness.
6 Societal and environmental well-being.
7 Accountability.

It is clear from the above overview that they are pretty broad and could only be fully applicable in some cases – particularly in the context of the financial system. The EIOPA guidelines already have somewhat more practical principles, which nevertheless still reflect the underlying principles of trustworthy AI. These include:

1 Human oversight.
2 Robustness and performance.
3 Data governance and record keeping.
4 Transparency and explainability.
5 Fairness and non-discrimination.
6 Principle of proportionality.

However, when creating a catalogue of underlying principles for Ethical Fintech, it should be noted that it covers not only solutions based on the so-called AI but also those technological solutions that are not related to the "intensive" processing of data, including personal data, although in practice it is difficult to imagine solutions present in the financial sector that will not be related to such processing. It is also worth noting that these are not the only examples of principles that may constitute the basis for creating a new set of standards (OECD, 2019), and they are subject to constant evolution. Therefore, the examples above are only meant to outline some general directions.

Arguably, in creating a framework for *Ethical Fintech, a* distinction should be made between two sets of principles, viz:

1 Of a technological nature [relating to the technology used].[11]
2 Of a strictly financial nature [characteristic of regulated activities].

By combining these two dimensions, an institution's actions can be considered ethical – at least in the sense of the relevant standards.

The technical part should be based on the following principles:

1 Privacy and data protection by design and default.
2 Human oversight.
3 Data governance and management.
4 Transparency and explainability.
5 Bias prevention, non-discrimination and fairness.
6 Proportionality.
7 Technical robustness, effectiveness and performance.

Another element that may complement the above is the principle of *ethics by design and default*. These principles should be understood and applied jointly, as the relations between them are very significant, which means that a failure to comply with one direction may result in a breach of another. The principle of proportionality requires a special explanation here, which should be understood as the application of solutions adequate to the identified threat level (risk) of using specific instruments, including products or services. The application of keys similar to those expressed in Regulation 2016/679 (GDPR), that is, Data protection impact assessment, and in this case, Technology Risk Impact Assessment,[12] which process may significantly contribute to the selection of adequate measures to the identified risks, may be helpful in this respect.

The above principles should also be subject to detail from the perspective of the specifics of the financial sector. However, creating a uniform catalogue in this respect seems to be a challenging task, although some foundations can be identified. The Securities Exchange Commission proposes ten fundamental principles, that financial professionals should be obliged to apply.[13] The scope is quite broad, it can be reduced to the following summary:

1 Honesty and integrity, as well as acting by relating to avoiding conflicts of interest.
2 Transparency and accuracy in the provision of information [including to customers].
3 Acting in accordance with laws, regulations and standards, including ISO.
4 Acting in good faith and with the utmost care and professionalism.
5 Respect for privacy and confidentiality [including of clients].
6 Upgrading skills and updating knowledge, as well as sharing knowledge.
7 Active promotion of ethical attitudes.
8 Exercising supervision and control over the respect of standards and obligations and reporting to the competent entities and authorities in the event of infringements and incidents.
9 Taking responsibility for one's actions as well as the actions of subordinates.

To this catalogue, we can also add some obligations to act by social responsibility [including environmental responsibility] and promote innovation, which can improve the quality and safety of services provided. Nowadays, this is undoubtedly an issue that financial institutions must not forget.

A catalogue of principles constructed in this way, which may also be supplemented with regulations specific to a given organization, should constitute a model for the behavior of the institution's employees and the institution itself, and what is crucial – management.

6.7 How to Demand?

The issue of choosing the "form" of implementing ethical solutions is the subject of discussion, which seems to be difficult to be resolved (Yudkin et al., 2021), and the effectiveness of different solutions varies (Boddington, 2020). This is an important issue as the choosing appropriate instruments will have consequences on many levels, not only for the institution itself but also for the people within it.

One of the most important challenges to be solved is the decision about WHO should shape ethical requirements, and *how* should be *perceived* by the addressees of these standards (Coeckelbergh, 2020). The matter may become further complicated when using (semi-)autonomous systems based on some form of learning that may interfere with the predefined goals (Russel, 2020).

From the perspective of the financial sector, there is a precise combination of law (complex law) and regulation (soft law), such as guidelines, positions and opinions. Some general assumptions (and goals) are set out in the relevant rules based on technological neutrality and a risk-based approach. Some ambiguities resulting from these (flexible) requirements are clarified through interpretation by supervisory and regulatory authorities. At the same time, international organizations (Weber, 2012) also produce their own guidelines (FSB, 2018), recommendations or reports, which are no less important than those of national authorities.

It is worth noting here the approach applied by for example, the European Banking Authority, where Article 16 of Regulation 1093/2010 sets out the powers for the authority to issue guidelines and recommendations.[14] At the same time, Article 16(3) provides those competent authorities, and financial institutions shall use their best endeavors to comply with those guidelines and recommendations [by the *comply or explain* principle]. This approach has the effect of, on the one hand, indicating certain expectations of the supervisor and regulator, but does not impose a rigid framework in this respect, giving some leeway and flexibility. A similar solution could be applied to Ethical FinTech.

At the other extreme, however, is one of the recent proposals to amend the draft AI Act,[15] which, in Article 4a, would make it mandatory for providers of AI systems to apply the requirements of the Charter of Fundamental Rights and to ensure that such systems are law-abiding, ethical and resilient. The proposed provision implies even more far-reaching obligations, with some standards to be issued by both the European Commission and standardization organizations. While the fate of these assumptions is not a foregone conclusion, there is a need for a firmer statement of requirements for ethical AI and other new technologies. However, it is still uncertain whether this is a desirable direction that will fulfill its purpose, especially since ethical standards tend to be associated with less binding obligations.

In the proposed wording of the Article 4a provision, the "ethical" value of AI systems should be understood as "(...) AI system is developed taking into account the specific benefits of the AI system while respecting the freedom and autonomy of human beings, human dignity as well as mental and physical integrity, and to be fair and explicable". Essentially, this coincides with the already cited ethical standards for trustworthy AI.

Introducing an Ethical FinTech requirement in the form of "hard" legislation – in addition more broadly – not just about AI, may not only be challenging but impossible due to the multitude of assumptions, challenges and risks that may be specific to different applications of innovative finance, such as DeFi and distributed ledger and blockchain technologies.

Therefore, it seems that the most effective approach to Ethical FinTech would be for all the supervisory and regulatory authorities concerned (as well as ENISA) to try to develop an ethical standard in this area, either as a guideline or as a code of good practice (in which case a more intensified participation of industry organizations and financial market players' associations would also be necessary). There is nothing to prevent a general requirement for ethical behavior, also in the application of new technologies in finance, from being included in the relevant legislation governing a particular segment or segments of the financial market. This may be of particular importance, for example, in the emerging crypto-asset market, characterized by a particular vulnerability to unethical behavior.

In the context of the consequences of a possible non-application of the Ethical FinTech Guidelines, two similar principles can essentially be adopted:

1 An analogous approach to the EBA guidelines and recommendations – comply or explain principles.
2 It is taking into account the (in)application of these standards when assessing a possible violation (and its scale, including the actor's contribution) and during supervisory inspections (for example, under the SREP).

Such an approach may be effective in that, on the one hand, it will not impose excessively rigid rules, leaving supervised institutions with some margin and flexibility. On the other hand, it will promote an ethical approach to the use of new technologies and innovative financial solutions. It will be a kind of hard and soft law (Weber, 2012) and ethical standards of even less "soft" character (see also Hagemann et al., 2018).

This direction, however, will require, and this should be strongly emphasized, a strong commitment on the part of both EU and national regulatory and supervisory authorities, including the extension of powers and going beyond the purely supervisory and regulatory role that such sources play. Education will be crucial in this context, both within authorities and institutions obliged to apply the "new" rules and to some point – customers that should also demand from institutions and regulators a more ethical approach.

6.8 Other Issues at the Intersection of Ethics, Law and Regulation

The above analysis does not exhaust all the threads that "orbit" around the concept of ethics of new technologies in finance but is only meant as a contribution to the discussion that is slowly developing also in the context of the financial sector, as evidenced by the already mentioned principles developed by EIOPA. I have not elaborated here, among others, on the issue of *responsibility for using new technologies* (Wendechorst, 2021), which is currently the subject of intense work in the European Commission, or the issue of *governance of new technologies,* also in the context of broadly understood authority.

Another important topic is the availability of RegTech and SupTech solutions, which will make it possible, on the one hand, to meet some of the ethical-legal-regulatory requirements (also in the context of fundamental rights or product management) and, on the other hand, to monitor them effectively. There is also an educational issue, which is also of systemic importance. However, this subject goes far beyond the framework of this publication. The ESG and CSR threads have also been highlighted and should be analyzed in depth in the context of the already existing legal framework in this area.

However, these are undoubtedly issues that need to be looked at more closely, including in the context of Ethical FinTech especially exploring the possibility and need for an appropriate framework by regulators and supervisors or even legislators themselves.

6.9 Conclusions

The above analysis was intended, on the one hand, to point out the (new) risks associated with the use of new technologies in the area and, on the other hand, to highlight the role of regulators and supervisors in creating conditions for financial institutions to develop more ethical products and services. The development of new technologies is already generating numerous benefits for both these bodies and supervised entities, as well as customers. Still, it can also be a source of severe and systemic risks for the entire financial system. Therefore, the implementation of appropriate organizational and technical solutions specific to the area of Ethical FinTech seems to be the only direction that can help minimize the possible negative impact on the financial system.

At the same time, the mere implementation of policies, procedures or regulations is undoubtedly insufficient and requires the building of certain attitudes within the (culture) of the organization. In this respect, the "new" ethics of modern technology in the financial sector is not so different from the "classic" ethics for the financial industry. At the same time, new risks emerge such as overreliance, and such risks will require more attention and extraordinary measures.

For this reason, a recommended approach is to work intensively on the model framework for ethics in finance. There are many options for these standards, but the specificity of the financial services may hamper the development of such frameworks. Still, the financial sector, however, requires a tailored and proportional approach, also in the context of specific segments of the financial market. Action is needed today to at least minimize systemic risk, also on a global scale and to ensure that products and services are ethically appropriate, and end-users are protected.

Notes

1 According to the BCBS Committee of the Bank for International Settlements, "[b]anks are increasingly exploring opportunities for using AI/ML. AI/ML technology is expected to increase banks' operational efficiency and facilitate improvements in risk management". This is just one example of the benefits that new technologies may create for the financial sector (see https://www.bis.org/publ/bcbs_nl27.htm).
2 https://unesdoc.unesco.org/ark:/48223/pf0000380455
3 This includes "human" costs, which are often overlooked in analyses of the impact of new technologies on workplaces and employee well-being. See Crawford (2021).
4 Gilbert (2022, p. 5) defines Web3 as "the putative next generation of the web's technical, legal, and payments infrastructure - including blockchain, smart contracts and cryptocurrencies". However, there is no consensus as to the proper definition of Web3 and it may change over time (Nath & Iswary, 2015).

5 https://eur-lex.europa.eu/legal-content/EN/TXT/?uri=CELEX:52020DC0591
6 For example, will what is ethical under Sharia law be ethical in the EU order? (See Said & Elangkovan, 2014).
7 https://eur-lex.europa.eu/legal-content/PL/TXT/PDF/?uri=CELEX:32019L0878&from=PL
8 For example, the so-called global stablecoins are currently not identified as having adverse impact on global financial stability, however, according to the FSB it may change in the future (see Financial Stability Board, 2022).
9 One example of such guidance is European Commission's Ethics Guidelines for Trustworthy AI, available on: https://ec.europa.eu/newsroom/dae/document.cfm?doc_id=60419
10 https://baselgovernance.org/blog/how-effective-are-jurisdictions-preventing-money-laundering-insights-10th-basel-aml-index
11 The European Banking Authority has proposed four pillars for a development, implementation, and adoption of certain machine learning applications within the banking sector. Those pillars are data management, technological infrastructure, organisation and governance, and analytics methodology (see EBA, 2021c).
12 A similar approach has been proposed by EIOPA (2021) in relation to the application of artificial intelligence within insurance sector.
13 https://www.sec.gov/Archives/edgar/data/1396279/000119312507083128/dex141.htm
14 Regulation (EU) No 1093/2010 of the European Parliament and of the Council of 24 November 2010 establishing a European Supervisory Authority (European Banking Authority), amending Decision No 716/2009/EC and repealing Commission Decision 2009/78/EC, OJ 2010 L-331/12.
15 Draft Opinion of the Committee on Legal Affairs for the Committee on the Internal Market and Consumer Protection and the Committee on Civil Liberties, Justice and Home Affairs on the proposal for a regulation of the European Parliament and of the Council laying down harmonised rules on artificial intelligence (Artificial Intelligence Act) and amending certain Union Legislative Acts (COM(2021)0206 – C9-0146/2021 – 2021/0106(COD)).

References

Albrechtslund, A. (2007). Ethics and technology design. *Ethics and Information Technology*, 9, 63–72. https://doi.org/10.1007/s10676-006-9129-8

Amigoni, F., Schiaffonati, V., (2005). *Machine Ethics and Human Ethics: A Critical View.* https://www.aaai.org/Papers/Symposia/Fall/2005/FS-05-06/FS05-06-016.pdf

Arbizu, E. (2018). *Ethics in the Financial System: A Compliance System.* 8 September. https://www.bbva.com/en/ethics-in-the-financial-system-a-compliance-system/

Awad, E., Levine, S., Anderson, M., Anderson, S.L., Conitzer, V., Crockett, M.J., Everett, J.A.C., Evgeniou, T., Gopnik, A., Jamison, J.C., Kim, T.W., Liao, S.M., Meyer, M.N., Mikhail, J., Opoku-Agyemang, K., Borg, J.S., Schroeder, J., Sinott-Armstrong, W., Slavkovik, M., Tenenbaum, J.B. (2022). Computational ethics. *Trends in Cognitive Science*, 26, 5, 388–405.

BaFin (2021). *Big Data and Artificial Intelligence: Principles for the Use of Algorithms in Decision-Making Processes.* https://www.bafin.de/SharedDocs/Downloads/EN/Aufsichtsrecht/dl_Prinzipienpapier_BDAI_en.html?nn=9866146

BBC. (2012). https://www.bbc.com/news/magazine-19214294.

Bernards, N., Campbell-Verduyn, M. (2019). Understanding technological change in global finance through infrastructures. *Review of International Political Economy*, 26, 5, 773–789. https://doi.org/10.1080/09692290.2019.1625420

Boatright, J.R. (2010). Ethics in finance. In J.R. Boatright (Ed.), *Critical Issues in Theory and Practice*(pp. 3–20). John Wiley & Sons.

Boddington, P. (2020). Normative modes: Codes and standards. In M.D. Dubber, F. Pasquale, S. Das, (Eds.), *The Oxford Handbook of Ethics of AI*, (pp. 125–140). Oxford University Press.

Bossu, W., Itatani, M., Margulis, C., Rossi, A., Weenink, H., Yoshinaga, A. (2020). *Legal Aspects of Central Bank Digital Currency: Central Bank and Monetary Law Considerations*. IMF Working Paper, WP/20/254, November.

Brendel, A.B., Birbabaie, M., Lembcke, T-B. (et al.) (2021). Ethical management of artificial intelligence. *Sustainability*, 13, 1974, 1–18.

de Bruin, B. (2014). Ethics management in banking and finance. In N. Morris, D. Vines (Eds.), *Capital Failure. Rebuilding Trust in Financial Services* (pp. 255–276). Oxford University Press.

Callejas-Albinana, F.E., Martinez-Rodriguez, I., Callejas-Albinana, A.I., Vidales-Carrasco, I.M. (2017). Assessing the growth of ethical banking: Some evidence from Spanish customers. *Frontiers in Psychology,* 8,782, 1–12.

Carroll, A.B. (1979). A three-dimensional conceptual model of corporate social performance. *Academy of Management Review*, 4, 4, 497–505.

Chen, Y., Bellavitis, C. (2020). Blockchain disruption and decentralized finance: The rise of decentralized business models. *Journal of Business Venturing Insights*, 13, https://doi.org/10.1016/j.jbvi.2019.e00151

Climent, F. (2018). Ethical versus conventional banking: A case study. *Sustainability*, 10, 2152. https://www.mdpi.com/2071-1050/10/7/2152/pdf?version=1529912854

Coeckelbergh, M. (2020). *AI Ethics*. Cambridge: MIT Press.

Crawford, K. (2021). *Atlas of AI*. Yale University Press.

EBA (2021a). *Guidelines on Internal Governance Under Directive 2013/36/EU*. EBA/GL/2021/05.

EBA (2021b). Draft Guidelines on the Use of Remote Customer Onboarding Solutions Under Article 13(1) of Directive (EU) 2015/849. EBA/CP/2021/40, 10 November.

EBA (2021c). Discussion Paper on Machine Learning for IRB Models. EBA/DP/2021/04, 11 November.

EIOPA (2019). https://www.eiopa.europa.eu/media/news/eiopa-establishes-consultative-expert-group-digital-ethics-insurance_en

EIOPA (2021). https://www.eiopa.europa.eu/eiopa-publishes-report-artificial-intelligence-governance-principles-2021-06-17_en

European Banking Authority (2021). *Analysis of RegTech in the EU Financial Sector*. EBA/REP/2021/17/ June.

European Commission (2022). https://ec.europa.eu/info/publications/210421-sustainable-finance-communication_pl

Federwisch, A. (2015). Ethical issues in the financial services industry. https://www.scu.edu/ethics/focus-areas/business-ethics/resources/ethical-issues-in-the-financial-services-industry/

Financial Stability Board (2022). *Assessment of Risks to Financial Stability from Crypto-Assets*. 16 February.

FSB (2018). https://www.fsb.org/wp-content/uploads/P090318-1.pdf

Gilbert, S. (2022). *Crypto, Web3 and the Metaverse*. University of Cambridge Policy Brief, March.

Goyal, K.A., Joshi, V. (2011). A study of social and ethical issues in banking industry. *International Journal of Economics and Research*, 2, 5, 49–57.

Hagemann, R., Huddlestone Skees, J., Thrierer, A. (2018). Soft law for hard problems: The governance of emerging technologies in an uncertain future. *Colorado Technology Law Review*, 17, 37, 58–59.

Hajizadeh, P., Hajizadeh, A. (2020). Benefits and challenges of cloud computing for financial sector. *International Journal of Academic Accounting, Finance & Management Research*, 4, 5, 73–79.

Harris, L., Spence, L.J. (2002). The ethics of eBanking. *Journal of Electronic Commerce Research*, 3, 2, 59–66.

Lentner, C., Szegedi, K., Tatay, T. (2015). Corporate social responsibility in the banking sector. *Public Finance Quarterly*, 60, 95–103.

Liu, X. (2018). Study on the integration of financial ethics education in financial institutions. In *4th International Conference on Arts, Design and Contemporary Education (ICADCE 2018)* (pp. 747–749). Atlantis Press.

Marcinkowska, M. (2013a). Regulation and self-regulation in banking: In search of optimum. *Bank i Kredyt*, 44, 2, 119–158.

Marcinkowska, M. (2013b). *Kapitał relacyjny banku. Tom 1. Kształtowanie relacje banku z otoczeniem.* Wydawnictwo Uniwersytetu Łódzkiego.

Matsuda, T., Wolff, J., Yanagawa, T. (Eds.). (2021). *Risks and Regulation of New Technologies*. Springer.

Mele, D., Rosanas, J.M., Fontrodona, J. (2017). Ethics in finance and accounting: Editorial introduction. *Journal of Business Ethics*, 140, 609–613.

Michalikova, K.F., Polyakova, A. (2021). Decentralized finance. *Globalization and Its Socio-Economic Consequences*, 129, 03008. https://doi.org/10.1051/shsconf/202112903008

Nath, K., Iswary, R. (2015). What comes after Web 3.0? Web 4.0 and the future. *International Conference on Computing and Communication Systems (I3CS'15)*.

Ocone, R. (2020). Ethics in engineering and the role of responsible technology. *Energy and AI*, 2, 1000019. https://reader.elsevier.com/reader/sd/pii/S266654682-0300197?token=5017D20DFA14B4338D3A9DE0C09DF34857EDFE974ED0FC3C4118518EC8829599CAC9C7F1F2652044679C1957ABDD82FB&originRegion=eu-west-1&originCreation=20220402183028

OECD (2019). https://oecd.ai/en/ai-principles

Ozili, P.K. (2021). Big data and artificial intelligence for financial inclusion: benefits and issues. *Artificial Intelligence Fintech, and Financial Inclusion*, January 14. http://dx.doi.org/10.2139/ssrn.3766097

Raab, C.D. (2020). Information privacy, impact assessment, and the place of ethics. *Computer Law & Security Law*, 37, 1–16. https://doi.org/10.1016/j.clsr.2020.105404

Ragatz, J.A, Duska, R.F. (2010). Financial codes of ethics. In J.R. Boatright (Ed.), *Finance Ethics. Critical Issues in Theory and Practice* (pp. 297–323). John Wiley & Sons. https://doi.org/10.1002/9781118266298.ch16

Russel, S. (2020). Artificial intelligence. A binary approach. In S.M. Liao (Ed.), *Ethics of Artificial Intelligence* (pp. 327–341). Oxford University Press.

Said, M.M., Elangkovan, K. (2014). Prosperity and social justice consequences of applying ethical norms of Islamic finance: Literature review. *Journal of Economics and Sustainable Development*, 5, 2, 99–107.

Shanmuganathan, M. (2020). Behavioural finance in an era of artificial intelligence: Longitudinal case study of robo-advisors in investment decisions. *Journal of Behavioral and Experimental Finance*, 27, 100297.

Spence, L.J. (2002). The ethics of eBanking. *Journal of Electronic Commerce Research*, 3, 2.
Stix, C. (2021). Actionable principles for artificial intelligence policy: Three pathways. *Science and Engineering Ethics*, 27, 15, 1–15. https://doi.org/10.1007/s11948-020-00277-3
Varma, J.R. (2019). Blockchain in finance. *The Journal for Decision Makers*, 44, 1, 1–11.
Wang, J.S. (2021). Exploring biometric identification in FinTech applications based on the modified TAM. *Financial Innovation*, 7, 42, 1–24. https://doi.org/10.1186/s40854-021-00260-2
Weber, R.H. (2012). Overcoming the hard law/soft law dichotomy in times of (financial) crises. *Journal of Governance and Regulation*, 1, 1, 8–14.
Wendechorst, C. (2021). Safety and liability related aspects of software, Luxembourg. https://ec.europa.eu/newsroom/dae/redirection/document/77327
Yudkin, D.A., Gantman, A.P., Hofmann, W. et al. (2021). Binding moral values gain importance in the presence of close others. *Nature Communications*, 12, 2718, 1–12. https://doi.org/10.1038/s41467-021-22566-6

7 Gender Disparity in the FinTech Sector

Systematic Literature Review

Błażej Prusak and Łukasz Wacławek

7.1 Introduction

It is indisputable that the importance of the FinTech sector in the global economy is growing. According to the Business Research Company (2019), the value of the global FinTech market in 2018 was US$127.66 billion, and it is expected to reach around US$310 billion in 2022, that is, an annual growth rate of nearly 25%. In particular, the growth in the digital payments sector is driving the global FinTech market. The sector has made payments for goods and services much faster, more convenient and cheaper for customers. Consumers today can pay for goods with cryptocurrencies, loyalty points and other forms of alternative cash. The growth of digital commerce and the steady proliferation of mobile technologies have contributed to the development of the digital payments sector. Global financial technology companies are increasingly using blockchain technology to enhance transaction security and operational efficiency. The use of blockchain technology increases the accuracy of transactions, speeds up the settlement process and reduces risk (The Business Research Company, 2019). Analyses also show that the FinTech sector is becoming more profitable, competitive, and its potential for growth is undeniable. In response, banks are looking for innovative technological solutions, which they often implement in newly created digital branches. Increasing importance is being attached to ESG-focused FinTechs (World FinTech Report, 2021; Pulse of FinTech, H2'21 2022).

With the growth of the FinTech sector, the question of female and male participation is becoming one of the most relevant issues. In the global economy, as evidenced by the World Economic Forum's 2022 report, experts say that real gender parity will not be achieved until as many as 132 years from now (Global Gender Gap Report, 2022, p. 5). A gender gap in different areas of economic activity has been noted for many years. The most common is the existence of a gender gap in entrepreneurship, employment, wages and working hours (Báez, Báez-García, Flores-Muñoz, & Gutiérrez-Barroso, 2018; Guzman & Kacperczyk, 2019; Petrongolo, 2019; Global Gender Gap Report 2021). As a rule, men are more likely to be top managers (Haveman & Beresford, 2012). A gender gap in financial literacy has also been identified

DOI: 10.4324/9781003340454-7

by several studies (Rani & Goyal, 2021). Moreover, data shows the IT sector is going to be male dominated (Gender Equality Index, 2020).

Given the last two characteristics mentioned above, one can assume that the FinTech sector will be particularly vulnerable to gender disparity. Some of the limited data in this area show that only 1.5% of global FinTech companies are founded solely by women and that they receive only 1% of total FinTech funding. The FinTech Diversity Radar 2021 research among over 1,000 private FinTech firms reveals that women make up barely 11% of all board members and 19% of company executives. The majority of women (26%) in the sector hold the titles of Chief People Officer or head of HR, followed by Chief Marketing Officer and Chief Financial Officer. Of all FinTech CEOs globally, only 5.6% are women, while less than 4% of women globally hold the title of Chief Innovation or Technology Officer (FinTech Diversity Radar, 2021). These figures show how large the gender gap can be in the FinTech Sector. It is therefore important to conduct research on gender disparity in the FinTech sector.

This chapter attempts to fill this research gap. On the basis of the research carried out, we were able to verify whether and in which areas related to FinTech activities gender disparity is present. The main aims of the chapter are to identify areas related to FinTech activities where gender disparity can be observed and answer the question of how FinTechs influence the gender gap. As the research method, we adopt a systematic literature review using the PRISMA concept (Page, McKenzie, Bossuyt, Boutron, Hoffmann, Mulrow, et al., 2021).

7.2 Methodology

The chapter employs the PRISMA concept (Page, McKenzie, Bossuyt, Boutron, Hoffmann, Mulrow, et al., 2021) to present the choice of literature in the analytical process in a clear and understandable way. As the first step, we use the most recognised global scientific databases, namely, Web of Science (WoS) and Scopus. The search was performed on 9 May 2022. Texts considered were ones in which the words "FinTech" and "gender" both appeared. Therefore, we searched for the following: "*FinTech AND gender*", which we entered in the *Topic* field in WoS (searching for specific words in titles, abstracts and keywords) and in the "*Article title, Abstract, Keywords*" field in Scopus. In addition, as few publications were retrieved from WoS and Scopus, we also searched for publications in the Google Scholar (GS) database using the Publish or Perish 8 software. The search was conducted on 11 May 2022 by entering the words "*FinTech AND gender*" in the *Keywords* field. Many more texts can be found on Google Scholar, but the scientific level of some texts is inadequate. Therefore, we set "100" as the citation threshold for inclusion of publications in the analysed records. Figure 7.1 shows the detailed process of selecting the final number of publications subject to final analysis. After identifying over 1,000 records, most of which were from GS, 976 were excluded due to failure to achieve the number of citations set for publications from the GS database. Further analyses only confirmed that many of the publications retrieved from the GS database according to the original search system were characterised by a lack of relevance to the topics under study. In the next stage, 63 records were screened. 14 records were removed due to duplication, three publications could not be accessed, and 24 studies showed no relevance to the subject matter. Consequently, we could analyse 22 publications in detail.

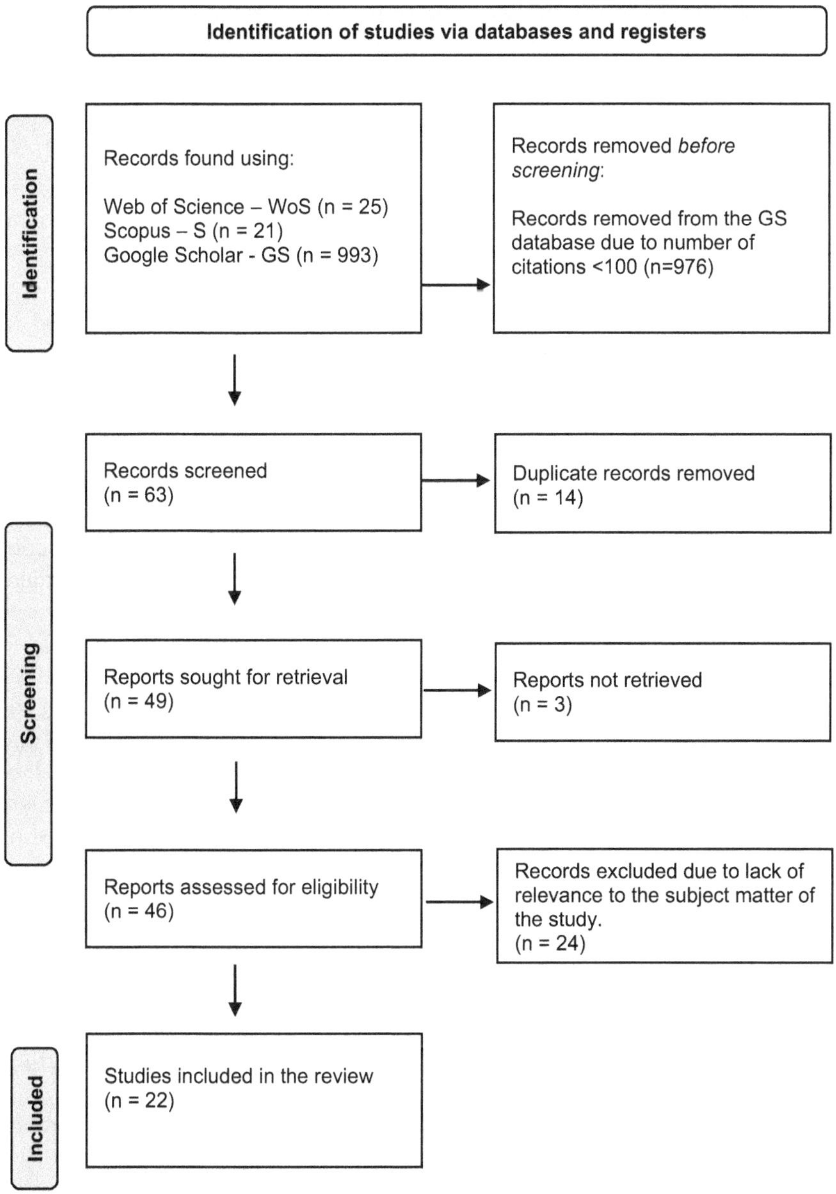

Figure 7.1 PRISMA Flow Chart of the Systematic Literature Review

Source: Own elaboration based on Page, McKenzie, Bossuyt, Boutron, Hoffmann, Mulrow, et al. (2021).

7.3 Results

Table 7.1 shows the results from the systematic literature review. Five areas were identified in which research on the relationship between FinTech and gender disparity was conducted, namely, FinTech and entrepreneurship, FinTech and wages/earnings, FinTech and CEOs/managers, FinTech and the role of women in society, FinTech and users. Within each area, publications have been sorted by year of publication.

The largest number of studies were conducted on FinTech and users, without being homogeneous, that is, the analyses concerned:

1 Potential gender disparity among FinTech users.
2 The intentions of individuals of each gender concerning the use of FinTech offers.
3 The impact of FinTechs on financial inclusion.
4 The development of appropriate software used by FinTechs adapted to people of both genders.

Regarding the analysis of FinTech users, the results are mixed. Gender disparity can be observed in only some of the services offered by FinTechs. In addition, it varies according to geographic location and is seen mainly in poorer countries. Cultural differences also play an important role in access to FinTech services. The results of studies concerning point 2 are also inconclusive and depend mainly on the type of services provided. One of them shows that gender is not a determinant of intentions to use FinTech services, while other studies produce results showing that women and men are driven by different factors when it comes to making decisions regarding the use of FinTech services. Given the diversity in these services, it is important for FinTech firms to prepare an appropriately structured offer for both men and women. Regarding point 3, we find clear results proving that the development of FinTechs has a positive impact on the financial inclusion of women. Regarding point 4, research shows that the algorithms used to develop software used by the FinTech sector can discriminate against users on the basis of gender, among other factors.

In other areas, single publications were found, and they show that:

1 The development of FinTechs can contribute to reducing the gender wage gap and have a positive impact on increasing earnings among women with low social status, among others. Moreover, it can significantly strengthen the role of women in society, including in the labour market.
2 The development of FinTechs can have a positive impact on the growth of entrepreneurship, including for women. It is worth noting, however, that a study using data from Cameroon and Burkina Faso finds a correlation between these factors, but the effect of gender disparity is not observed.
3 Men predominate among managers of FinTech firms. This implies the presence of a strong gender disparity effect in this area.

Table 7.1 Results from the Systematic Literature Review on Gender Disparity in FinTech

Publication	*Conclusions of Research on Gender Disparity in the FinTech Sector*	*Areas of Interest*
Kedir and Kouame (2022)	Based on studies conducted in Cameroon and Burkina Faso, the evidence shows that the use of mobile money positively influences the level of self-employment and entrepreneurship among women. However, the results allude to an analogous effect among men. Thus, in this case, the effect of gender disparity cannot be observed.	FinTech and entrepreneurship
Guo, Chen and Zeng (2021)	Research in China shows that the development of FinTechs causes: (1) A reduction of the gender wage gap. This is a consequence of, among other things, increasing the efficiency of the labour market, raising wages among disadvantaged groups, and supporting transparency and fairness in the employment process. (2) An increase in entrepreneurship and, concomitantly, in earnings among women through the reduction of capital constraints (increased access to financing) and of operating costs of business activities. (3) A reduction in the earnings gap between women and men within households, and consequently the increase in the bargaining power of women within a household. (4) Increase in the earnings of mainly women with low social status and, concomitantly, low level of human capital. Furthermore, this reduces the risk of decreasing earnings among women giving birth and raising children.	FinTech and wages/ earnings FinTech and entrepreneurship
Sannino, Di Carlo and Lucchese (2020)	Based on a study of the demographic characteristics of corporate leaders (CECs) in FinTech sector, in firms that have introduced the concept of CSR (corporate social responsibility) 94% of CEOs are male and only 6% were female. The research sample consisted of 100 main FinTech entities identified in 2018 by the annual KPMG Report.	FinTech and CEOs/ managers
Saputra, Burnia, Shihab, Anggraini, Purnomo and Azzahro (2019)	Efforts in women's economic empowerment have been undertaken by various parties including the FinTech sector, and now they are mushrooming. Amartha.com, one of the FinTechs operating in Indonesia, engages in peer to peer (P2P) lending business that claims to contribute to women's empowerment. Based on data from the Central Bureau of Statistics, the female labour force participation rate in Indonesia is 51.7%, while the male labour force participation rate reaches 88.5%. In this society, women's empowerment becomes critical because it can create conditions, atmosphere, climate that will potentially allow the community to grow. Moreover, women's empowerment and gender equality are one of the development priorities that must be achieved in 2030 under the Sustainable Development Goals. One of the conclusions is that increasing women's capacity increases the institutional capacity of the community, both apparatus and citizen. Women are key managers of natural resources and powerful agents of change. FinTech's P2P lending technology can also increase the role of women in employment opportunities, organising experience, improving skills and engaging in community development.	FinTech and the role of women in society

(*Continued*)

Table 7.1 (*Continued*)

Publication	*Conclusions of Research on Gender Disparity in the FinTech Sector*	*Areas of Interest*
Caglayan, Talavera, Xiong and Zhang (2022)	One of the conclusions is that borrowers with better credit scores and those who can offer higher rates are likely to reapply for funds after a failed attempt – females with better education are discouraged quickly. There is no evidence of gender discrimination from the perspective of investors and most importantly, the evidence shows that gender does not play a significant role in lenders' decision-making process. This result is crucial, as it shows that the gender of an applicant does not affect P2P lenders' funding behaviour in China (contrary to evidence in earlier empirical studies, which suggests that institutional lenders are prone to stereotyping consumers in their lending decisions). Female applicants are not discriminated against on the basis of gender.	FinTech and users
Kim (2022)	Mobile money does not address many of the structural drivers of financial gender inequality, but it does improve levels of financial inclusion by increasing women's access to various financial channels from which they were previously excluded. Moreover, in some societies around the world, women are often treated as inferior and constitute a vulnerable group. Because of entrenched gender roles and gender discrimination, women traditionally have a lower level of education and are subordinated to male family members, which creates many restrictions in terms of their economic activities.	FinTech and users
Kim (2022), Nel and Boshoff (2023)	The evidence shows that the existence of and resistance to innovation may be related to gender. Designing separate advertisements to target gender-specific perceptions could be effective. FinTech could also design advertisements that target the perceptions of both genders as, for example, satisfaction with a traditional bank is a more substantial factor contributing to the usage barrier for males than females, but it also influences females' perception of the usage barrier. Such advertisements should include male and female images to appeal to both genders. Advertisements could also include gender-neutral language to avoid gender-specific bias. Lastly, demonstrations and use-case scenarios included in advertisements to change consumer perceptions could also be gender-neutral. Research investigating gender differences shows that usefulness is a more important factor influencing behavioural intention for males than for females, while perceived ease of use more strongly influences behavioural intention for females than for males. The value barrier is a stronger determinant of non-adoption intention for males than females. Also, the results show that the opposite is true for the risk barrier – the risk barrier is a stronger determinant of non-adoption for females than males. Moreover, gender differences are noted in the influence of the value barrier, risk barrier and the image barrier on the perception of the barrier to using online banking.	FinTech and users

Noreen, Mia, Ghazali and Ahmed (2022)	The government of Pakistan launched the banking on equality programme to enhance gender equality in financial inclusion. Studies report that FinTech has a great potential to provide access to financial and non-financial institutions for underprivileged segments of society. There is a crucial need for a well-established FinTech ecosystem in the country to make use of the potential benefits of FinTech. The State Bank of Pakistan encourages women to participate in financial inclusion through the policy entitled "Banking on Equality: Reducing the Gender Gap in Financial Inclusion". Several relevant organisations provide initial feedback on the level of increase in financial inclusion among men while it remains stagnant among women.	FinTech and users
Flavián; Pérez-Rueda, Belanche and Casalo (2022)	One of the important moderating factors in the adoption and use of emergent technologies is gender. This is attributable to differences between men's and women's decision-making processes. The research identifies different factors as more important when evaluating behaviours. Men are more motivated by the need for achievement than women, therefore, with identical levels of technological optimism, men may be more likely to adopt new technologies to achieve gains. Studies suggest that, traditionally, men are more associated with innovative behaviour than women, thus, following role congruity, innovativeness may be a more important factor for men than for women. On the other hand, women tend to exhibit higher anxiety and lower self-efficacy than men when dealing with new technologies to the extent that they avoid technologies that cause them discomfort. As a result, with identical levels of discomfort and insecurity, women may be less likely than men to adopt new technologies. Similarly, women may value awareness more than men because it reduces their anxiety levels and increases their perceived self-efficacy. Indeed, as a means of increasing their confidence in their use of a given technology, women tend to acquire relevant knowledge by consulting additional information sources before making decisions, which suggests that awareness may be more important for women than for men.	FinTech and users

(*Continued*)

Table 7.1 (Continued)

Publication	*Conclusions of Research on Gender Disparity in the FinTech Sector*	*Areas of Interest*
Boamah, Murshid and Mozumder (2021)	Research from Bangladesh indicates that there is unequal access to FinTech services, such as mobile money due to social norms. The male's role in this society is to manage the household budget, which consequently leads to women generally not having their own savings and not acquiring personal properties. This, in turn, is the reason why women are less likely to use FinTech services compared to men.	FinTech and users
Museba, Ranganai and Gianfrate (2021)	In this study, 59% of the respondents are male and 41% were female, which represents the gap in women's access to FinTech services. In Uganda, the female ratio is 49% to 51%, which is representative of the Ugandan population. However, there is room for improvement of gender equality in access to financial technology.	FinTech and users
Fu, Huang and Singh (2021)	The study concludes that a machine is biased in terms of gender even when it does not use gender information as an input. The authors propose a general and effective "debiasing" method that can be applied to any prediction focused ML (machine learning) application. Any bias against occupations or locations with a high concentration of individuals from a particular gender group suggests gender bias. Although using occupation and location that are highly correlated with gender to discriminate against borrowers may not necessarily be illegal, it is still concerning.	FinTech and users
Nurlaily, Aini and Asmoro (2021)	This study shows that gender can moderate the impact of perceived risk on the intention to continue using FinTech, especially in the female user group.	FinTech and users
Li, Hanna and Kim (2020)	Based on US research using 2015 data, men are more likely to use mobile payments compared to women.	FinTech and users
Singh, Sahni and Kovid (2020)	Evidence obtained from a group of 439 users shows that gender, as a demographic characteristic, has no influence on decision-making when using FinTech services. Men as well as women have similar beliefs when deciding to use FinTech services.	FinTech and users

Stancu, Panait, Raimi and Palazzo (2020)	The study analyses the values of two indicators by gender for 48 countries from Europe and Central Asia, which fall within all income levels. One of the final conclusions is that credit institutions must have a policy of attracting financial consumers differentiated according to their certain characteristics like gender. That is why the FinTech sector must focus on increasing financial inclusion and attracting vulnerable groups to the financial circuit.	FinTech and users
Varkey (2020)	This research examines both the overall and category-specific financial literacy of scheduled tribes in Kerala with special emphasis on gender. There are drastic differences in the financial literacy of scheduled tribes across categories of services and gender. The tribal community is unable to find satisfactory literacy in FinTech services, but has healthy knowledge on other basic financial and banking services – women often outperform men in this regard.	FinTech and users
Sahay, Allmen, Lahreche, Khera, Ogawa, Bazarbash and Beaton (2020)	FinTech is contributing toward closing gender gaps in financial inclusion in most countries, but there is a concern that gaps could rise in the post-COVID era. Stakeholders note several barriers that may be higher for women: cultural or social norms, financial literacy, safety and disparity in access to resources. Given these structural barriers, concerns remain that the gender gap may widen as the shift toward digital financial services accelerates during the COVID-19 crisis. FinTech is contributing toward closing the gender gap in financial inclusion albeit with differences across regions. Gender gaps tend to be slightly lower for FinTech-driven financial inclusion than for traditional financial inclusion. There is variation across countries with FinTech playing a positive role in closing gender gaps in the Middle East and African countries. Conversely, gaps are lower for traditional financial inclusion in the Asian and Latin American countries. Cross-country variation can be explained by obstacles that FinTech cannot address, such as cultural or social norms and barriers in financial and digital literacy.	FinTech and users
Belanche, Casalo and Flavian (2019)	The research was conducted on a group of potential users of financial robo-advisors from North America, Great Britain and Portugal. It shows that gender is not a determinant of intention to use financial robo-advisors, meaning that both men and women base their decisions on similar grounds.	FinTech and users

(*Continued*)

Table 7.1 (Continued)

Publication	*Conclusions of Research on Gender Disparity in the FinTech Sector*	*Areas of Interest*
Katyayani and Varalakshmi (2019)	Financial corporations are also adopting digital tools when providing services to their customers. This study accounts for various demographic factors, such as gender. It finds this demographic factor impacts on users' interest in adopting FinTech. One of the hypotheses of the study is "There is no impact of gender on users' intention to adopt the FinTech". Accordingly, gender does not influence the adoption of financial technology by users.	FinTech and users
Lui and Lamb (2018)	The authors point out that algorithms built using artificial intelligence and applied to banking or FinTechs could discriminate against users on the basis of, for example, gender or race.	FinTech and users
Demirguc-Kunt, Klapper, Singer, Ansar and Hess (2018)	The authors conclude that the introduction of mobile money accounts can reduce the gender gap when it comes to bank account ownership. In only two (Burkina Faso and Tanzania) out of eight African countries (Burkina Faso, Tanzania, Côte d'Ivoire, Gabon, Kenya, Senegal, Uganda, Zimbabwe) is there a gender gap in mobile money account ownership (pp. 25–26). The use of bank accounts for digital payments is similar between men and women in high-income countries. In contrast, a gender gap is noted in developing countries, as men are more likely to make digital payments than women. These differences can be significant depending on the individual country (pp. 56–57).	FinTech and users

Source: Own elaboration based on literature indicated in the table.

7.4 Conclusions

The analysis indicates that the topic of gender disparity in the FinTech sector has only recently been addressed. The oldest publications date back to 2018, while the majority were published between 2020 and 2022. Moreover, in many articles, gender disparity is seen as a side issue when conducting other research on the FinTech sector. This implies there is an important research gap in terms of analyses of gender disparity in the FinTech sector.

Using a systematic literature review method, the chapter has identified five areas relating to gender disparity in FinTech, i.e.: FinTech and entrepreneurship, FinTech and wages/earnings, FinTech and CEOs/managers, FinTech and the role of women in society, FinTech and users.

The studies reviewed were often carried out on very diverse samples from different countries. Furthermore, services provided by FinTech firms are heterogeneous suggesting that the problem of gender disparity may only apply to the use of some services. In fact, gender discrimination cannot be observed in the case of certain services. Relatively ambiguous results were obtained regarding the intention to use FinTech services. For some services, no gender disparity was identified, while in other cases characteristics that differentiate men from women were observed. It should be mentioned here that the issue of cultural diversity, and the level of economic development and financial literacy play an important role in both areas. These factors have a very significant impact on gender disparity. The dominance of men among managers can also be mentioned as a disadvantageous feature of the FinTech sector. This is mainly the result of lower levels of financial literacy among women and the fact that men dominate the IT industry. Elements that are discriminating based on gender are also present in the software used by FinTech institutions. In this case, it is important to take action to raise awareness among developers to draw attention to this problem and to remove such discriminatory elements from software in use as soon as possible. The analysis also showed the positive impact of FinTech development on reducing the gender wage gap, increasing the level of entrepreneurship and the social status of women.

From a general economic point of view, one can argue that action should be taken to reduce the gender gap in the various areas of the FinTech sector, because of the many positive effects mentioned above. These effects are particularly evident in poorer countries, where women's social status is low, and their role is limited to raising children and being a housewife. Some of the key actions leading to the reduction of this gap could include increasing financial literacy among women; encouraging women to work in the IT sector through, for example, re-branding, adapting study and course offers to women's expectations and promoting them; and adapting FinTech companies' service and product offers to different genders.

References

Báez, A.B., Báez-García, A.J., Flores-Muñoz, F., Gutiérrez-Barroso, J. (2018). Gender diversity, corporate governance and firm behavior: The challenge of emotional management. *European Research on Management and Business Economics,* 24, 3, 121–129. https://doi.org/10.1016/j.iedeen.2018.07.001

Belanche, D., Casalo, L.V., Flavian, C. (2019). Artificial intelligence in FinTech: Understanding robo-advisors adoption among customers. *Industrial Management & Data Systems*, 119, 7, 1411–1430. https://doi.org/10.1108/IMDS-08-2018-0368

Boamah, E.F., Murshid, N.S., Mozumder, M.G.N. (2021). A network understanding of FinTech (in)capabilities in the global South. *Applied Geography*, 135, 1–11. https://doi.org/10.1016/j.apgeog.2021.102538

Caglayan, M., Talavera, O., Xiong, L., Zhang, J. (2022). What does not kill us makes us stronger: The story of repetitive consumer loan applications. *European Journal of Finance*, 28, 1, 46–65. https://doi.org/10.1080/1351847X.2020.1793792

Demirguc-Kunt, A., Klapper, L., Singer, D., Ansar, S., Hess, J. (2018). *Global Findex Database 2017: Measuring Financial Inclusion and the Fintech Revolution.* Washington, DC: World Bank. https://openknowledge.worldbank.org/handle/10986/29510

FinTech Diversity Radar (2021). The FinTech promise for an even recovery. https://findexable.com/diversity-radar/

Flavián, C., Pérez-Rueda A., Belanche D., Casaló L.V. (2022). Intention to use analytical artificial intelligence (AI) in services – the effect of technology readiness and awareness. *Journal of Service Management*, 33, 2, 293–320. https://doi.org/10.1108/JOSM-10-2020-0378

Fu, R.S., Huang, Y., Singh, P.V. (2021). Crowds, lending, machine and bias. *Information Systems Research,* 32, 1, 72–92. https://doi.org/10.1287/isre.2020.0990

Gender Equality Index 2020: Digitalisation and the future of work. https://eige.europa.eu/publications/gender-equality-index-2020-report/men-dominate-technology-development

Global Gender Gap Report (2021). World Economic Forum.

Global Gender Gap Report (July 2022). World Economic Forum.

Guo, Q., Chen, S.Y., Zeng, X.Q. (2021). Does FinTech narrow the gender wage gap? Evidence from China. *China & World Economy*, 29, 4, 142–166. https://doi.org/10.1111/cwe.12382

Guzman, J., Kacperczyk, A. (2019). Gender gap in entrepreneurship. *Research Policy*, 48, 7, 1666–1680. https://doi.org/10.1016/j.respol.2019.03.012

Haveman, H.A., Beresford, L.S. (2012), If you're so smart. Why aren't you the boss? Explaining the persistent vertical gender gap in management. *The Annals of the American Academy of Political and Social Science*, 639, 1, 114–130. https://doi.org/10.1177/0002716211418443

Katyayani J., Varalakshmi C.H. (2019). Influence of consumer profile on adoption of FinTech products with reference to Vijayawada city, Ap. *International Journal of Recent Technology and Engineering*, 7, 5S4, 455–457.

Kedir, A., Kouame, E. (2022). FinTech and women's entrepreneurship in Africa: The case of Burkina Faso and Cameroon. *Journal of Cultural Economy*, 15, 4, 452–467. https://doi.org/10.1080/17530350.2022.2041463

Kim, K. (2022). Assessing the impact of mobile money on improving the financial inclusion of Nairobi women. *Journal of Gender Studies*, 31, 3, 306–322. https://doi.org/10.1080/09589236.2021.1884536

Li, B., Hanna, S.D., Kim, K.T. (2020). Who uses mobile payments: FinTech potential in users and non-users. *Journal of Financial Counseling and Planning*, 31, 1, 83–100. https://doi.org/10.1891/JFCP-18-00083

Lui, A., Lamb, G.W. (2018). Artificial intelligence and augmented intelligence collaboration: Regaining trust and confidence in the financial sector. *Information & Communications Technology Law*, 27, 3, 267–283. https://doi.org/10.1080/13600834.2018.1488659

Muscba, T.J., Ranganai, E., Gianfrate, G. (2021). Customer perception and use of digital financial services and mobile money services in Uganda. *Journal of Enterprising Communities – People and Places in the Global Economy*, 15, 20, 177–203. https://doi.org/10.1108/JEC-07-2020-0127

Nel, J., Boshoff, C. (2023). Unraveling the link between status quo satisfaction and the rejection of digital-only banks. *Journal of Financial Services Marketing*, 28, 189–207. https://doi.org/10.1057/s41264-022-00146-z

Noreen, M., Mia, M.S., Ghazali, Z., Ahmed, F. (2022). Role of government policies to FinTech adoption and financial inclusion: A study in Pakistan. *Universal Journal of Accounting and Finance*, 10, 10, 37–46. https://doi.org/10.13189/ujaf.2022.100105

Nurlaily, F., Aini, E.K., Asmoro, P.S. (2021). Understanding the FinTech continuance intention of Indonesian users: The moderating effect of gender. *Business: Theory and Practice*, 22, 2, 290–298. https://doi.org/10.3846/btp.2021.13880

Page, M.J., McKenzie, J.E., Bossuyt, P.M., Boutron, I., Hoffmann, T.C., Mulrow, C.D., et al. (2021). The PRISMA 2020 statement: An updated guideline for reporting systematic reviews. *BMJ*, 372, 71. https://doi.org/10.1136/bmj.n71

Petrongolo, B. (2019). The gender gap in employment and wages. *Nature Human Behaviour*, 3, 316–318. https://doi.org/10.1038/s41562-019-0558-x

Pulse of FinTech H2'21 (2022). KPMG, https://assets.kpmg/content/dam/kpmg/xx/pdf/2022/02/pulse-of-fintech-h2-21.pdf

Rani, S., Goyal, N. (2021). Gender gap in financial literacy: Literature review. *Journal of Tianjin University Science and Technology*, 54, 8, 339–354. https://doi.org/10.17605/OSF.IO/SF8MA

Sahay, R., Eruksson von Allmen, U., Lahreche, A., Khera, P., Ogawa, S., Bazarbash, M., Beaton, K. (2020). The promise of FinTech: Financial inclusion in the post COVID-19 era. *International Monetary Fund*, Departmental Paper No. 20/009.

Sannino, G., Di Carlo, F., Lucchese, M. (2020). CEO characteristics and sustainability business model in financial technologies firms: Primary evidence from the utilization of innovative platforms. *Management Decision*, 58, 8, 1779–1799. https://doi.org/10.1108/MD-10-2019-1360

Saputra A.D., Burnia I.J., Shihab, M.R., Anggraini, R.S.A., Purnomo, P.H., Azzahro, F. (2019). Empowering women through peer to peer lending: Case study of Amartha.com. Proceedings of 2019 International Conference on Information Management and Technology, ICIMTech 2019. https://doi.org/10.1109/ICIMTech.2019.8843721

Singh, S., Sahni, M.M., Kovid, R.K. (2020). What drives FinTech adoption? A multi-method evaluation using an adapted technology acceptance model. *Management Decision*, 58, 8, 1675–1697. https://doi.org/10.1108/MD-09-2019-1318

Stancu, A., Panait, M., Raimi, L., Palazzo, M. (2020). Financial consumers - promoters of sustainable development? Evidences from Europe and central Asia. Innovative models to revive the global economy, Proceedings of the 3rd international conference on economics and social sciences, 841–850. https://doi.org/10.2478/9788366675162-083

The Business Research Company (2019). Global FinTech market value is expected to reach $309.98 billion at a CAGR of 24.8% through 2022. https://www.prnewswire.com/news-releases/global-FinTech-market-value-is-expected-to-reach-309-98-billion-at-a-cagr-of-24-8-through-2022--300926069.html

World FinTech Report (2021). Capgemini Research Institute. https://FinTechworldreport.com/

Varkey, J. (2020). Financial literacy in the FinTech era: A study of scheduled tribes in Kerala. *International Journal of Advanced Science and Technology*, 29, 5, 2904–2915.

8 FinTech and Sustainability

Does FinTech Firms' SDG-Orientation Play a Role in the Bank-FinTech Relationship?

Stefano Cosma and Daniela Pennetta

8.1 Introduction: Sustainability, Financial and Social Inclusion and Financial Institutions

The increase of extreme environmental and climatic disasters, both in frequency and intensity, and the growing social imbalances that impact on the lives of people around the world as well as the recent COVID-19 pandemic have increased the attention paid to the adverse side effects of unsustainable economic growth. The UN has defined sustainable development as "*development that meets the needs of the present without compromising the ability of future generations to meet their own needs*". In 2015, the United Nations introduced Agenda 2030, a plan of action for people, planet and prosperity, that integrates economic, environmental and social issues (UN, 2015). Agenda 2030 aims to end poverty, fight inequality, address climate change and build peaceful societies that respect human rights, by simultaneously ensuring that nobody is left behind. The goals set for sustainable development have global validity and require a strong cooperation between countries, institutions, governments, the private sector and citizens (Kara et al., 2021).

Even if there is not any explicit mention about the role of the financial system in achieving a sustainable development path, there is strong consensus that it can directly or indirectly support the transition to a sustainable economic model (Linciano et al., 2021).

One possible way is through the integration of social and environmental considerations in financial institutions' culture, strategy and decision-making processes (Ferrata, 2019). More specifically, the Final Report of the HLEG on Sustainable Finance (2018), and the "Action Plan: Financing Sustainable Growth" released by the European Commission in 2018, highlight the importance of the commitment of financial institutions to redirect existing resources toward sustainable uses through their investment, lending and insurance activities, serving Agenda 2030 over the medium to long term (European Commission, 2018). The role of the governance of financial institutions is crucial in aligning their activity to Agenda 2030 by ensuring the inclusion of sustainability issues in the decision-making process, highlighting the interdependency between sustainable development, Sustainable Development Goals

DOI: 10.4324/9781003340454-8

(SDGs) and ESG factors (*Environmental, Social, Governance*) (Sciarelli et al., 2021).

The second possible contribution of the financial system to the achievement of SDGs is the mitigation of financial exclusion. The European Commission (2008) defined financial exclusion as "*a process whereby people encounter difficulties accessing and/or using financial services and products in the mainstream market that are appropriate to their needs and enable them to lead a normal social life in the society in which they belong*". Therefore, there is a strong relationship between the difficulty in accessing financial services and being socially excluded (Carbó et al., 2007). Financial inclusion, and in particular fostering access to payments, credit, savings and insurance services, supports poverty reduction, enables people to reduce vulnerability through the stabilization of their cash flows, to invest in education and health, and to cope with unforeseen emergencies (Mehrotra, 2019); also, it improves the fulfillment of financial obligations and supports economic growth through the financing of entrepreneurship, in particular start-ups and small enterprises (Ozili, 2018; Moufakkir & Mohammed, 2020; Arner et al., 2020).

To such ends, FinTechs, as natural digital firms, leverage on the advantages allowed by the implementation of new technologies: (1) a better collection, management and analysis of data, (2) the reduction of intermediation costs and (3) the possibility to introduce new forms of intermediation and customer-centric business models (UN Task Force on Digital Financing of the SDGs, 2020). Overall, this brings to the market more affordable, better and personalized financial services, which can satisfy the unmet needs of customers, particularly underserved, excluded and unsatisfied segments, such as vulnerable households, Micro Small and Medium-sized Enterprises (MSMEs) and digital natives (Salampasis & Mention, 2018).

In this chapter, we investigate if FinTech firms' SDG-orientation facilitates bank-FinTech relationships and if there are differences among various types of agreement (equity or non-equity agreements). More specifically we seek answers to two research questions:

RQ1. Does FinTechs' SDG-orientation determine the presence of relationships with banks?
RQ2. Does FinTechs' SDG-orientation determine the type of bank-FinTech relationship?

This specific theme is unexplored in the extant literature but is important to investigate. If a significant relation emerges between FinTechs firms' SDG-orientation and their relationship with banks, then we can better understand whether, beyond the pressures emanating from regulators, authorities and public opinion, being SDG-oriented may be strategy for FinTechs in establishing strategic alliances with banks. Indeed, since FinTech firms are mainly innovative start-ups, they often struggle to survive because of the economic and financial weakness typical of this stage of life (Carbó-Valverde et al., 2022).

Cooperation with traditional financial institutions like banks can help FinTechs in their development and growth path (Hornuf et al., 2020). On the other side, through strategic alliances with FinTechs, banks may not only improve their innovation capacity (Bömer & Maxin, 2018; Klus et al., 2019) but also make more effective their journey toward sustainability. In general, we explore if bank-FinTech relationships may strengthen the role of the overall financial system in underpinning of Agenda 2030.

The chapter is structured as follows. In Section 8.2, we explore how FinTech can contribute to sustainability, by separately consider the different specialization area of FinTechs (payments, financing, investments and insurance). In section 8.3, we explain data and methods. Section 8.4 presents results and discussion. Section 8.5 concludes with managerial and regulatory implications.

8.2 FinTech and Its Contribution to Sustainability

8.2.1 Payment Services

Fuelled by the spread of internet and mobile devices even among the poorest (Ozili, 2018), the increasing consumer comfort with online financial transactions and the general acceptance of new technologies (Committee on the Global Financial System and Financial Stability Board, 2017; Financial Stability Board, 2019), FinTech firms are contributing to the expansion of mobile money, that is, the use of mobile phones to affordably deposit, transfer and withdraw money without having a bank account (Suri, 2017). By promoting affordable access to payment accounts (Ozili, 2018), FinTechs are enhancing the financial inclusion of individuals, households and micro and small firms (Gautam, 2019). Having a payment account allows people to store, send and receive money, also in the form of remittances (Gomber et al., 2018; Gautam, 2019), by accumulating savings and producing the necessary information for their assessment and to access other financial services, in particular credit and insurance products. These are crucial in starting a business, investing or saving for education, managing risk and coping with unexpected financial distress, which could facilitate an overall improvement of financial resilience, quality of life and income equality (Ouma et al., 2017; Gosavi, 2018; Bongomin & Ntayi, 2019; Demir et al., 2020). Furthermore, payment services provided by FinTech firms help to reduce risks of loss, theft, corruption and other financial crimes associated with cash-based transactions (Mhlanga, 2020).

8.2.2 Financing Services

In the financing field, FinTech firms contribute to SDGs through financial inclusion in two ways. First, the implementation of sophisticated credit risk assessment algorithms that consider non-traditional, unstructured and accurate customer data (Berg et al., 2020), also known as *digital footprints*, can lead to a better understanding of the financial position of each customer. This could reduce information asymmetries and credit rationing, or financial exclusion caused by the application of traditional and standard risk assessment and management methods typical of banks (Donald, 2020; Hua & Huang, 2021; Mhlanga, 2020). Some argue that the ability to consider more information in creditworthiness assessment may also lead to lower interest rates for borrowers (see Jagtiani & Lemieux, 2019).

Secondly, crowdfunding platforms, in particular equity- and lending-based crowdfunding platforms, have introduced a new intermediation model aimed at facilitating a direct financial exchange between investors and individuals or firms seeking funds. This provides the latter an opportunity to realize their projects through a new financing channel able to serve untapped customer segments and which can complete the market (Gomber et al., 2018; Jagtiani & Lemieux, 2018; Dai, 2020). The streamline activity of crowdfunding platforms, as well as their possibility to not undertake credit and financial risks, allow them to offer cheaper financing products to individuals and MSMEs (Lee & Shin, 2018; Odinet, 2018). The contribution of FinTech firms to financial inclusion can, in turn, stimulate entrepreneurial activity with a positive effect on job creation, innovation and economic growth (Kara et al., 2021). If fundraising is also intended to, for example, female entrepreneurship (Saputra et al., 2019), the development of sustainable and circular production systems, the financing of education, medical or other unexpected expenses or other charitable initiatives in support of environmental and social causes, then FinTech firms also contribute to redirect financial resources toward more sustainable uses (Macchiavello & Siri, 2020).

8.2.3 Investment Services

Turning to investment services, FinTech firms are contributing to sustainable development by offering affordable and innovative digital solutions focused on MSMEs' resource planning. These include business financial manager software and treasury management services, that, for example, allow MSMEs to create and archive invoices, receipts and other documents, track income and expenses, calculate and manage tax declarations and payroll and check comprehensive reports on business performance. All these functionalities are aimed to gain real time visibility of cash flows, to easily identify potential problems and quickly determine the appropriate action to take, reducing the risks to which MSMEs are exposed (Pooley, 2020). Also, these tools are important sources of reliable information to be used for loan application purposes, allowing MSMEs to be more likely to be eligible (Donald, 2020).

In the investments field, FinTech firms contribute also to financial inclusion by enlarging the range of affordable saving options available to investors, allowing them to invest small amounts of money for short periods of time (Chuen, 2018). Particularly, robo-advisors could target underserved investors, providing web-based portfolio management services with almost zero human intervention and using algorithms powered by artificial intelligence that reduce the cost for personalized advice, thus meeting the needs of investors with few assets available for investments (Schwinn & Teo, 2018). The digitalization of investment services may also strengthen capital markets through enhanced savings rates (Arner et al., 2020) and improve the asset allocation of retail investors, especially for those with low financial literacy and with limited knowledge of investing who are more likely to held unfruitful cash holdings (Agarwal & Chua, 2020). The expansion of saving options may reduce poverty and inequalities by allowing people to invest and cope with unexpected financial shocks and to shift excess wealth for retirement purposes, with an improvement in consumption smoothing (Schwinn & Teo, 2018). This also means that saving rates may increase, bringing new financial resources into the financial system, which can in turn support innovation, MSMEs development, human capital and infrastructure. It is worth noting that some FinTechs offer to investors the possibility to allocate their resources in ESG-related investment products, thereby underpinning attainment of the UN SDGs (Arner et al., 2020).

8.2.4 Insurance Services

Finally, FinTech firms operating in the insurance segment, so-called InsurTech firms, contribute to SDGs by introducing new and cost-effective insurance products targeting unserved markets. InsurTech products include microinsurance, that is, low-priced tailored products to low-income people and peer-to-peer insurance, which makes individuals pool together to share risks, making insurance more inclusive and affordable to high-risk groups that are difficult to cover in traditional insurance (Abdikerimova & Feng, 2021). Also, specific products are addressed to customers that are not continuously exposed to risks, such as on-demand insurance and usage-based insurance, which fulfill the need of temporary and less expensive coverage (Nicoletti, 2021). Furthermore, InsurTech firms play an important role in widening the spectrum of insurable risks and customers thanks to their ability to incorporate new and innovative sources of data in their actuarial assessments of customers. For example, through the inclusion of meteorological information, images, geospatial and other ESG-related risks information, they can offer coverage against weather events, allowing households, farmers, entrepreneurs and MSMEs operating in climate-sensitive sectors to manage climate risk and increase their resilience to negative economic shocks caused by climate change (Volz et al., 2020). Also, the possibility to exploit data retrieved from networked devices (that is, IoT technology), such as drive behavior, sport and dietary habits, data breaches and other risk expositions, reduces information asymmetries and allows InsurTech firms to accurately assess every kind of customers. This enables insurers to serve people and MSMEs without insurance history or which are traditionally associated to riskier groups through personalized and fairly priced life and non-life insurance products (McFall & Moor, 2018). Overall, InsurTech firms' activity is contributing to reduce the risks to which households and firms are exposed and, consequently, to build more resilient societies.

8.3 Data and Methods

Our analysis focuses on Italy. Even though Italy is a developed country, its sustainability performance is not completely satisfying and none of the SDG goals has been reached yet (Sachs et al., 2021). Furthermore, in Italy, the diffusion of digital financial services may be hindered by the general low level of digital competences (Istat, 2021) and financial literacy (OECD, 2020) and the high incidence of elderly population (Eurostat, 2020). In this framework, bank-FinTech relationships may be fundamental in fostering FinTech initiatives and in spreading the use of digital financial products among individuals and MSMEs, with positive effects on sustainability performance.

8.3.1 Samples

To answer our research questions, we first identify 124 Italian FinTech firms through the Italian FinTech ecosystem report elaborated by Ernst and Young (2020). All the selected FinTechs are in Italy, have an active website, which is fundamental in retrieving qualitative information, and are available in the Aida database, which is the largest source of financial information for Italian firms.

Subsequently, we construct two different samples. One is functional to study the role of FinTechs' SDG-orientation in determining the presence of relationships with banks (RQ1) and consists of an unbalanced panel in which the 124 identified FinTech firms are observed over the period 2007–2019, thereby realizing a total of 528 data points.

The second sample, which allows us to explore if the SDG-orientation of FinTech firms affects the type of relationship established with banks (RQ2), is a cross-sectional dataset at a relationship level that we construct in three steps. First, we construct the treatment sample that includes all equity investments and partnership agreements in which FinTechs are involved. We identified equity investments through FinTech firms' shareholding structures and partnership agreements through FinTechs' websites. We end up with a treatment sample of 72 records (45 equity agreements and 27 partnership agreements), involving 30 out of 124 FinTech firms. Second, we construct the control sample, which consists of 94 non-treated FinTech firms. Third, we apply the Propensity Score Matching (PSM) technique to match to each observation in the treatment sample three cases from the control sample through the nearest neighbor technique. The matching is based on all control variables concerning the business model and economic and structural features – see Section 3.4. The final cross-sectional dataset comprises 288 observations: 27 partnership agreements and their 81 matched control cases; and 45 equity agreements and their 135 matched control cases.

8.3.2 *Dependent Variables*

The first sample (RQ1) includes the dependent variable (1) *Rel*, a binary year-specific indicator equal to one when least a relationship with a bank is established for a specific FinTech, zero otherwise (Hornuf et al., 2020).

The second sample (RQ2), instead, includes the dependent variable (2) *Type_Rel*, an ordinal categorical variable taking the value of one when there are no bank-FinTech relationships (that is, control cases), two for partnership agreements and three for equity agreements. The order reflects the increasing degree of integration between parties that occurs when moving toward equity agreements.

8.3.3 *Independent Variables*

We assess FinTechs' SDG-orientation through a qualitative approach. First, we rate FinTechs' contribution to SDGs relying on the information available on their website and assigning a score from 0 to 3 for each sustainability pillar (economic, social and environmental). Here, zero indicates the absence of a substantial contribution, while one, two and three points refer to, respectively, low, medium and high contribution. The choice to qualitatively assess SDG-orientation mainly comes from the unavailability of non-financial declarations or social reports published by FinTechs. Aware that this data-collection methodology may lead to subjectivity bias, we overcome this problem by engaging a panel of four independent experts who individually and independently assess the SDG-orientation of our sample of FinTechs. To obtain comparable evaluations, our experts were provided with the same supporting materials: a list of the 17 SDGs and the related pillars, and the literature review on FinTech and its contribution to sustainability (that is, Section 2). After collecting the evaluations, we construct our measures of FinTechs' SDG-orientation. We also consider possible discrepancies in score assignment, and for each sampled FinTech, we compute the following variables:

1 *Economic_Score*: the mean of the scores assigned by the experts on the contribution to the economic pillar less half of its variance.
2 *Social_Score*: the mean of the scores assigned by the experts on the contribution to the social pillar less half of its variance.
3 *Environmental_Score*: the mean of the scores assigned by the experts on the contribution to the environmental pillar less half of its variance.
4 *Sustainability_Score*: which measures the overall contribution to SDGs and is computed as the mean of all the assigned scores less half of the variance.

In this way, the average assigned scores decrease as the discordance between them increases.

8.3.4 Control Variables

We also consider some components of FinTech firms' business models for control purposes, since their *modus operandi* may be in line with the cooperation deemed ideal by banks (Schmidt et al, 2018). We collect information about:

1. *Customers*: a categorical variable representing the type of customers to whom financial products are offered; there are three possible levels, namely, "Business", "Consumer" and "All". We consider the latter as the base level (Laidroo et al., 2021).
2. *Products*: a categorical variable representing the type of financial services offered. It has five possible levels: "Payments", "Financing", Investments", "Insurance" and "Diversified" (Tanda and Schena, 2019), where the last level refers to FinTech firms operating in more than one segment and "Payments" is the base level.
3. *Distribution*: a categorical variable based on distribution channel strategy that has two possible levels: "Website Only", if the FinTech firm distributes products and services only through their website (base level); and "Multichannel" if the FinTech also exploits other distribution channels (such as mobile applications, APIs and devices) (Laidroo et al., 2021).
4. *Intermediation_Model*: a categorical variable representing the adopted intermediation model and consisting in three possible levels: "Direct", if the FinTech directly offers to customers its own financial products; "Platform", if the FinTech offers an online marketplace where two opposite side of the market can meet, thus satisfying opposite needs; and "Broker", if the FinTech distributes third parties' products. The latter is the base level (Gimpel et al., 2018).

Finally, we include some economic and structural features as control variables. More specifically, for a specific FinTech firm observed in a specific year we considered the logarithms of:

1. $Avg\_Rev\_Growth_{3Y}$: measures the previous three years average revenue growth.
2. $Avg\_Intangibles_{3Y}$: measures the average incidence of intangibles-on-total assets of the previous three years. A proxy of technological innovation developed by FinTech firms.
3. Avg_Size_{3Y}: the average total assets of the FinTech firm in the previous three years.
4. *Age*: the years of business activity.

Table 8.1 provides definitions and sources of our variables, while Tables 8.2 and 8.3 provide descriptive statistics of the variables in our panel and cross-sectional databases.

Table 8.1 Definition and Sources of Variables

Variable	*Description*
Dependent Variables	
Rel	Binary variable equal to 1 if the FinTech firm cooperates with at least one bank in a certain year, 0 otherwise.
Type_Rel (*)	Ordinal categorical variable equal to 1 if the FinTech firm is not engaged in a relationship with a bank, 2 if the FinTech firm becomes partner of a bank and 3 if the FinTech firm receives equity investments from a bank.
	Source: Aida, FinTech firms' website.
Independent Variables	
Economic_Score	Average contribution to economic SDGs based on scores assigned by a panel of four experts, adjusted by subtracting half of the variance.
Social_Score	Average contribution to social SDGs based on scores assigned by a panel of four experts, adjusted by subtracting half of the variance.
Environmental_Score	Average contribution to environmental SDGs based on scores assigned by a panel of four experts, adjusted by subtracting half of the variance.
Sustainability_Score	Average overall contribution to SDGs based on scores assigned by a panel of four experts, adjusted by subtracting half of the variance.
	Source: panel of experts.
Control Variables	
Customers	Categorical variable with three possible levels according to type of customers served: "Business", "Consumer" and "All". Base level: "All".
Products	Categorical variable with five possible levels according to type of products offered: "Payments", "Financing", "Investments", "Insurance" and "Diversified". Base level: "Payments".
Distribution	Categorical variable with two possible levels according to type of distribution channel exploited: "Website Only" and "Multichannel". Base level: "Website Only".
Intermediation_Model	Categorical variable with three possible levels according to type of intermediation model adopted: "Direct", "Platform" and "Broker". Base level: "Broker".
	Source: FinTech firms' website.
$Avg\_Rev\_Growth_{3Y}$	Logarithm of previous three years revenue growth for an individual FinTech and year.
$Avg\_Intangibles_{3Y}$	Logarithm of previous three years average incidence of intangibles-to-total assets for a FinTech firm and year.
Avg_Size_{3Y}	Logarithm of previous three years average total assets.
Age	Age of the FinTech firm in years in a respective year.
	Source: Aida.

(*) Available only for cross-sectional database.

Table 8.2 Summary Statistics of Panel Dataset: 582 FinTech-Year Observations, 2007–2019

Continuous Variables	*Mean*	*Median*	*Standard Deviation*	*Minimum*	*Maximum*
Rel	0.165	0	0.371	0	1
Economic_Score	1.179	0.958	0.688	-0.375	3
Social_Score	0.582	0.625	0.544	-0.375	3
Environmental_Score	0.169	0	0.369	0	2.333
Sustainability_Score	0.494	0.364	0.402	-0.091	2.273
Avg_Rev_Growth$_{3Y}$	0.383	0.301	0.381	0	2.513
Avg_Intangibles$_{3Y}$	0.078	0.057	0.081	0	0.301
Avg_Size$_{3Y}$	4.217	5.114	2.308	0	7.333
Age	2.991	2	2.835	0	19

Categorical variables (% of cases in the sample)

Customers:	**Products:**	**Distribution:**	**Intermediation Model:**
Business 31.45%	Payments 13.71%	Website Only 68.55%	Direct 46.77%
Consumer 20.16%	Financing 49.19%	Multichannel 31.45%	Platform 45.97%
All 48.39%	Investments 26.61%		Broker 7.26%
	Insurance 6.45%		
	Diversified 4.03%		

Table 8.3 Summary Statistics of Cross-Sectional Dataset: 288 Observations: 27 Partnership Agreements, 45 Equity Agreements and a Total of 144 Control Cases

Continuous Variables	*Mean*	*Median*	*Standard Deviation*	*Minimum*	*Maximum*
Economic_Score	1.110	0.792	0.645	0	3
Social_Score	0.579	0.333	0.516	-0.375	2.333
Environmental_Score	0.151	0	0.312	0	2.333
Sustainability_Score	0.471	0.364	0.359	0	2.273
Avg_Rev_Growth$_{3Y}$	0.422	0.301	0.392	0	2.208
Avg_Intangibles$_{3Y}$	0.075	0.057	0.078	0	0.301
Avg_Size$_{3Y}$	4.208	5.056	2.363	0	7.106
Age	3.319	3	3.207	0	19

Categorical variables (% of cases in the sample)

Type Rel:	**Customers:**	**Products:**	**Distribution:**	**Intermediation Model:**
1 75%	Business 28.82%	Payments 27.08%	Website Only 61.11%	Direct 51.04%
2 9.38%	Consumer 14.58%	Financing 43.75%	Multichannel 38.89%	Platform 45.14%
3 15.62%	All 56.6%	Investments 20.48%		Broker 3.82%
		Insurance 3.13%		
		Diversified 5.56%		

8.3.5 *Methods*

To answer RQ1 we implement a random-effects logistic panel regression, where the dependent variable is *Rel.* Thus, we model the probability of the ith FinTech in year t to establish at least a relationship with banks through the logistic function:

Model 1

$$\pi_{i,t} = \text{Prob}(y_{i,t}=1|x) = \frac{1}{1+\exp(\beta_0 + \sum_{j=1}^{J} \beta_j S_i + \sum_{k=1}^{K} \beta_k BM_i + \sum_{c=1}^{C} \beta_c FC_{i,t} + \varepsilon_{i,t})}$$

where S_i are the time-invariant SDG-orientation measures of the ith FinTech firm, BM_i are the time-invariant business model features of the ith FinTech firm, and $FC_{i,t}$ are the economic and structural features of the ith FinTech firm in t.

To answer RQ2, we use the cross-sectional sample and an ordinal logistic regression, where the dependent variable is *Type_Rel.* Thus, we model the probability for the ith FinTech firms to fall within the m ordered outcome through the ordinal logistic function:

Model 2

$$\pi_{m,i} = \text{Prob}(y_{m,i} = m \mid x) = \frac{1}{1+\exp(-\kappa_m + \beta X_i)} - \frac{1}{1+\exp(-\kappa_{m-1} + \beta X_i)}, \; m = (1, 2, 3)$$

where $\kappa_0 = -\infty$ and $\kappa_2 = +\infty$.

$$\text{Here } \beta X_i = \left(\beta_0 + \sum_{j=1}^{J} \beta_j S_i + \sum_{k=1}^{K} \beta_k BM_i + \sum_{c=1}^{C} \beta_c FC_i + \varepsilon_i\right)$$

where S_i, BM_i and FC_i are, respectively, SDG-orientation measures, business model components and economic and structural features of the ith FinTech firm.

In both models, the log-likelihood function is maximized by the BFGS (Broyden, Fletcher, Goldfarb & Shanno) second-order optimization. We compute average partial effects (APEs) for all independent and control variables (Wooldridge, 2009).

8.4 Results and Discussion

We report the results obtained from Models 1 and 2 in Tables 8.4 and 8.5, respectively. We provide two versions for each model, which consider separately the overall contribution of FinTech firms to SDGs, and the single contribution to the economic, social and environmental pillars.

The overall contribution to SDGs positively influences on probability to establish at least one relationship with a bank (Model 1a); in particular, for a one-unit increment in *Sustainability_Score*, the likelihood to observe a bank-FinTech relationship increases by 5.4%. If we consider separately the three sustainability pillars introduced by Agenda 2030, we can see that being committed to social and environmental issues positively influences the likelihood to observe a bank-FinTech relationship (Model 1b). In particular, the average effect of a one-unit increment in *Social_Score* and *Environmental_Score* are 9.3% and 6.7% respectively. *Economic_Score* has a neutral effect.

The overall contribution to sustainability has a positive effect on the establishment of both partnership and equity agreements (Model 2a, Table 8.5). The effect is stronger for the latter – the coefficient equals 15.1%. However, when we separately consider the contribution to the three pillars, we cannot observe significant differences between the two types of relationship, except for *Economic_Score*, which exerts a statistically significant effect at the 10% level for equity investments and partnership agreements (coefficients equal to 2.3% and 5.9%, respectively (Model 2b).

Overall, the SDG-orientation of FinTech firms positively affects the probability of some relationships with banks. These results provide evidence that bank-FinTech relationships, which may be beneficial for the resilience of FinTech firms, represent an additional avenue through which both parties can enhance the contribution of the financial system to sustainability. This holds particularly for social and environmental dimensions. Also, FinTech firms which contribute the most to sustainability, and especially to the economic pillar, are more likely to relate with banks through the highest degree of integration between parties, namely, equity investments. This usually implies a strong commitment by banks to provide new financial resources and enlarge the market share of the participated FinTech firm through reputational spillovers, the access to a wide customer base and distribution network, beyond the possibility to exploit synergies arising from the integration of tangible and intangible assets. This can further enhance the underpinning of Agenda 2030 and its SDGs.

Other interesting results concern the components of FinTech's business models. In particular, firms that offer financial products to both businesses and individuals seem to have a higher probability (from 2.9% to 9.8%) to establish a strategic alliance with a bank compared to firms that serve only one customer segment (Models 1a and 1b). Furthermore, specialization in the business segment is more negatively related to equity investments than partnership agreements (Models 2a and 2b). FinTech firms operating in payments have a greater probability to cooperate with a bank with respect to those operating in financing, insurance or investments segments; the opposite occurs if the comparison is made with diversified FinTech firms, for which coefficients range between 9% and 27.6% in Models 1a and 1b, respectively. Financing, insurance and investments segments show a greater negative effect for equity than partnership agreements (Models 2a and 2b).

There is also evidence that FinTech firms opting for a distribution channel strategy only based on their internet presence (i.e., if they distribute products and services only through their website) have a 4.9 to 12.1% higher probability to cooperate with at least a bank (Models 1a and 1b), even if there is not a significant effect on *Type_Rel*. Finally, *Intermediation_Model*, which has "Broker" as base level, shows that FinTech firms that do not distribute third parties' products, that is, direct model, are less likely to establish relationships with banks particularly through equity investments (Models 2a and 2b).

Table 8.4 Results of Logistic Panel Regressions (*Rel*)

Variable	*Rel*	
Model	*(1a)*	*(1b)*
Intercept	0.206 ***	0.181 ***
	(0.003)	(0.002)
SDG-orientation		
Sustainability_Score	0.054 ***	–
	(0.009)	
Economic_Score	–	-0.004
		(0.01)
Social_Score	–	0.093 ***
		(0.006)
Environmental_Score	–	0.067 ***
		(0.007)
Customers		
Business	-0.029 ***	-0.097 ***
	(0.012)	(0.007)
Consumer	-0.042 ***	-0.098 ***
	(0.011)	(0.009)
Products		
Diversified	0.09 *	0.276 ***
	(0.048)	(0.045)
Financing	-0.355 ***	-0.271 ***
	(0.0468)	(0.038)
Insurance	-0.335 ***	-0.283 ***
	(0.046)	(0.041)
Investments	-0.273 ***	-0.093 ***
	(0.035)	(0.028)
Distribution		
Multichannel	-0.049 **	-0.121 ***
	(0.025)	(0.014)
Intermediation Model		
Direct	-0.023	0.037
	(0.025)	(0.035)
Platform	0.065 **	0.028
	(0.03)	(0.04)
Economic and structural features		
$Avg\_Rev\_Growth_{3Y}$	-0.005	-0.004
	(0.004)	(0.004)
$Avg\_Intangibles_{3Y}$	0.02 ***	0.003
	(0.005)	(0.004)
Avg_Size_{3Y}	0.062 ***	0.05 ***
	(0.011)	(0.012)
Age	0.023 ***	0.017 ***
	(0.002)	(0.002)
N° observations	582	582
Wald χ^2	43.31 ***	64.39 ***
McFadden's R2	0.343	0.348
Nagelkerke's R2	0.415	0.421
AIC	270.997	272.657
BIC	340.861	351.253
Firm effects	Yes	Yes

Note: Random effects regressions for the dependent variable *Rel*. In Model 1a we implement the overall measure of SDG-orientation. In Model 1b we separately consider the contribution to economic, social and environmental pillars. Average Partial Effects (APEs) are shown. Robust standard errors are in parenthesis. Significance levels: *, **, *** for 10%, 5% and 1% respectively.

Table 8.5 Results of Ordered Logit Regressions (Dependent Variable *Type_Rel*). Using the Cross-Sectional Dataset – Model 3

Variable	*Type_Rel*		
	Outcome Level	*Model 2a*	*Model 2b*
Intercept	No relationship	0.754 *** (0.022)	0.753 *** (0.022)
	Partnership agreement	0.095 *** (0.017)	0.096 *** (0.017)
	Equity agreement	0.151 *** (0.02)	0.15 *** (0.02)
	SDG-orientation		
Sustainability_Score	No relationship	-0.154 ** (0.071)	–
	Partnership agreement	0.043 * (0.023)	–
	Equity agreement	0.111 ** (0.051)	–
Economic_Score	No relationship	–	-0.082 * (0.047)
	Partnership agreement	–	0.023 * (0.014)
	Equity agreement	–	0.059 * (0.034)
Social_Score	No relationship	–	0.123 (0.089)
	Partnership agreement	–	-0.034 (0.024)
	Equity agreement	–	-0.089 (0.066)
Environmental_Score	No relationship	–	-0.118 (0.085)
	Partnership agreement	–	0.033 (0.024)
	Equity agreement	–	0.085 (0.062)
	Customers		
Business	No relationship	0.149 ** (0.063)	0.211 *** (0.059)
	Partnership agreement	-0.043 ** (0.0195)	-0.061 *** (0.019)
	Equity agreement	-0.106 ** (0.046)	-0.15 *** (0.046)

(Continued)

Table 8.5 (Continued)

Variables		*Type_Rel*	
	Outcome Level	*Model 2a*	*Model 2b*
Consumer	No relationship	0.123	0.136
		(0.108)	(0.121)
	Partnership agreement	-0.034	-0.035
		(0.032)	(0.034)
	Equity agreement	-0.088	-0.101
		(0.077)	(0.089)
	Products		
Diversified	No relationship	-0.021	-0.02
		(0.092)	(0.112)
	Partnership agreement	-0.001	-0.001
		(0.004)	(0.089)
	Equity agreement	0.021	0.021
		(0.096)	(0.118)
Financing	No relationship	0.575 ***	0.554 ***
		(0.065)	(0.086)
	Partnership agreement	-0.078 ***	-0.087 ***
		(0.022)	(0.022)
	Equity agreement	-0.497 ***	-0.467 ***
		(0.077)	(0.098)
Insurance	No relationship	0.593 ***	0.612 ***
		(0.128)	(0.084)
	Partnership agreement	-0.085	-0.112 **
		(0.065)	(0.051)
	Equity agreement	-0.507 ***	-0.5 ***
		(0.089)	(0.084)
Investments	No relationship	0.266 ***	0.336 ***
		(0.101)	(0.105)
	Partnership agreement	-0.008	-0.026
		(0.012)	(0.034)
	Equity agreement	-0.258 ***	-0.31 ***
		(0.092)	(0.085)
	Distribution		
Multichannel	No relationship	0.031	0.047
		(0.094)	(0.095)
	Partnership agreement	-0.008	-0.013
		(0.025)	(0.024)
	Equity agreement	-0.022	-0.035
		(0.07)	(0.071)
	Intermediation Model		
Direct	No relationship	0.363 **	0.496 ***
		(0.159)	(0.191)
	Partnership agreement	-0.048 **	-0.047**
		(0.021)	(0.024)
	Equity agreement	-0.315 **	-0.448 **
		(0.147)	(0.209)

(Continued)

Table 8.5 (Continued)

Variable		*Type_Rel*	
	Outcome Level	*Model 2a*	*Model 2b*
Platform	No relationship	0.122	0.305
		(0.229)	(0.27)
	Partnership agreement	-0.008	-0.009
		(0.017)	(0.019)
	Equity agreement	-0.115	-0.296
		(0.214)	(0.278)
	Economic and structural features		
$Avg\_Rev\_Growth_{3Y}$	No relationship	-0.131 *	-0.149 *
		(0.078)	(0.078)
	Partnership agreement	0.037 *	0.041 *
		(0.022)	(0.022)
	Equity agreement	0.095 *	0.107 *
		(0.057)	(0.058)
$Avg\_Intangibles_{3Y}$	No relationship	0.263	0.291
		(0.519)	(0.525)
	Partnership agreement	-0.074	-0.081
		(0.147)	(0.149)
	Equity agreement	-0.19	-0.21
		(0.373)	(0.378)
Avg_Size_{3Y}	No relationship	-0.016	-0.016
		(0.018)	(0.017)
	Partnership agreement	0.005	0.005
		(0.005)	(0.005)
	Equity agreement	0.012	0.012
		(0.013)	(0.012)
Age	No relationship	-0.024 **	-0.024 ***
		(0.009)	(0.009)
	Partnership agreement	0.007 **	0.007 **
		(0.003)	(0.003)
	Equity agreement	0.017 **	0.017 **
		(0.007)	(0.007)
N° observations		288	288
Wald χ^2		40.81 ***	38.93 ***
McFadden's R2		0.126	0.1433
Nagelkerke's R2		0.169	0.191
AIC		398.294	398.917
BIC		456.902	464.85

Note: Ordered logit regressions for the dependent variable *Type_Rel*. In Model 2a we implement the overall measure of SDG-orientation. In Model 2b, we separately consider the contribution to economic, social and environmental pillars. The Table shows the Average Partial Effects (APEs) of each independent variable on the three levels of *Type_Rel* (1 = No partnership; 2 = Partnership agreement; 3 = Equity agreement). Robust standard errors are in parenthesis. Significance levels: *, **, *** for 10%, 5% and 1% respectively.

These results show that the diversification of customer segments and product range are factors that positively influence the establishment of bank-FinTech relationships. This is probably because it implies more collaboration opportunities, thus increasing the attractiveness of FinTech firms for banks keen on strategic alliances. From the opposite perspective, the results also justify why cooperation with banks for specialized FinTech firms has a large and negative probability to occur in equity form. Among product specializations, the payment segment seems to be the most targeted by banks, probably because it represents the most mature field in which FinTech firms operate. Finally, FinTech firms that distribute their products via multiple channels are less likely to cooperate with banks, probably because they are already able to reach a large market share. As concerns economic and structural features, it seems that the likelihood to establish at least one relationship with a bank is higher for FinTech firms that, in the previous three years, are characterized by larger size and market experience as indicated by the positive and statistically significant coefficients of Avg_Size_{3Y} and *Age* in Models 1a and 1b. Only in Model 1a we find a positive and statistically significant effect of $Avg\_Intangibles_{3Y}$, used to proxy FinTechs' innovativeness, with a coefficient equal to 2%. Furthermore, in Models 2a and 2b, we observe that high-growth and older FinTech firms are more likely to receive investments from banks rather than establishing partnership agreements.

Overall, our results show that more structured and experienced FinTech firms, that had the opportunity to create, test and implement their technological innovations and that are gaining market shares appear more attractive to banks, especially when the latter opt for equity investments.

8.5 Conclusions, Implications and Further Research

Since the release of Agenda 2030 in 2015, the transition to a sustainable economic model has become a more urgent and priority objective. Financial institutions have an important role in achieving a sustainable economic model. In particular, FinTech firms, by leveraging on new technologies, contribute to Agenda 2030 thanks to their ability to redirect financial resources toward more sustainable uses and to mitigate financial exclusion (Arner et al., 2020).

We have examined if FinTech firms' SDG-orientation has a strategic potential in establishing strategic alliances with banks. More specifically, if FinTech firms' SDG-orientation facilitates bank-FinTech relationships and if there are differences among various types of agreement (equity or non-equity agreements).

We find that FinTech firms' SDG-orientation positively affects the probability to observe relationships between FinTechs and banks. This holds for social and environmental dimensions introduced by Agenda 2030. This conclusion is strengthened by the evidence that FinTech firms that contribute the most to sustainability, and particularly to the economic pillar, are more likely to strongly cooperate with banks through equity agreements, which usually imply a firm commitment of banks in sustaining FinTech firms' activity. FinTechs' business models and other economic and structural feature also influence the presence and type of bank-FinTech relationships.

These results confirm that SDG-orientation should be considered as a strategic choice by FinTech managers, since it is positively associated to the probability of establishing relationships with banks, which can support their development and growth path. On the other side, cooperation with SDG-oriented FinTech firms may represent a part of banks' journey toward sustainability. Furthermore, SDG-orientation of FinTech firms, on one side, and the support of banks to sustainable FinTech initiatives, on the other side, could be useful for both in improving reputation, as well as in acquiring and retaining customers, who are increasingly concerned about sustainability and interested in financial products embodying economic, social and environmental issues.

From a social perspective, bank-FinTech relationships may contribute to the efficiency and completeness of the financial market by delivering cheaper, innovative, of greater quality and personalized financial products to customers, thus tapping underserved, excluded and unsatisfied market segments.

Regulators should promote the spread of digital financial services because these are commonly recognized to offer strong support to the transition toward a more inclusive financial system (Arner et al., 2020) and foster the development of ecosystems where FinTechs can be fostered through interactions with traditional financial institutions. More specifically, bank-FinTech relationships, when involving sustainability-oriented initiatives, may strengthen the role of the overall financial system in the underpinning of Agenda 2030 and should be considered by regulators in setting guidelines, regulations and assessment procedures.

We acknowledge that our study has a limitation. We measured FinTechs' SDG-orientation through a qualitative approach, based on the opinions and evaluations of four independent experts. Even if the presence of more experts reduces possible subjectivity bias, the processed information could still be incomplete, particularly as concerns the integration of sustainability issues in FinTechs' internal processes and policies. Future research can certainly benefit from the release of FinTechs' non-financial declarations or social reports.

Future research may extend the analysis to an international sample to explore possible differences between advanced, developed and developing countries, in which digital finance and its contribution to financial inclusion and sustainability can be more or less pronounced.

References

Abdikerimova, S., Feng, R. (2021). Peer-to-Peer multi-risk insurance and mutual aid. *European Journal of Operational Research,* 299, 2, 735–749. https://doi.org/10.1016/j.ejor.2021.09.017

Agarwal, S., Chua, Y.H. (2020). FinTech and household finance: A review of the empirical literature. *China Finance Review International,* 10, 4, 361–376. https://doi.org/10.1108/CFRI-03-2020-0024

Arner, D.W., Buckley, R.P., Zetzsche, D.A., Robin, V. (2020). Sustainability, FinTech and financial inclusion. *European Business Organization Law Review*, 21, 1, 7–35. https://doi.org/10.1007/s40804-020-00183-y

Berg, T., Burg, V., Gombović, A., Puri, M. (2020). On the rise of fintechs: Credit scoring using digital footprints. *The Review of Financial Studies*, 33, 7, 2845–2897. https://doi.org/10.1093/rfs/hhz099

Bömer, M., Maxin, H. (2018). Why fintechs cooperate with banks—evidence from Germany. *Zeitschrift für die gesamte Versicherungswissenschaft*, 107, 4, 359–386. https://doi.org/10.1007/s12297-018-0421-6

Bongomin, G.O.C., Ntayi, J. (2019). Trust: Mediator between mobile money adoption and usage and financial inclusion. *Social Responsibility Journal,* 16, 8, 1215–1237. https://doi.org/10.1108/SRJ-01-2019-0011

Carbó-Valverde, S., Cuadros-Solas, P.J., Rodríguez-Fernández, F. (2022). Entrepreneurial, institutional and financial strategies for FinTech profitability. *Financial Innovation,* 8, 1, 1–36. https://doi.org/10.1186/s40854-021-00325-2

Carbó-Valverde, S., Gardener, E.P.M., Molyneux, P. (2007). Financial Exclusion in the UK. In *Financial Exclusion*, 14–44. Palgrave Macmillan, London. https://doi.org/10.1057/9780230508743_3

Committee on the Global Financial System & Financial Stability Board (May, 2017). FinTech credit: Market structure, business models and financial stability implications. *Financial Stability Board, Basel.* https://www.fsb.org/wp-content/uploads/CGFS-FSB-Report-on-FinTech-Credit.pdf

Chuen, D.L.K. (2018). Invited editorial comment: FinTech and alternative investment. *The Journal of Alternative Investments*, 20, 3, 6–15. https://doi.org/10.3905/jai.2018.20.3.006

Dai, R.M. (2020). Fintech as a catalyst for growth of micro, small and medium enterprises in Indonesia. *Academy of Strategic Management Journal*, 19, 5, 1–12.

Demir, A., Pesqué-Cela, V., Altunbas, Y., Murinde, V. (2020). Fintech, financial inclusion and income inequality: A quantile regression approach. *The European Journal of Finance,* 28, 1, 86–107. https://doi.org/10.1080/1351847X.2020.1772335

Donald, D.C. (2020). Smart precision finance for small businesses funding. *European Business Organization Law Review*, 21, 1, 199–217. https://doi.org/10.1007/s40804-020-00180-1

Ernst & Young (2020). FinTech waves - Italian FinTech ecosystem 2020. https://assets.ey.com/content/dam/ey-sites/ey-com/it_it/generic/generic-content/ey-fintech-ecosystem.pdf

European Commission. (2008). Financial services provision and the prevention of financial exclusion. https://www.bristol.ac.uk/geography/research/pfrc/themes/finexc/ec-financial-exclusion.html

European Commission. (2018). Action plan: Financing sustainable growth. https://eur-lex.europa.eu/legal-content/EN/TXT/?uri=CELEX%3A52018DC0097

Eurostat (2020). Ageing Europe. Looking at the lives of older people in the EU. https://ec.europa.eu/eurostat/documents/portlet_file_entry/3217494/KS-02-20-655-EN-N.pd f/9b09606c-d4e8-4c33-63d2-3b20d5c19c9

Ferrata, L. (2019). Digital financial inclusion–an engine for "leaving no one behind". *Public Sector Economics*, 43, 4, 445–458. https://doi.org/10.3326/pse.43.4.6

Financial Stability Board (2019). FinTech and market structure in financial services: Market developments and potential financial stability implications. https://www.fsb.org/wp-content/uploads/P140219.pdf

Gautam, D.P. (2019). Do remittances promote financial inclusion? In *Economic and Political Institutions and Development*, 91–108. Springer, Cham. https://doi.org/10.1007/978-3-030-06049-7_6

Gimpel, H., Rau, D., Röglinger, M. (2018). Understanding FinTech start-ups–a taxonomy of consumer-oriented service offerings. *Electronic Markets*, 28, 3, 245–264. https://doi.org/10.1007/s12525-017-0275-0

Gomber, P., Kauffman, R.J., Parker, C., Weber, B.W. (2018). On the fintech revolution: Interpreting the forces of innovation, disruption, and transformation in financial services. *Journal of Management Information Systems*, 35, 1, 220–265. https://doi.org/10.1080/07421222.2018.1440766

Gosavi, A. (2018). Can mobile money help firms mitigate the problem of access to finance in Eastern sub-Saharan Africa? *Journal of African Business*, 19, 3, 343–360. https://doi.org/10.1080/15228916.2017.1396791

High-Level Expert Group on sustainable finance. (2018). Financing a sustainable European economy. https://ec.europa.eu/info/sites/default/files/180131-sustainable-finance-final-report_en.pdf

Hornuf, L., Klus, M.F., Lohwasser, T.S., Schwienbacher, A. (2020). How do banks interact with fintech startups? *Small Business Economics,* 57, 3, 1505–1526. https://doi.org/10.1007/s11187-020-00359-3

Hua, X., Huang, Y. (2021). Understanding China's fintech sector: development, impacts and risks. *European Journal of Finance*, 27, 4–5, 321–333. https://doi.org/10.1080/1351847X.2020.1811131

Istat (2021). Rapporto annuale 2021. https://www.istat.it/storage/rapporto-annuale/2021/Rapporto_Annuale_2021.pdf

Jagtiani, J., Lemieux, C. (2018). Do fintech lenders penetrate areas that are underserved by traditional banks? *Journal of Economics and Business*, 100, 43–54. https://doi.org/10.1016/j.jeconbus.2018.03.001

Jagtiani, J., Lemieux, C. (2019). The roles of alternative data and machine learning in fintech lending: Evidence from the LendingClub consumer platform. *Financial Management*, 48, 4, 1009–1029. https://doi.org/10.1111/fima.12295

Kara, A., Zhou, H., Zhou, Y. (2021). Achieving the United Nations' sustainable development goals through financial inclusion: A systematic literature review of access to finance across the globe. *International Review of Financial Analysis,* 77, 1, 101833. https://doi.org/10.1016/j.irfa.2021.101833

Klus, M.F., Lohwasser, T.S., Holotiuk, F., Moormann, J. (2019). Strategic alliances between banks and fintechs for digital innovation: Motives to collaborate and types of interaction. *The Journal of Entrepreneurial Finance*, 21, 1, 1. https://doi.org/10.57229/2373-1761.1346

Laidroo, L., Koroleva, E., Kliber, A., Rupeika-Apoga, R., Grigaliuniene, Z. (2021). Business models of FinTechs–Difference in similarity? *Electronic Commerce Research and Applications*, 46, 1, 101034. https://doi.org/10.1016/j.elerap.2021.101034

Lee, I., Shin, Y.J. (2018). Fintech: Ecosystem, business models, investment decisions, and challenges. *Business horizons*, 61, 1, 35–46. https://doi.org/10.1016/j.bushor.2017.09.003

Linciano, N., Cafiero, E., Ciavarella, A., Di Stefano, G., Levantini, E., Mollo, G., Nocella, S., Santamaria, R., Taverna, M., Taverna, M. (2021). Sustainable finance: Trends, issues and perspectives amid the evolution of the EU regulatory framework. *CONSOB Quaderno finanza sostenibile* (no. 1). https://www.consob.it/documents/1912911/1972319/fs_1.pdf/cd935bf5-f395-d36b-732c-068399d7a308

Macchiavello, E., Siri, M. (2020). Sustainable finance and Fintech: Can technology contribute to achieving environmental goals? A preliminary assessment of 'Green FinTech'. *European Banking Institute Working Paper Series 2020* (no. 71). https://ssrn.com/abstract=3672989 or http://dx.doi.org/10.2139/ssrn.3672989

McFall, L., Moor, L. (2018). Who, or what, is insurtech personalizing?: Persons, prices and the historical classifications of risk. *Distinktion: Journal of Social Theory*, 19, 2, 193–213. https://doi.org/10.1080/1600910X.2018.1503609

Mehrotra, A. (2019, April). Financial inclusion through FinTech–A case of lost focus. In *2019 International Conference on Automation, Computational and Technology Management (ICACTM)*, 103–107, IEEE. https://doi.org/10.1109/ICACTM.2019.8776857

Mhlanga, D. (2020). Industry 4.0 in finance: The impact of artificial intelligence (ai) on digital financial inclusion. *International Journal of Financial Studies*, 8, 3, 45. https://doi.org/10.3390/ijfs8030045

Moufakkir, M., Mohammed, Q. (2020). The nexus between FinTech adoption and financial inclusion. In *Impact of financial technology (FinTech) on Islamic finance and financial stability*, 193–209. IGI Global. https://doi.org/10.4018/978-1-7998-0039-2.ch010

Nicoletti B. (2021). Propositions of value for the customer in insurance 4.0. In: *Insurance 4.0*. Palgrave Studies in Financial Services Technology, 69–99. Palgrave Macmillan, Cham. https://doi.org/10.1007/978-3-030-58426-9_4

Odinet, C.K. (2018). Consumer Bitcredit and Fintech lending. *Alabama Law Review*, 69, 4, 781–858.

OECD (2020). 2020 International survey of adult financial literacy. https://www.oecd.org/financial/education/oecd-infe-2020-international-survey-of-adult-financial-literacy.pdf.

Ouma, S.A., Odongo, T.M., Were, M. (2017). Mobile financial services and financial inclusion: Is it a boon for savings mobilization? *Review of Development Finance*, 7, 1, 29–35. https://hdl.handle.net/10520/EJC-83159723e

Ozili, P.K. (2018). Impact of digital finance on financial inclusion and stability. *Borsa Istanbul Review*, 18, 4, 329–340. https://doi.org/10.1016/j.bir.2017.12.003

Pooley, H. (2020). Why banks are missing an opportunity to capture the lucrative small and medium enterprise market. *Journal of Payments Strategy & Systems*, 13, 4, 337–351.

Sachs, J., Kroll, C., Lafortune, G., Fuller, G., Woelm, F. (2021). *Sustainable Development Report 2021*. Cambridge University Press. http://dx.doi.org/10.1017/9781009106559

Salampasis, D., Mention, A.L. (2018). FinTech: Harnessing innovation for financial inclusion. In D.L. Kuo Chuen and R. Deng (Eds.), *Handbook of Blockchain, Digital Finance, and Inclusion, Volume 2*, 451–461. Academic Press. https://doi.org/10.1016/B978-0-12-812282-2.00018-8

Saputra, A.D., Burnia, I.J., Shihab, M.R., Anggraini, R.S.A., Purnomo, P.H., Azzahro, F. (2019, August). Empowering women through peer to peer lending: Case study of Amartha. com. In *2019 International Conference on Information Management and Technology (ICIMTech)*, 1, 618–622. IEEE. https://doi.org/10.1109/ICIMTech.2019.8843721

Schmidt, J., Drews, P., Schirmer, I. (2018). Charting the emerging business ecosystem of fintechs and banks: Seven types of collaborative business models. In *Proceedings European Conference on Information Systems 2018*.

Schwinn, R., Teo, E.G.S. (2018). Inclusion or Exclusion? Trends in Robo-advisory for Financial Investment Services. In D. L. Kuo Chuen ans R. Deng (Eds.), *Handbook of Blockchain, Digital Finance, and Inclusion, Volume 2*, 451–461. Academic Press. https://doi.org/10.1016/B978-0-12-812282-2.00018-8

Sciarelli, M., Cosimato, S., Landi, G., Iandolo, F. (2021). Socially responsible investment strategies for the transition towards sustainable development: The importance of integrating and communicating ESG. *The TQM Journal*, 33, 7, 39–56. https://doi.org/10.1108/TQM-08-2020-0180

Suri, T. (2017). Mobile money. *Annual Review of Economics*, 9, 497–520.
Tanda, A., Schena, C.M. (2019). *FinTech, BigTech and Banks: Digitalisation and Its Impact on Banking Business Models*. Springer, Cham. https://doi.org/10.1007/978-3-030-22426-4
Task Force on Digital Financing of the SDGs. (2020). People's money. Harnessing digitalization to finance sustainable future. https://unsdg.un.org/resources/peoples-money-harnessing-digitalization-finance-sustainable-future
United Nations. (2015). Transforming our world: The 2030 agenda for sustainable development. *New York: United Nations, Department of Economic and Social Affairs*. https://sdgs.un.org/2030agenda
Volz, U., Knaack, P., Nyman, J., Ramos, L., Moling, J. (2020). Inclusive green finance: From concept to practice. *Kuala Lumpur and London: Alliance for Financial Inclusion and SOAS*, University of London. https://eprints.soas.ac.uk/34540/1/AFI_IGF _SOAS_digital.pdf
Wooldridge, J. (2009), *Introductory Econometrics: A Modern Approach*, 4th ed., South-Western Cengage Learning, Mason, Ohio, Chapter 17.

9 FinTech and ESG

A Happy Union?

Timothy King

9.1 Introduction

This chapter provides the reader with an overview of the emergent Environmental, Social and Governance (ESG) FinTech landscape detailing the extent to which ESG factors are beginning to become important considerations for the FinTech sector. The chapter begins with an overview of some of the recent academic literature that generally highlights the growing importance of ESG. The chapter then proceeds to review key recent developments in FinTech that relate to treatment of ESG factors – organised according to two dedicated sections: *FinTech: the climate and the environment* which discusses how FinTech can address major challenges relating to climate change, and *RegTech and ESG*, which discusses how RegTech can be used successfully in the future to help firms identify, report and comply with increasing disclosure requirements around ESG. Finally, the chapter concludes.

9.2 Why Should We Care About ESG? Evidence from Academic Literature

A growing body of academic literature focuses on whether and how ESG and corporate social responsibility (CSR) activities can impact a firm's performance. First, a number of studies question whether ESG/CSR impacts various risks relevant to the firm. For example, Bozos et al. (2022) analyse non-binding shareholder proposals in US firms to investigate how the extent of voting support from shareholders on CSR issues is associated with changes in firms' underlying systematic risks. The main finding is there is a non-linear effect of voting support whereby proposals that attract low voting support result in increasing risk, while those with high support reduce risk. Additionally, the authors demonstrate that the effect of voting support on risks varies according to whether firms operate in consumer-sensitive or non-consumer-sensitive industries. Moreover, at least several other studies also look at the how ESG/CSR influences systematic risk (e.g., Albuquerque et al., 2019; El Ghoul et al., 2016; Oikonomou et al., 2012), firm-specific risk (e.g., Becchetti et al., 2015; Humphrey et al., 2012) or the cost of equity- (Chava, 2014; El Ghoul et al., 2011; Hong & Kacperczyk, 2009; Ng & Rezaee, 2015) or debt

DOI: 10.4324/9781003340454-9

capital (e.g., Chava, 2014; Goss & Roberts, 2011; Zerbib, 2019). Findings are largely mixed with respect to risk. For instance, while Becchetti et al. (2015) report that ESG and CSR are associated with increased firm-specific risk, Humphrey et al. (2012) report no significant differences for low or high CSR firms. However, the existing literature typically supports the finding that firms have access to lower costs of capital when they have stronger environmental profiles implying that an ESG focus can benefit firms in terms of access to both debt and equity capital.

A larger strand of literature examines the impact of ESG and CSR on firm value and measures of traditional firm performance. Much of this literature reports a positive relationship between ESG/CSR and firm performance. For instance, at least several studies report a clear positive link between firm ESG/CSR performance and firm value (e.g., Albuquerque et al., 2019; Fatemi et al., 2015), as well as other performance outcomes, such as profitability (Borghesi et al., 2014; Liang & Renneboog, 2017; Lins et al., 2017) and short- and long-run returns (e.g., Deng et al., 2013; Edmans, 2011; Flammer, 2015, 2021; Masulis & Reza, 2015;). Conversely, some other studies suggest, for example, that relevant news about a firm's CSR can be met with negative market reactions irrespective of whether firm CSR events are positive or negative (Krüger, 2015), or that the impact on firm value can be positive or negative depending on firm characteristics including the level of a firm's customer awareness (Servaes & Tamayo, 2013).

Relatedly, a small number of recent research papers study spillover effects from firms' ESG activities. Cao et al. (2019) find that there are positive spillover effects to peer firms from the adoption of close-call shareholder proposals on ESG/CSR issues, with peer group firms adopting comparable ESG/CSR practices. Similarly, Dai et al. (2021) demonstrate that there are unilateral spillover effects of CSR from customers to suppliers. Rind et al. (2022) focus on firms' employee welfare policies and find that peer group firms mimic one another's employee welfare decisions, which can have positive implications for firm value and innovation in firms.

Another stand of the extant literature on ESG links the characteristics of firm managers with the ESG and CSR performance of their companies. As highlighted by Gillan et al. (2021) one of the key questions to arise from this research stream, is whether firms' ESG and CSR performance and activities stem directly from the intentions of managers to act in a certain way, or, alternatively, whether they are the product of prevailing governance frameworks within firms. For instance, several papers show that managerial gender matters for firms' ESG/CSR. Borghesi et al. (2014) find that female CEOs are more likely to invest in CSR. Cronqvist and Yu (2017) present evidence of a female socialisation effect whereby the daughters of (male) CEOs transmit their stronger natural preferences for ESG and CSR concerns, which manifests as significantly higher ESG/CSR scores at the firm level. However, Aabo and Giorici (2022) caution that the apparent effect of female CEOs on a firm's ESG performance depends on the specific ESG scores being used with the effect varying from a strong, significant positive relationship to no association at all, depending on data provider. More recently, King et al. (2023) show that female led firms are associated with better workplace conditions and that this effect is strongest when firms operate in more competitive industries and in environments where agency costs facing firms are lower.

Finally, a very small nascent literature considers whether firms' ESG and CSR performance can be used to forecast firm financial distress. Li et al. (2021) show that corporate governance factors, including firm ownership structure and the composition of the corporate board, have explanatory power in predicting firm financial distress, while Citterio and King (2023) demonstrate for the first time that ESG factors can have significant explanatory power in models designed to predict bank financial distress.

9.3 FinTech: The Climate and the Environment

One of the biggest global grand challenges relates to climate change. Illuminating the gravity of this issue, Oxfam (2022) reports that the number of climate-related disasters has increased threefold over the past thirty years and that in the ten years between 2006 and 2016 global sea levels rose at a rate 2.5 times greater than virtually all of the 20th century. Although clearly the impacts of climate change are already being felt – as the previous examples illustrate, worryingly the impacts of climate change are predicted to become even more severe in the future. Research by Woods Hole Research Centre and McKinsey Global Institute Analysis predicts that from 2020 to 2050 global average temperatures will increase between 1.5 and 5°C, while a report from the United Nations Convention to Combat Desertification (2022) estimates that by 2050 as much as three-quarters of the world's population will be affected by droughts, water scarcity, rising sea levels, which, combined with other factors including overpopulation, extreme temperatures and declining crop productivity, could lead to as many as 216 million people being displaced.

Although the entire planet will experience the effects of climate change, the most severe impacts are expected to be felt more strongly by some of the poorest nations given that many such countries are geographically located close to higher natural risks, as well as lacking relative development, infrastructure and capital compared to developed nations to address and to adapt to increasing threats. This is highlighted by the Financial Stability Oversight Council (FSOC, 2021, p. 4) who warn that the adverse effects of climate change are likely to be disproportionately borne by financially vulnerable communities, including low-income communities, communities of colour, and Native-American communities. These communities may also have fewer resources to recover from, or adapt to, adverse impacts.

Increasingly firms in many jurisdictions are required to provide more meaningful disclosure around risks relating to the climate, which are commonly referred to as climate change risk (CCR). Such enhanced disclosure is designed to provide investors and wider stakeholders with more accurate and increased information regarding the extent of firm operations and specifically how operations are impacted by CCR. Salient examples include violations of environmental regulations, such as those relating to emissions of harmful chemicals, to more positive actions taken by firms, including investments in renewable energy.

9.3.1 How Can FinTech Help Address Fundamental Climate Change Challenges?

FinTech innovations that are environmental and climate focused are often labelled as "Green FinTech". These are often focused on providing innovative solutions to address key United Nations Sustainable Development Goals (SDGs), such as 7 (Affordable and Clean Energy), 11 (Sustainable Cities and Communities), 12 (Responsible Consumption and Production), 13 (Climate Action), 14 (Life Below Water), 15 (Life on Land) and 17 (Partnerships for the Goals).

An important way that Green FinTech can help address these goals is through ensuring that the financial sector supports the financing of sustainable and green investments via the allocation of private finance to support governmental spending. This is outlined in the Paris Agreement, which calls for countries to ensure that "*finance flows consistent with a pathway toward low greenhouse gas emissions and climate-resilient development*" (Paris Agreement Article 2.1(c)). Private finance is expected to be particularly valuable in helping channel funds towards green investments given restrictions on governmental expenditures, which also impact taxpayers and can lead to underinvestment in certain areas. Yet, analysis of recent data suggests that private-sector finance is growing at approximately half the rate of the public sector – 4.8% compared to 9.1% according to a report by the Climate Policy Initiative (2022). More alarmingly, the same report reveals that there is still considerable support for fossil fuels in many countries, with total fossil fuel subsidies in just 51 major countries over 40% greater than levels of total investment in climate finance between 2011 and 2020.

A positive development, as a side to FinTech, is that there is now considerable commitment from the banking sector under initiatives like the Principal for Responsible Banking, which seeks to ensure that banks take measurable action towards addressing UN SDGs, as well as key multilateral financial institutions like the European Investment bank that since 2021 no longer funds any fossil fuel energy projects. Additionally, the 2022 Climate Change Conference (COP 27) outlined out a new pooled fund to help countries that have suffered substantial loss and damage from events relating to climate change, which as previously noted are often the poorest countries. However, at the time of writing the sources of funding, the size of the fund and the triggers for payout are key issues yet to be resolved. In sum, although there is growing commitment within the banking sector there is still a considerable way to go as inferable from a 2022 blog post by Frank Elderson, (a member of the European Central Bank (ECB)), on the ECB's blog who argues that

> *banks must adapt the way they do business to account for climate-related and environmental risks... simply put, the glass is filling up slowly but it is not yet even half full. Yes, climate change has made it to the top levels within banks and some first steps have been taken. But there is a difference between talking about steps and beginning to act; and there is an even bigger difference in doing what is needed.*

Within the taxonomy of Green FinTech, there are also more specific terms including "Climate FinTech", which relates to innovations in the financial sector that help manage climate change risks, support investments in climate-friendly actions that reduce the output of harmful emissions and improve the resilience of firms and countries to climate change. Encouragingly, Climate FinTech is already helping in this respect as well as SDGs in several notable areas.

9.3.1.1 Assessment of Climate Risk

This is an important area of development for at least three principal reasons. First, because of the increasing value relevance and importance of climate risks to investors; research by International Data Corporation (who specialise in providing market intelligence to the information technology, telecommunications and consumer technology markets) estimates that physical assets worth in excess of $2.5 trillion US dollars are at risk due to climate change, with this figure set to reach $23 trillion by 2050 (International Data Corporation, 2022). Furthermore, climate risk represents a particularly important challenge for the financial sector. A 2021 article published in the ECB's Macroprudential Bulletin highlights this issue: "*The unique and complex features of climate risks, with their potential tipping points and non-linearities, represent a major challenge in terms of accurately capturing the impact of climate risks on the financial system*" (Baranović et al., 2021).

Second, given observations by regulators and policymakers that current tools in use within the financial sector are largely inadequate for the provision of accurate and timely assessment of climate-related risks. For instance, this is a point stressed in a 2021 report by the FSOC who consider that "*current data, measurement tools, and expertise are not sufficient to fully assess these* [climate] *risks*" (p. 10) and advocates the "*critical importance of taking prompt action to improve the availability of data and measurement tools, enhance assessments of climate-related financial risks and vulnerabilities, and incorporate climate-related risks into risk management practices and supervisory expectations for regulated entities, where appropriate*" (p. 3).

Third, because of increased threat from litigation for banks (and other firms) who do not accurately disclose ESG risks. As highlighted in a 2022 keynote address by Anneli Tuominen, a member of the Supervisory Board of the ECB, at the 9th Conference on the Banking Union:

> *If banks* [and non-financial firms] *do not meet the targets they have announced or follow the climate strategy they have communicated, they expose themselves to litigation and reputational risks ... and there has been a clear increase in climate-related cases being filed around the world in recent years, and this trend is likely to continue.*

Despite this, as highlighted in Anneli Tuominen's speech, over the last couple of years the ECB has highlighted that although there have been improvements in climate risk disclosure by banks since 2020, there are still many banks who still fail to report whether climate and environmental risks have a material impact on their risk profile even if many consider themselves exposed to these risks.

So how can FinTech help? Innovative new tools, such as an artificial intelligence (AI)-driven climate intelligence platform and recent flagship product called EarthScan by UK company Cervest, as well as GIS Connect developed by Aquaoso Technologies in 2021 are already helping firms better identify and manage their climate-related risk.[1] For example, Cervest's EarthScan applies data modelling and machine learning on climate data to provide firms, governments and non-government agencies (NGO) tailored and real-time assessment of the predicted effects of climate risks (including the impact of multiple severe hazards including heatwaves, flooding and precipitation, wind, drought and wildfire) on clients' physical risk and allows sophisticated forecasting across entire portfolios. Users can then choose from both detailed views as well as a simplified risk rating scores ranging from A to F, where a rating of A represents "very low climate-related risk" and F an "extremely high climate-related risk".

Insurance companies worldwide are also increasingly turning to FinTech solutions to address climate change risks. One example is the People's Insurance Company of China Property and Casualty (PICC P&C), a major Chinese insurance company. The company has developed a new platform called the Remote Damage Assessment and Claim Settlement Platform to help manage such risks that threaten the area around the city of Ningbo – a city on the coastal plain on the Yong River in the Eastern province of Zhejiang. The platform makes use of big data and geospatial data including data on building plans to provide fast mapping of areas hit by water sourced disaster and to produce automated assessments of the likely number of insurance claims, as well as an anticipated value for these claims, meaning that insurance claims can be settled quickly and efficiently.

9.3.1.2 Reallocation of Capital towards Sustainable Investments

Sophisticated uses of non-standard datasets combined with distributed ledger technology and big data analytics, including AI and machine learning techniques, are only just starting to become more common in helping to draw out complex insights from ESG data to better inform investors and wider stakeholders. This is an important development, especially when considering a growing regulatory push towards enhanced disclosure of ESG risk and performance in many regions – with increasing adoption of international frameworks including the Global Reporting Initiative (GRI), Sustainability Accounting Standards Board (SASB), Task Force on Climate-Related Financial Disclosures (TCFD) and the Carbon Disclosure Project (CDP). For example, in Europe, the March 2021 introduction of the Sustainable Finance Disclosure Regulation (SFDR) mandates that all asset managers selling financial products into the EU detail how they incorporate sustainability into their investment choices, as well as disclosing any potentially negative impacts their investments could have on social or environmental objectives.

There are at least several key areas in which FinTech can help. With such initiatives and regulatory changes, there is great potential in this area to increase the transparency of firms' ESG activities, especially given difficulties in considering ESG holistically across divergent business units and in firms that operate across sectors for instance. FinTech solutions can play a role here in helping increasing transparency with potentially positive implications for fund flows as well as filter down benefits that should help firms' and industries improve ESG performance. Despite this, there remains "*no globally mandatory standard for ESG reporting, nor is there a single process for collecting and calculating results*" (KPMG and the Monetary Policy of Singapore, 2022, p.26).

Clearly there is a need for improvement in ESG reporting and disclosure. Here FinTech is expected to play a key role in providing automated and integrated ESG reporting that can provide real-time insights. Current systems in a majority of firms are slow and cumbersome and do not support quick and accurate dissemination of relevant information. The March 2021 Pulse Survey by PwC of company CFOs infers that this is a particular priority for the financial industry with 74% (60%) of (non) financial sector CFOs stating that "*Producing investor-grade ESG information*" is a prime concern with respect to ESG reporting. Figure 9.1, from the same report, shows the wider results of this survey, which highlights a need for more robust ESG data gathering, analysis and reporting from the perspectives of both financial- and non-financial sector CFOs.

Some notable examples of innovations in this area currently referred to as "ESGTech", include a Singapore-based company also called "ESGTech", which offers a global platform for financial and non-financial firms as well as regulators from which they can gather, verify and disclose ESG data in standardised and transparent reporting formats. Another example is the US-located "Clarity AI", which combines big data with machine learning to help investors make informed investment decisions that consider ESG thereby helping to channel investments towards firms with the greatest (positive) social and environmental impact.

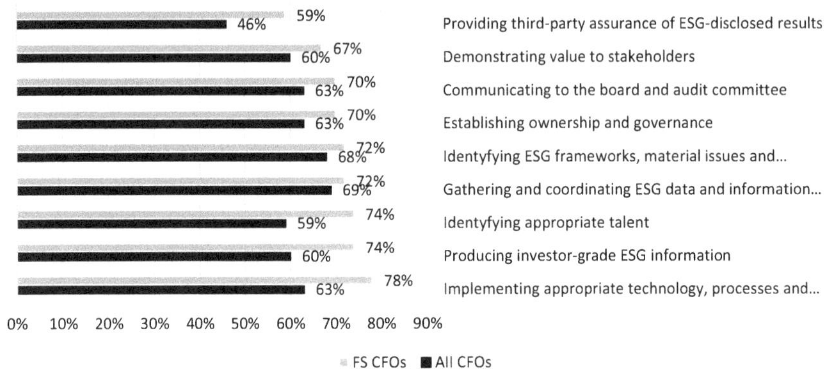

Figure 9.1 CFO Priorities with Respect to ESG Reporting

There is also the wider adoption of new digital technologies. Notably, the COVID-19 pandemic has helped in accelerating demand for digital technologies to provide new solutions to existing problems facing societies. So-called "Social FinTechs" are already having a significant impact worldwide and particularly so in developing economies, where their potential for impact is typically greatest. Latin America has witnessed particularly impressive growth in recent years with 36% of FinTech startups in the region offering products aimed at the unbanked or individuals partially excluded from the financial system, according to research by venture development firm Finnovista. This is particularly germane given that the World Bank reports that 65% of Mexican adults to not have a bank account of any kind. Against this backdrop, there have been some major FinTech success stories for helping address financial inclusion. One example is the firm Kueski whose app Kueski Pay allows customers to make payments across thousands of retailers and stores in Mexico, while also allowing for flexible payment options including periods of interest-free payments. One of the key drivers of this regional success is the high rates of technology adoption in Latin America; the World Bank reports that half of the unbanked population of Mexico owns a smartphone and has internet access while approximately 62% of the population own a smartphone.

Another area of development is the growth in connected and integrated platforms, which can help firms understand ESG across the entire supply chain. This is an increasingly salient issue, not only because of increased demand by end consumers and investors to know the extent of firms' ESG commitment and wider performance but also because of a rapidly developing regulatory environment that pushes firms to improve their practices. For example, in Germany the introduction of the Supply Chain Due Diligence Act (SDDA) of 2021 requires firms to improve the human rights and reduce the environmental risks in their supply chains or face financial penalties as high as 2% of annual turnover. Here supply chain finance can provide financial incentives for firms within a supply chain (buyers and suppliers) to commit to, and/or improve, ESG performance. One important idea, given the above regulatory as well as growing stakeholder pressure, is that supply chain finance can reduce the costs associated with ESG for smaller firms as larger firms are increasingly incentivised to commit resources to help them improve their practices. FinTechs in this area generally specialise in helping firms obtain the best funding solutions based on their detailed networks of banks and other providers of capital. Arguably to be most effective, these platforms need to be integrated or closely connected to platforms, such as the Coriolis ESG platform, that offers ESG scoring for firms of all sizes measured against SDGs.

9.4 RegTech and ESG

Regulatory technology, commonly referred to as "RegTech", is an important area of FinTech, which can be classified under reporting and analytics, and more specifically risk management (Bowden et al., 2021). The first, and most widely accepted, definition is by the UK's Financial Conduct Authority (FCA) (2016, p. 3) which defines RegTech as "*a subset of fintech that focuses on technologies that may facilitate the delivery of regulatory requirements more efficiently and effectively than existing capabilities*". More granularly, RegTech assists firms in meeting compliance requirements by leveraging innovative technologies, such as blockchain, cloud computing, machine learning, AI, big data, Application Program Interface (API), Analytics, and Voice and Text Recognition. Going forward, RegTech is expected to play a key role in helping firms meet the increasing and evolving compliance requirements relating to ESG. However, RegTech is still in its infancy and especially so in relation to compliance around ESG.

As might be expected, the adoption of RegTech differs across countries and regions. To take the example of the banking sector within the European Union, and not limited to the use of RegTech for ESG, Figure 9.2 taken from a 2021 report by the European Banking Authority (EBA), shows some significant differences in both the geographical coverage and deployment rate of RegTech providers solutions.

As can be seen from Figure 9.2, France and Germany have significantly higher deployment rates combined with leading rates of geographical coverage, whereas Eastern European countries within the EU tend to have both much lower deployment rates and geographical spread.

Figure 9.3, taken from the same 2021 EBA report, highlights key areas in which RegTech providers perceive advantages over traditional solutions. Adaptability to new regulatory requirements, accuracy, increased speed, cost reduction and scalability are all thought to be "very relevant".

Although Figures 9.2 and 9.3 focus on the banking sector, which may be thought apt given that RegTech was originally largely confined to the financial sector, it is important to note that regulatory compliance is not just

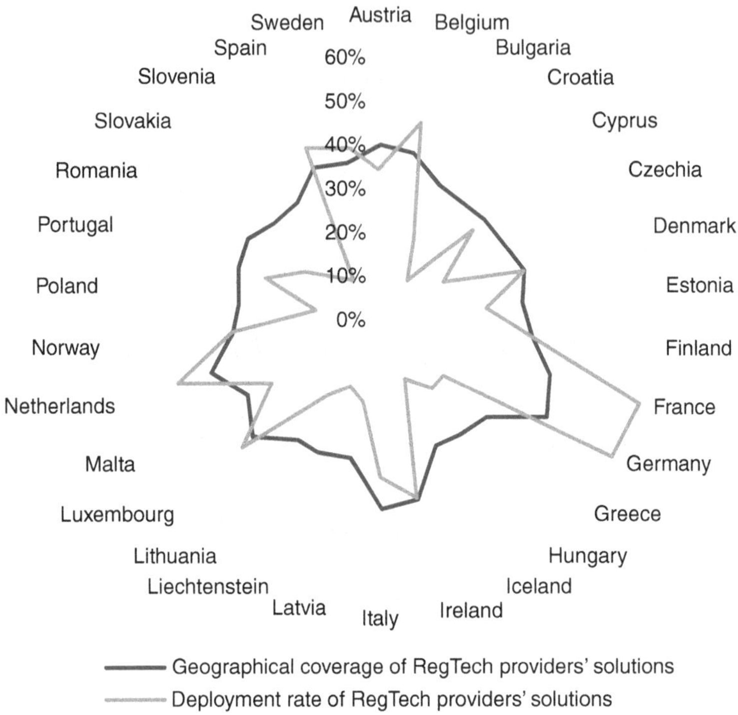

Figure 9.2 Geographical Coverage & Deployment Rate of RegTech Providers Solutions

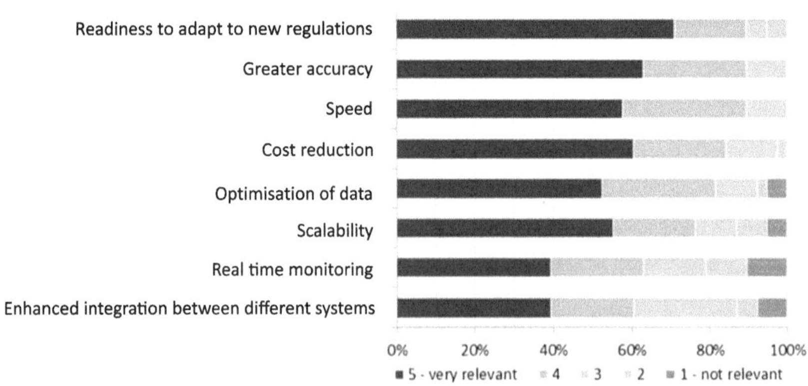

Figure 9.3 How RegTech Providers Perceive Their Advantages Over Traditional Solutions

limited to financial sector firms. Instead, it also increasingly important in many other sectors. In this vein, RegTech can now be seen as existing outside of the confines of a standard FinTech definition, which relates to the innovative use of technology specifically within the financial sector. Indeed, RegTech is predicted to play an increasingly important role in helping all firms meet evolving regulatory ESG requirements.

An important way that RegTech solutions can help firms operating in environments faced with onerous compliance requirements is in meeting real-time compliance without having to invest in expensive and extensive compliance and operations infrastructure; such benefits are particularly germane to smaller companies (Larsen & Gilani, 2017). More specifically, RegTech can help assist firms in not only meeting evolving compliance requirements but also facilitating the easier entry of small- and medium-sized firms into new business areas (characterised by higher compliance requirements) with benefits felt by individual firms as well as potential benefits for competition and consumer choice. A good example relates to companies selling vaping products who are required to comply with various regulations surrounding the sale of tobacco and vaping products. In the US, such companies are subject to increasingly onerous tobacco regulations at the federal level, from the United States Food and Drug Administration (FDA), as well as additional state-level regulations, which can vary by state. For small- and medium-sized companies especially, which vaping companies tend to be, RegTech is providing firms with an important means to ensure efficient compliance with requirements, such as verifying a customer's age and identity. This is not a straightforward process given key differences across US states: for instance, the age at which tobacco products can be purchased varies between 18 and 23 years; similarly, some states regulate vaping products the same as tobacco products whereas others have regulations for the vaping juice; finally, some states require that only a customer's age be verified whereas others also require an identity document like a driver licence be shown. Consequently, in the absence of real-time RegTech solutions, regulatory compliance would typically involve considerable human labour at a considerable cost to firms; furthermore, the additional time required to verify customers may also have led to lost repeat business.

A further example specific to the banking sector is the company "Regnology", which, through its Abacus360 Banking product, is helping national and international European banks to comply with evolving reporting requirements from different regulators and authorities, such as banks with securities traded on a regulated market of any EU member state who from 2022 have had to comply with the EBA ESG risks disclosure reporting Implementing Technical Standards (ITS)[2]. This enhanced disclosure around ESG risks represents a binding part of Pillar 3 disclosures on ESG risks. Another related example is the Singapore firm "Regtank" which utilises blockchain technology as well as machine learning and AI to assist financial institutions, venture capital and crowdfunding firms in managing their compliance and regulatory requirements more effectively.

9.5 Concluding Remarks

This chapter has focused on the intersection between ESG and FinTech. First, it discussed the growing importance placed on ESG both in terms of value relevance and risk. Second, across two main sections, it provides the reader with an overview of the extent to which FinTech can help in addressing key challenges facing the world and its people today and in the future. One important conclusion to come from this chapter is that although the FinTech sector has grown tremendously in recent years, the potential for FinTech to help address important issues such as climate change remains largely untapped. It is very much hoped that FinTech can evolve with the growing latent demand for technological-driven solutions to issues, such as ESG reporting and compliance, with positive implications for addressing SDG.

Notes

1 See: https://aquaoso.com/press-release/aquaoso-launches-groundbreaking-gis-connect-part-of-data-acclimation-platform/
2 For further details, please refer to the EBA website: https://www.eba.europa.eu/implementing-technical-standards-its-prudential-disclosures-esg-risks-accordance-article-449a-crr

References

Aabo, T., Giorici, I.C. (2022). Do female CEOs matter for ESG scores? *Global Finance Journal*, 56, 100722, 1–9. https://doi.org/10.1016/j.gfj.2022.100722

Albuquerque, R., Koskinen, Y., Zhang, C. (2019). Corporate social responsibility and firm risk: Theory and empirical evidence. *Management Science*, 65, 10, 4451–4469.

Baranović, I., Busies, I., Coussens, W., Grill, M., Hempell, H.S. (2021). The challenge of capturing climate risks in the banking regulatory framework: Is there a need for a macroprudential response? *Macroprudential Bulletin*, 15. https://www.ecb.europa.eu//pub/financial-stability/macroprudential-bulletin/html/ecb.mpbu202110_1~5323a5baa8.en.html

Becchetti, L., Ciciretti, R., Hasan, I. (2015). Corporate social responsibility, stakeholder risk, and idiosyncratic volatility. *Journal of Corporate Finance*, 35, 297–309.

Borghesi, R., Houston, J.F., Naranjo, A. (2014). Corporate socially responsible investments: CEO altruism, reputation, and shareholder interests. *Journal of Corporate Finance*, 26, 164–181.

Bowden, J., King, T., Koutmos, D., Loncan, T., Stentella Lopes, F.S. (2021). A Taxonomy of FinTech Innovation. In T. King, F.S. Stentella Lopes, A. Srivastav, J. Williams (Eds.), *Disruptive Technology in Banking and Finance* (pp. 47–91). Palgrave Studies in Financial Services Technology. Palgrave Macmillan, Cham.

Bozos, K., King, T., Koutmos, D. (2022). CSR and firm risk: Is shareholder activism a double-edge sword? *Journal of Risk and Financial Management*, 15, 11, 543.

Cao, J., Liang, H., Zhan, X. (2019). Peer effects of corporate social responsibility. *Management Science*, 65, 12, 5487–5503.

Chava, S. (2014). Environmental externalities and cost of capital. *Management Science*, 60, 9, 2223–2247.

Citterio, A., King, T. (2023). The role of Environmental, Social, and Governance (ESG) in predicting bank financial distress. *Finance Research Letters*, 51, 103411.

Climate Policy Initiative. (2022). *Global Landscape of Climate Finance a Decade of Data: 2011-2020.* https://www.climatepolicyinitiative.org/wp-content/uploads/2022/10/Global-Landscape-of-Climate-Finance-A-Decade-of-Data.pdf

Cronqvist, H., Yu, F. (2017). Shaped by their daughters: Executives, female socialization, and corporate social responsibility. *Journal of Financial Economics*, 126, 3, 543–562.

Dai, R., Liang, H., Ng, L. (2021). Socially responsible corporate customers. *Journal of Financial Economics*, 142, 2, 598–626.

Deng, X., Kang, J.K., Low, B.S. (2013). Corporate social responsibility and stakeholder value maximization: Evidence from mergers. *Journal of Financial Economics*, 110, 1, 87–109.

Edmans, A. (2011). Does the stock market fully value intangibles? Employee satisfaction and equity prices. *Journal of Financial Economics*, 101, 3, 621–640.

El Ghoul, S., Guedhami, O., Kwok, C.C., Mishra, D. (2011). Does corporate social responsibility affect the cost of capital? *Journal of Banking & Finance*, 35, 9, 2388–2406.

El Ghoul, S., Guedhami, O., Wang, H., Kwok, C.C. (2016). Family control and corporate social responsibility. *Journal of Banking & Finance*, 73, 131–146.

Elderson, F. (2022, November 2). Banks need to be climate change proof. *ECB Blog*. Retrieved January 24, 2023, from https://www.ecb.europa.eu/press/blog/date/2022/html/ecb.blog221102~7599e5851e.en.html

European Banking Authority. (2021). *EBA ANALYSIS OF REGTECH IN THE EU FINANCIAL SECTOR* (EBA/REP/2021/17). https://www.eba.europa.eu/sites/default/documents/files/document_library/Publications/Reports/2021/1015484/EBA%20analysis%20of%20RegTech%20in%20the%20EU%20financial%20sector.pdf

Fatemi, A., Fooladi, I., Tehranian, H. (2015). Valuation effects of corporate social responsibility. *Journal of Banking & Finance*, 59, 182–192.

Financial Conduct Authority. (2016). *Feedback Statement: Call for Input on Supporting the Development and Adopters of RegTech* (FS16/4). https://www.fca.org.uk/publication/feedback/fs-16-04.pdf

Flammer, C. (2015). Does corporate social responsibility lead to superior financial performance? A regression discontinuity approach. *Management Science*, 61, 11, 2549–2568.

Flammer, C. (2021). Corporate green bonds. *Journal of Financial Economics*, 142, 2, 499–516.

FSOC Report on Climate-Related Financial Risk. (2021). Financial stability oversight council. https://home.treasury.gov/system/files/261/FSOC-Climate-Report.pdf

Gillan, S.L., Koch, A., Starks, L.T. (2021). Firms and social responsibility: A review of ESG and CSR research in corporate finance. *Journal of Corporate Finance*, 66, 101889.

Goss, A., Roberts, G.S. (2011). The impact of corporate social responsibility on the cost of bank loans. *Journal of Banking & Finance*, 35, 7, 1794–1810.

Hong, H., Kacperczyk, M. (2009). The price of sin: The effects of social norms on markets. *Journal of Financial Economics*, 93, 1, 15–36.

Humphrey, J.E., Lee, D.D., Shen, Y. (2012). Does it cost to be sustainable? *Journal of Corporate Finance*, 18, 3, 626–639.

International Data Corporation. (2022). *Today and the Future Market Perspective*. https://cervest.earth/e-book/climate-intelligence-idc-report
King, T., Nica, M., Oberoi, J., Srivastav, A. (2023). Compassionate Leaders: Implications of CEO social preferences for employment quality. Working Paper.
KPMG and the Monetary Policy of Singapore. (2022). *Enabling Tomorrow: The Emergent ESG Fintech Ecosystem*. Retrieved January 24, 2023, from https://assets.kpmg/content/dam/kpmg/sg/pdf/2022/11/enabling-tomorrow-the-emergent-esg-fintech-ecosystem.pdf
Krüger, P. (2015). Corporate goodness and shareholder wealth. *Journal of Financial Economics*, 115, 2, 304–329.
Larsen, K., Gilani, S. (2017). RegTech is the new black—the growth of RegTech demand and investment. *Journal of Financial Transformation*, 45, 22–29.
Li, Z., Crook, J., Andreeva, G., Tang, Y. (2021). Predicting the risk of financial distress using corporate governance measures. *Pacific-Basin Finance Journal*, 68, 101334.
Liang, H., Renneboog, L. (2017). Corporate donations and shareholder value. *Oxford Review of Economic Policy*, 33, 2, 278–316.
Lins, K.V., Servaes, H., Tamayo, A. (2017). Social capital, trust, and firm performance: The value of corporate social responsibility during the financial crisis. *The Journal of Finance*, 72, 4, 1785–1824.
Masulis, R.W., Reza, S.W. (2015). Agency problems of corporate philanthropy. *The Review of Financial Studies*, 28, 2, 592–636.
McKinsey Global Institute. (2020). *Climate Risk and Response: Physical Hazards and Socioeconomic Impacts*. https://www.mckinsey.com/~/media/mckinsey/business%20functions/sustainability/our%20insights/climate%20risk%20and%20response%20physical%20hazards%20and%20socioeconomic%20impacts/mgi-climate-risk-and-response-full-report-vf.pdf
Ng, A.C., Rezaee, Z. (2015). Business sustainability performance and cost of equity capital. *Journal of Corporate Finance*, 34, 128–149.
Oikonomou, I., Brooks, C., Pavelin, S. (2012). The impact of corporate social performance on financial risk and utility: A longitudinal analysis. *Financial Management*, 41, 2, 483–515.
Oxfam (2022, May 25). *5 Natural Disasters that Beg for Climate Action*. Oxfam International. https://www.oxfam.org/en/5-natural-disasters-beg-climate-action
Paris Agreement Article 2.1(c)).
PwC. (2021). *PwC's US Pulse Survey of C-suite Executives*. https://www.pwc.com/us/en/library/pulse-survey/c-suite-leaders-pursuing-growth-in-2021.html
Rind, A.A., Akbar, S., Boubaker, S., Lajili-Jarjir, S., Mollah, S. (2022). The role of peer effects in corporate employee welfare policies. *British Journal of Management*, 33, 3, 1609–1631.
Servaes, H., Tamayo, A. (2013). The impact of corporate social responsibility on firm value: The role of customer awareness. *Management Science*, 59, 5, 1045–1061.
Tuominen. (2022, September 22.). *The Way Towards Banks' Good Climate Change Risk Management*. 9th Conference on the Banking Union, Frankfurt, Germany. https://www.bankingsupervision.europa.eu/press/speeches/date/2022/html/ssm.sp220922~bb043aa0bd.en.html
United Nations Convention to Combat Desertification. (2022). *Drought in Numbers*. https://www.unccd.int/resources/publications/drought-numbers
Zerbib, O.D. (2019). The effect of pro-environmental preferences on bond prices: Evidence from green bonds. *Journal of Banking and Finance*, 98, 39–60.

10 Sustainability, Public Security, and Privacy Concerns Regarding Central Bank Digital Currency (CBDC)

Robert Rybski

10.1 Introduction

Currently, over 100 central banks research or develop their own central bank digital currency (further CBDC) (Stanley, 2022). Four projects have already moved into production: DCash in March 2019 (issued by the Eastern Caribbean Central Bank), the Bahamian Sand Dollar in October 2020 (Central Bank of Bahamas), the eNaira in Nigeria in October 2021 (Central Bank of Bahamas) and Jam-Dex in August 2021 (Bank of Jamaica). One major central bank – The People's Bank of China – currently undertakes an advanced pilot project of CBDC (Bansal & Singh, 2021). Considering this overall development, introducing CBDC by at least one major central bank in the coming years seems unavoidable. This would form a tipping point for the massive spread of CBDC implementations. From that moment, CBDC would stop occupying a niche and would rather enter the mainstream of the banking sector.

For those reasons, it is worth assessing CBDC projects broader than the central banks often tend to. This chapter considers potential concerns regarding the introduction of CBDC – not only whether to introduce it but also what design criteria should be considered. Vocalizing those concerns (and potentially addressing them) at an early stage allows appropriately adjusting the design of CBDC projects. Potential changes at the level of CBDC projects will also bring results at the macro level. Changes suggested by this chapter will generally influence the banking sector's economic and social effects that this book focuses on – either by extending and reinforcing them or mitigating some of them.

The most obvious concern concerning CBDC concerns central bank money's public security in the era of growing cyber threats. The other evident concern concerns privacy issues towards the state and keeping information on individual finances secret. However, one particular angle of discussions on CBDC does not get enough attention – sustainability.

Thus, this chapter aims to assess whether and how currently developed projects of CBDC include issues of sustainability, public security, and privacy. Prioritizing the sustainability issue might not have been the case within the

DOI: 10.4324/9781003340454-10

projects currently developed. This chapter assesses different areas of CBDC from the broad perspective of sustainability, with conclusions addressing areas worth further development to increase the implementation of sustainability by the central banks. It then reconstructs a design of CBDC that would be most desired from the perspective of sustainability, public security, and privacy.

Central banks are faced with a hard decision – whether they go forward with their scoping projects on CBDC (or even go live with their pilot projects). Including at every level of CBDC projects, sustainability issues, public security, and privacy concerns might be a trump card for those projects. As a result, CBDC projects might gain economic significance and social acceptance provided that central banks can show through those projects full inclusion of sustainability, public security, and privacy.

10.2 CBDC as Financial Technology

Since this chapter concentrates on particular design aspects of CBDC, there is no need to further address basic questions concerning what money is (Gormez, 2019; Schnabel & Schin, 2018); forms of money exist nowadays (Board of Governors of the Federal Reserve System, 2022, p. 5); what is fiat money (Gormez, 2019); what forms good money (Schnabel & Schin, 2018); what currency (Bossu et al., 2020), or legal tender means (Bossu et al., 2020, pp. 31–33).

The Committee on Payments and Market Infrastructures Markets Committee of the Bank for International Settlements defines CBDC as a "digital form of central bank money that is different from balances in traditional reserve or settlement accounts" (CPMI-MC, 2018). As a result, CBDC bears no credit and no liquidity risk (Board of Governors of the Federal Reserve System, 2022, p. 16), because it has the status of central bank money. Nevertheless, not every CBDC is developed based on distributed ledger technology[1] (further DLT); apart from token-based CBDC (based on DLT), more traditional account-based CBDC can also be developed. With many pros and cons of each of the token-/account-based approaches, it is worth underlining that there is limited scalability of CBDC developed on a decentralized ledger (Ahnert et al., 2022), so developing it to offer this service to massive customers, brings as a result massive increase in ecological footprint. Quick implementations of the CBDC account-based retail system seem well-fitted, as it could mostly use technologies already in place at banks (Schwarcz, 2021). For example, Chinese CBDC does not use the DLT technology (Bansal & Singh, 2021, p. 6).

When considering accessibility, there are three basic types of CBDC (Bossu et al., 2020):

1 Wholesale CBDC – with direct access to central bank money limited mainly to banks – it's a form of business as usual CBDC model.

2 Retail CBDC (that is, without wholesale) – with access to central bank money enabled directly to individuals, including non-banking entities. In this scenario, "wholesale" entities keep direct access to central bank money based on existing infrastructural arrangements.
3 CBDC for general purposes – access to central bank money within the CBDC project enabled both for "retail" and for "wholesale" entities.

It is worth noting that digitalization is not a novel feature of CBDC because many forms of money have already been digital for years (Carstens, 2018). However, the innovation of CBDC does not come with its digital nature but rather with broad access (Bilotta & Botti, 2021) – retail CBDC has appropriate potential as an innovative financial technology (Cirasino, 2021), because banks already have access to central bank money (CPMI MC, 2018).

10.2.1 CBDC as Programmable Money

The final technical aspect of CBDC that requires presenting concerns the circumstance that CBDC can be programmable. This feature of CBDC became viral at some point, and discussions within public opinion steered in the direction as if the true aim of CBDC was to introduce money with an expiry date. This public notion misses the point as the basic function of introducing an expiry date for pre-defined amounts is to allow offline usage of CBDC and thus allow double spending of electronic money (Kahn et al., 2021). The expiry date for money issued in the form of CBDC could also have application in case of stimulating the domestic economy – either in *ad hoc* packages (helicopter money) – or in the case of a long process of restructuring the economy by stimulating consumption (e.g., Chinese attempts).

10.3 Why Do Central Banks Develop CBDC?

The motivation for central banks to develop CBDC projects is numerous and diversified. These motifs will not always appear jointly, but a general overview of those motivations explains their usefulness. Surprisingly motivational reasons are not that different for general-purpose CBDCs and wholesale CBDCs (Barontini & Holden, 2019, p. 9), and they will thus not be analysed separately. Similarly, also motivations for emerging economies and advanced economies share common grounds. However, in the case of advanced economies with efficient financial systems, the incentives to develop new technology (CBDC) with risks to be identified are not that strong (Chorzempa, 2021, p. 110).

The basic motivation for developing CBDC seems to be increased demand for electronic payment combined with a decline in usage of banknotes (cash) – either as a future projection (Boonstra, 2022; ECB, 2020, p. 10) or as an already happening scenario (Chorzempa, 2021; Barontini & Holden, 2019; Sirai, 2019). By developing CBDC, central banks can adapt to this megatrend of increasing cashless payments (Bilotta & Botti, 2021). Under this motivation is an attempt for the CBDC to allow using it the same way cash is used today (ECB, 2020, p. 11). That is why the central banks of Sweden and Uruguay, where increased demand for electronic payment and a decline in usage of banknotes (cash) occurred, developed the general-purpose version of CBDC (Barontini & Holden, 2019). This will guarantee the public with offering access to legal tender in the growing cashless transactions (Bilotta & Botti, 2021). More cashless transactions result in the currently growing exposure (in the areas of credit and liquidity risk) to commercial banks and especially to non-banking payment system operators – the introduction of CBDC results in shifting some of those risks back to the central bank (Cirasino, 2021; Bindseil, 2019). Reduction of credit and liquidity risk in the financial system would result from the settlement of securities (that is, cash legs of) transactions in CBDC (CPMI MC, 2018). Moreover, some CBDC implementations mimic cash characteristics, but in the end, CBDC will only have some characteristics of banknotes (Boonstra, 2022). A clear example of similarity to cash forms lack of charging users by the payment system operators in the Chinese pilot project (Bansal & Singh, 2021).

The other basic motivation concerns payments safety and efficiency (Barontini & Holden, 2019; Laboure et al., 2021; Ward & Rochemont, 2019). Surveys from central banks of emerging economies also show that CBDC aims to incorporate the informal economy and fight financial crime (Barontini & Holden, 2019). Further application of CBDC could be a transmission of monetary policy (ECB, 2020). This could be undertaken by appropriately setting the remuneration rate on CBDC (ECB, 2020).

Surprisingly, the motivation for the development of CBDC might also be very general – with a policy purpose for the whole financial system. The European Central Bank might decide to develop CBDC in order to "foster the digitalisation of the economy" (ECB, 2020), but such motivation is also present in the case of central banks from emerging economies (Barontini & Holden, 2019; Laboure et al., 2021). This digitalization could discourage using cash and supporting electronic payments (Barontini & Holden, 2019). This could even take the form of developing a "cashless" society (Barontini & Holden, 2019). Nevertheless, with digitalization, new features of central bank money can be applied. Chinese CBDC pilot programme explores the potential of programmable money (Bansal & Singh, 2021). Application for financial institutions could result in the central bank issuing inactive digital currency, which would be activated after meeting certain conditions – for example, keeping appropriate interest rates (Bansal & Singh, 2021). Applications for the general public have already tested limiting particular issuance of CBDC to enable spending it only on public transportation – without the possibility of re-converting it for general purposes (Bansal & Singh, 2021).

There is a further untold part of the story to CBDC. CBDC projects are developed because "many central bank-operated wholesale payment systems are at the end of their technological life cycles" and those systems "are programmed in obsolete languages" or they "use database designs that are no longer fit for purpose and are costly to maintain" (Bech and Garratt, 2017, p. 66). It must be noted, however, that few central banks have implemented a new interbank settlement system (Eurozone, Australia, Hong Kong, Brazil) or are implementing it – like US Federal Reserve and Swedish Sveriges Riksbank. But there is another cost: the central banks do not thematize that much in their reports on CBDC, which the CBDC projects can address. Providing constant access to physical cash is a high cost that CBDC, a less costly version of currency, could lower (Allen, 2022; Chorzempa, 2021; Cirasino, 2021). At the same time, introduction of CBDC could lead to increases in seignorage revenue for central banks (Bindseil, 2019; Cirasino, 2021) – although opinions in this regard are mixed (Ward & Rochemont, 2019).

Materialization of a scenario in which foreign central banks offer CBDC has three dimensions that motivate the development of its own CBDC. Firstly, such a scenario brings currency substitution risk and increases the economy's FX risk (ECB, 2020). The development of its own CBDC is perceived as a factor supporting its currency's sovereignty and stability (ECB, 2020). Secondly, geopolitical considerations might also stand behind the development of its own CBDC (Boonstra, 2022; Chorzempa, 2021; Laboure et al., 2021). This is the case with the Chinese CBDC project (Allen, 2022; Knoerich, 2021). It is also clearly visible in the case of the US Dollar (further USD), as the potential development of the digital dollar in the form of CBDC is perceived as a measure to preserve the "dominant international role" of the USD (Board of Governors of the Federal Reserve System, 2022, p. 15). Thirdly, development by major central banks their CBDCs can be motivated by the issue of global usage of their currencies. This means preventing a scenario in which the international role of its currency decreases. This is a clear case of the Euro, which forms approximately 21% of foreign currency reserves – the lack of the Eurozone's CBDC will diminish the international position of the Euro (Boonstra, 2022). Developing CBDC could thus increase the demand for its currency (ECB, 2020, p. 14) or lead to its true internationalization (cf Bansal & Singh, 2021, pp. 10–15). The existing dominance of the USD representing around 60% of foreign currency reserves (Bansal & Singh, 2021) is based on "reliable rule of law, strong and transparent institutions, deep financial markets, and an open capital account" (Chorzempa, 2021, p. 112). The same foundations will also be present in the case of possible internationalization of national currencies offered in the form of CBDC (or lack of materialization of such scenarios).

CBDC could also be developed as an introduction of a parallel payment system (Cirasino, 2021; ECB, 2020). This parallel function is based on ensuring legal tender for CBDC (Ward and Rochemont, 2019). Scenarios in which such a backup system would be needed concern the materialization of emergency scenarios like cyberattacks on existing (private) infrastructure of payment systems or natural disasters (Cirasino, 2021; ECB, 2020). CBDC could also be used to immediately pay out support to the general public (helicopter money) – as in some jurisdictions during the COVID-19 crisis (Bindseil, 2019; Cirasino, 2021).

An interesting perspective on CBDC is one of central banks from emerging economies – for their development of CBDC brings a clear benefit of increasing financial inclusion across society (Barontini & Holden, 2019; Boonstra, 2022; Chorzempa, 2021; Laboure et al., 2021). Because of shortcomings in existing financial infrastructure, potential disruptions caused by CBDC would be limited in emerging economies, thus encouraging even more to use this new technology (Barontini & Holden, 2019). This is a clear example of leapfrogging concept because implementations of CBDCs (along with advanced pilot projects) have already happened solely in emerging economies. One must note that motivations concerning promoting financial inclusion are present in emerging economies, and the US Federal Reserve marks for further research potential gains from CBDC for economically vulnerable households and communities (Board of Governors of the Federal Reserve System, 2022, p. 16).

CBDC is also seen as a chance for simplifying, accelerating, and reducing cross-border payments costs (cf Bansal & Singh, 2021, pp. 7–10; Board of Governors of the Federal Reserve System 2022, p. 15; Cirasino, 2021; Laboure et al., 2021). Further motivation for central banks could be improving cross-currency payments thanks to improving interoperability among payment systems dealing with different currencies (ECB, 2020, p. 14). It must be noted in this regard that to increase interoperability, openness is required. For instance, Federal Reserve System committed to publishing as open-source all the codebase that will be developed (Chorzempa, 2021, p. 112). On the other hand, developing interoperability could mean avoiding sanctions enforced by the US, because cross-border transactions will bypass the SWIFT system (Boonstra, 2022).

Similarly, potential engagement in developing CBDC might be an intent to decrease the ecological footprint of the monetary and payment systems by introducing an energy-efficient CBDC and putting pressure on other payment system operators to do the same (ECB, 2020, p. 14).

The final motivation (that quickly gained traction) is connected with the massive deployment of private digital tokens (digital crypto-assets developed based on DLT technology in the form of global "stablecoins"). This covers a scenario in which a particular private global "stablecoin", developed by a foreign private entity (without financial supervision), acquires a global footprint and becomes popular for retail payments in a particular jurisdiction (ECB, 2020). In such a scenario, CBDC could be developed as a measure to prevent displacing central bank money in transactions (CPMI MC, 2018; Laboure et al., 2021), to keep payments under supervision in a given jurisdiction (ECB, 2020) as well as to keep control of what constitutes money intending to manage the economy effectively (Laboure et al., 2021) and to ensure financial stability (Boonstra, 2022). Of course, central banks became very interested in exploring the consequences of this scenario (and started working on their own CBDC) after Facebook announced in 2019 the developing Libra (Auer et al., 2020). Paradoxically, if any global stablecoin establishes itself, then potential benefits from introducing widely accessible CBDC might not be limited (Ward & Rochemont, 2019). For those reasons, the broad implementation of CBDC seems even more probable.

10.4 Legal Framework for Central Banks to Develop CBDC

Presented motivations must consider the legal frameworks within which the central banks operate. In a state governed by the rule of law, every action of state authorities (to which also central banks belong) requires an appropriate legal basis with doubtless competencies to act (in this case – to introduce CBDC). Initial assessments of legal frameworks (that cover central bank law and monetary law) show that domestic jurisdictions generally either lack a robust legal basis that would allow central banks to have a full flexibility on the scope of CBDC (wholesale/retail/for general purpose) and the technical (account-based/token-based) side (Bossu, 2020; Schwarcz, 2021) or... central banks "remain unsure" whether they have the authority to proceed with CBDC (Boar et al., 2020).

Those assessments bring us to three possible scenarios covering the implementation phase (stretching from pilot project to fully fledged implementation). The first scenario covers a situation where a central bank develops only such a CBDC for which it has a sound legal basis (in most cases, this would be wholesale CBDC). In the second scenario, a central bank either freezes or drops further work on CBDC (till domestic law is changed appropriately). In the third scenario, the national lawmaker changes the law to allow the central bank to introduce a particular type of CBDC.

From those three scenarios, the most desirable one seems to be the third scenario because the engagement of lawmakers gives a chance to win public acceptance for the CBDC project. Otherwise, CBDC might be perceived as a technocratic project without many benefits for Main Street (contrary to Wall Street).

10.5 Why Is CBDC Not Only About Central Bank Money and Monetary Policy?

Current discussions concerning CBDC concentrate on the policy angle and technological dimension. However, CBDC is not only a story of central banks entering the area of electronic payments, the realm of private financial institutions (with many FinTech enterprises active in this area), because CBDC will have brisk economic and social effects. Thus to properly perceive the development of CBDC, arises the need to assess whether and how currently developed CBDC projects include issues of sustainability, public security, and privacy.

10.6 Linking CBDC with Sustainability

The easiest starting point for assessing CBDC from the perspective of specific areas is the one that has recently become viral – sustainability, especially since School Strike for Climate (Wallis et al., 2021; Wehrden et al., 2019), almost every public and private entity started presenting its efforts towards sustainability. In this context of plenty, interesting results brought public consultation on a CBDC developed by Eurosystem (digital euro). Respondents await a few features of the digital euro: "privacy, security, usability, low cost and accessibility" (ECB, 2021). Not a particular word demanding the inclusion of sustainability seems to be coming out of this public consultation. However, this emptiness does not arise from the lack of interest of the general public in regard to sustainability but from the construction of the text that was shared then within public consultation (ECB, 2021, pp. 35–37). The template for public consultation lacked any reference towards sustainability and any potential different policy choices that could be taken on this front. Although authors of the text of public consultation were seeking feedback from future users of the digital euro on its preferred features, the lack of any gradation on this front is hard to follow. If that option was included, the general public might come back with a demand to implement strict changes supporting a high level of ambition regarding sustainability. An example of potential ecological gains already pops up during discussions regarding scoping the final design of Eurosystem's CBDC – choosing an offline payment tool results in lower energy consumption – compared to payment devices being non-stop connected (ECB, 2020, p. 31). However, public consultation – when it polls on whether payments through CBDC should be confirmed online or offline lacks any reference towards energy savings coming along with choosing offline functionality (ECB, 2021, pp. 35–37). Similar omission of sustainability issues also happened in public consultation undertaken by the Federal Reserve System (Board of Governors of the Federal Reserve System, 2022).

The lack of sustainability issues inclusion in the Eurosystem's public consultation and the US Federal Reserve System is remarkable. Already preliminary report on Eurosystem's CBDC discussed (a little) energy efficiency and ecological footprint of payment systems in regards to the potential introduction of digital euro in the form of CBDC (ECB, 2020, p. 15). ECB (2020, p. 15) has noted that "payment instruments and infrastructures may not always be energy-efficient" and it further underlined that a "well-designed digital euro may thus help to reduce the overall costs [...] and ecological footprint of euro area payment systems". This enigmatic statement (regarding reduction of overall costs) most probably refers to reducing overall costs thanks to the reduction of energy costs by increasing energy efficiency. ECB stressed further that the Eurosystem should

> play a catalyst role and lead by example [...] creating incentives and putting pressure on providers of payment services to reduce their costs

> and ecological footprint. This would be achieved by highlighting the cost and energy efficiency of the digital euro, compared with other payment solutions, when promoting its use.
>
> (ECB, 2020, p. 15)

Despite the lack of addressing the issue of ambitions regarding sustainability during public consultation, ECB confirmed that it treats the sustainability dimension seriously within its CBDC project by including two straightforward requirements in the design of the future Eurosystem's CBDC. According to ECB, digital euro should thus be (a) cost-saving[2] and (b) environmentally friendly.[3] This statement and those requirements on the design of the digital euro form a clear declaration that CBDC, developed by ECB, intends to compete with private payment providers on the front of ecological footprint (including its energy efficiency).

This particular development within Eurosystem has at least seven dimensions – and most of those findings are universal (that is, relevant to every jurisdiction). Firstly, offering a low-carbon payment system might open a new toolbox with measures to help achieve climate policy goals. Secondly, by introducing CBDC designed sustainably, central banks can give their input into climate policy.[4] The amount of this input will depend on two things:

1. How much priority will the central banks put into minimizing the ecological footprint of CBDCs and
2. the scope of CBDC – the broader the application of CBDC then, the more input they can bring.

Thirdly, this new climate policy measure (namely, using CBDC payment infrastructure with a lower carbon footprint) will vehemently open the market for new services: low-carbon payment services. Fourthly, this development, on the one hand, might be perceived as a partial squeeze-out of private actors out of the market of low-carbon payment services. This is the case because public authorities (i.e. central banks) will use public funds to develop and start offering this service (even if that is not the initial motivation of central banks developing CBDC). On the other hand, it must be noted that in the area of sustainability, this leading role of public bodies is much needed and welcomed to increase environmental standards. Fifthly, despite considerations regarding limiting access to CBDC developed by ECB for actors outside the Eurozone (ECB, 2021, p. 29), introducing the digital euro in this low-carbon form will attract an influx of assets handled by the actors willing to lower their ecological & carbon footprint. Global (payment) providers might want to switch to the broadest possible extent to using CBDC (instead of developing their low-carbon solutions). It becomes a policy question to what extent the central banks will be willing to welcome this influx of assets in seeking this low-carbon payment service. Sixthly, other central banks developing CBDC will need to follow the standard set by the Eurosystem. Otherwise, using their currencies for payment purposes might become much less attractive with further monetary consequences (already recognized by central banks). Seventhly, such an approach gives hope that CBDC developed by central banks will not one day be assessed as socially wasteful and environmentally bad – as nowadays central bankers assess mining bitcoins (Carstens, 2018). Taking into account the critical approach of central banks towards crypto-assets, it is thus important for central banks that CBDC differs from crypto-assets in a way that CBDC includes sustainability.

10.7 Designing CBDC in Accordance with Sustainability

Sustainability issues in the payment system (such as CBDC) are focused on the energy intensity and emitting greenhouse gases (further GHG). However, sustainability is much more than that because it influences the economic and social effects of the banking sector that this book analyses. Firstly, the sole concept of sustainability is diversified as there are different "shades of sustainability" (Rybski, 2022), which represent different levels of ambition – starting from the growth-oriented concept of green growth through just transition, sustainable development, and towards degrowth concepts. Secondly, sustainability covers direct environmental impacts and social and governance issues. This is especially visible in the case of the 17 United Nations Sustainable Development Goals[5] (further SDGs). For simplification purposes, the framework of SDGs will be used as a reference point to analyse CBDC's links to sustainability – with full awareness of criticism of SDGs (Spaiser et al., 2017). One must also note that because agencies of the United Nations traditionally promote the concept of green growth (Kasztelan, 2021), that is, decoupling economic growth from GHG emissions, the level of ambition represented in the 17 UN SDGs also remains strongly (green) growth-oriented. Out of all seventeen SDGs, eight (i.e. SDGs 1,[6] 5,[7] 8,[8] 9,[9] 10,[10] 12,[11] 13,[12] and 16[13]) remain relevant in the context of CBDC. Because the structure of SDGs is based on achieving them in 2030 – for that reason 169 indivisible targets were introduced. Thus further assessment of CBDC will include making connections of particular design features of CBDC that could help achieve particular SDG.

10.7.1 Maximizing Decreases in Energy Usage by Payment Systems

Implementing the assumption of achieving low energy intensity of CBDC (and low GHG emissions) and making it work in practice requires making a few choices already at the design phase. Two choices relating to the basics of the structure have to be made. The first concerns whether settlements will be undertaken within a centralized or distributed ledger infrastructure – where the centralized ledger lowers CBDC energy consumption (Lee & Park, 2022). Another vital characteristic is the potential usage of renewable energy (or carbon-neutral electricity).

In the case of a centralized system, it is relatively easy for the central bank also to decide (or leave it as an option for the future) to run CBDC on renewable energy (or on carbon-neutral electricity). In the case of distributed ledger infrastructure, the possibility of reducing ecological footprint by deciding on the energy consumption choice looks bleak. Within a CBDC based on distributed ledger infrastructure, the central bank would lose influence on the type of energy consumed because it would depend on particular energy consumed for processes within a particular ledger. In most cases, this would mean using electricity coming directly from the power grid – and GHG emissions of such a CBDC (based on the distributed ledger) would be fully dependent on the carbon intensity of the power grid in a particular country. Because the implementation of CBDC will probably be much ahead of carbon neutrality of power in most jurisdictions, then keeping energy intensity as low as possible is the most important issue in controlling the ecological footprint of CBDC. Despite some opinions regarding energy consumption of cryptocurrencies and future CBDC that "energy consumption, per se, is not an issue in the context of climate change" (Laboure et al., 2021), it must be noted that reducing energy consumption as fast as possible should be the highest priority (also in the case of CBDC), because lasting reduction of energy consumption is much more valuable than an effort to decarbonize the same amount of energy out of four reasons:

1 Renewable energy installations are not produced and transported currently with carbon neutral energy.
2 Before whole energy used for the purpose of cryptocurrencies or CBDC is carbon-neutral, already vast amounts of GHGs will be emitted (in regards to the amount of energy that could have been saved).
3 The same renewable energy (or other carbon neutral) capacity that was intended to be used for cryptocurrency or CBDC, could already be used for further decarbonizing the energy consumption.
4 Decarbonizing energy mix is an effort that is based on the (relative) share of renewables in global energy consumption – thus reducing energy consumption (without increasing the energy output of renewables that mostly generate energy one way or the other) – remains the most efficient way to decarbonize our energy mix. Those circumstances cause that while developing CBDC, central banks should decrease the energy usage of CBDC to the maximum and put pressure on all payment system operators to introduce such a new standard.

The second design choice concerns the consensus mechanism, which is an additional computation used to increase the resilience of the system in the case when some of its members act maliciously (Lee & Park, 2022). Although this choice is relevant only for systems based on the distributed ledger, it immensely influences the energy intensity of potential CBDC based on it, depending on the chosen method of proof and the number and distribution of entities participating in a system (Lee & Park, 2022; OSTP, 2022). This is why Bitcoin was intentionally designed to operate resiliently in a trustless environment, based on an energy-intensive computation process that secures its resilience (Lee & Park, 2022). However, this verification at every step of all the previously existing transactions results in absurd environmental impacts. Crypto-assets mining generated in 2022 around 110 to 170 million metric tons of carbon dioxide, with electricity usage in a range from 120 to 240 TWh per year (OSTP, 2022). This vast amount of yearly electricity usage is (for a lower estimate) equal to the electricity consumption of the whole economy of Argentina (around 0.5 USD trillion GDP in 2021) or (for a higher estimate) equal to Australia (around 1.5 USD trillion GDP in 2021).

Making design choices that will allow reducing energy usage – like limiting the number of participants – reduces system security level as it multiplies vulnerabilities to attack (Lee & Park, 2022). It must be noted that CBDC will not operate within an unfriendly environment in which trust has to be gained through the additional effort put into computation (as in the case of Bitcoin), but rather trust in CBDC stems from the sole fact that it is backed by a central bank (Lee & Park, 2022). Because of that, CBDC does not have to gain a resilience level similar to that of Bitcoin, so this already allows for lowering energy-usage thanks to a lack of computation or mining (Lee & Park, 2022). How low can energy consumption go regarding transactions with CBDC? This cannot be verified till a CBDC project of one of the main central banks goes into full swing, but some projections have already been made. Interesting findings compare electricity consumption per transaction, where Bitcoin required in 2020 around 700 kWh, Ethereum 30 kWh, USD paper money around 0.044 kWh, and credit card payment systems – Visa around 0.0008 kWh and Mastercard around 0.0006 kWh (Lee & Park, 2022; OSTP, 2022). Because a CBDC system can be designed with similar characteristics to the credit card network (Lee & Park, 2022), it could be estimated that the energy consumption of CBDC could be then located at the levels of the credit card payment system (instead of those energy consumption levels per transaction present in the case of Bitcoin). As a result, it would be very hard for central banks to develop a CBDC in such a way that it ends up as an ecological catastrophe. The proper design of CBDC is important to decrease its ecological footprint and to ensure social backing for CBDC because CBDC is a project developed by public authorities.

Payment systems developed by public authorities should not only consume excessive amounts of energy (and natural resources used for generating it) but also should rather use as low as possible. The potential to design CDBC in a way that should bring maximum decreases in energy usage by payment systems (which also brings pressure for other payment system operators to follow that central bank) has three strong anchor points in the UN SDGs. Firstly, such a design of CBDC would deliver towards the overall aim of doubling the "global rate of improvement in energy efficiency" (SDG 7 – target 7.3[14]).

Secondly, achieving as low as possible energy usage is also a sign of efficient use of natural resources that enables decoupling economic growth from environmental degradation (SDG 8 – target 8.4[15] and SDG 12 – target 12.2[16]). Thirdly, this kind of approach towards developing CBDC would mean input of central banks into global actions against climate change (SDG – targets 13.2[17] and 13.3[18]).

Summing up, if the CBDC is to be developed according to the sustainable development principles, it has to represent as low as possible energy usage.

10.7.2 Usage of Renewable Energy

The design of CBDC could also foresee that a CBDC runs solely on renewable energy (though not eligible for every form of CBDC). Taking such a policy choice would have an input into increasing renewable energy usage (SDG 7 – target 7.2[19]) as well measures that provide input of central banks into global climate action (SDG – targets 13.2[20] and 13.3[21]). This design postulates that central banks consider running CBDC on carbon-neutral and sustainable energy has rarely been expressed (G7, 2021; Lee and Park, 2022). However, as noted earlier, the most important thing is to keep energy usage at the maximum low level.

10.7.3 Input into Digitalization of the Economy

Some central banks perceive CBDC projects as an input into the digitalization of their economies. This approach plays along with the SDGs, as SDGs support achieving „higher levels of economic productivity through [...] technological upgrading" (SDG 8 – target 8.2[22]) and also encourage to adopt "development-oriented policies that support [...] decent job creation, entrepreneurship, creativity and innovation" (SDG – target 8.3[23]). As a result, only proceeding forward with the CBDC project to lower the amount of physical cash in the economy brings necessary input into the digitalization of the economy.

10.7.4 Reducing Costs of International Transfers due to Enhanced Interoperability

The common introduction of CBDCs by most central banks poses a chance to reduce costs of international. The condition for this constitutes developing CBDCs based on the interoperability of those systems. This feature should be developed by central banks from emerging and advanced economies. All those elements are crucial to achieving SDG 10, which directly requires to "reduce [by 2030] to less than 3% the transaction costs of migrant remittances and eliminate remittance corridors with costs higher than 5%" (target 10.c). Taking into account that remittances constitute significant capital influxes for many economies, all CBDCs should be developed to address this social aspect of sustainability.

10.7.5 *Fighting Financial Crime*

Sustainability (surprisingly) also includes the obligation to fight financial crime. This obligation has been directly phrased within SDG 16: "By 2030, significantly reduce illicit financial [...] flows, strengthen the recovery and return of stolen assets and combat all forms of organized crime" (target 16.4). CBDC projects should thus, from the beginning, include also an approach that requires fighting financial crime. On a practical level, this would mean the choice of introducing account-based CBDC (instead of token-based CBDC) to help fight illicit financing (Laboure et al., 2021).

Nevertheless, the sole introduction of CBDC should generally increase the standard of AML/CFTC compared to its current level (Sandner et al., 2020). This would also cope with SDG 10, which requires improvements in implementing already existing financial regulations (target 10.5), which also covers AML/CFTC regulations.

10.7.6 *Programmable CBDC*

Enhancing sustainability can also be approached from the most viral controversy around CBDC – from its... programmability. The programmable functionality of CBDC could be applied to increase the efficiency of measures undertaken within sustainable finance. In the case of Green Bonds, where proceeds should be spent on particular types of investments, using CBDC for that functionality could increase green bonds' transparency (Laboure et al., 2021). Such a design option could then be classified as a measure towards achieving SDG 7 (target 7.2) and SDG 13 (targets 13.2 and 13.3). However, full functionality will be achievable when developing CBDC based on DLT (Sandner et al., 2020). This is a problematic aspect from the perspective of sustainability. On the other hand, to increase social acceptance of CBDC policy, stakeholders might want to develop CBDC in a technique that does not allow programmable functions.

10.7.7 *Ensuring Social Inclusion*

The motivation of many central banks to develop CBDC is connected with increasing financial inclusion within society. This has a few dimensions. Firstly, this covers engaging unbanked people (Laboure et al., 2021). Secondly, in the case of persons that live in rural or remote areas, CBDC should also increase their access to financial services (G7, 2021; Sirai, 2019). Thirdly, this improves the efficiency of payments and, as a result, improves the cost of money transfers – internally and internationally (Laboure et al., 2021).

This inclusive functionality of CBDC is broadly reflected within different aspects of SDGs 1, 5, 8, 9, 10, and 16. The commitment to ensuring equal access to financial services (by 2030) is directly provided in numerous sub-targets: for all men and women, in particular from vulnerable groups (SDG 1 – target 1.4,[24] SDG 8 – target 8.10,[25] SDG 10 – target 10.2[26]); for women – that is, as a measure to ensure equal access to economic resources (SDG 5 – targets 5.a and 5.b combined[27]); for small-scale industrial and other enterprises (SDG 9 – target 9.3[28]). This vast amount of sub-targets clearly shows how important the perspective of sustainable development remains to ensure social inclusion. The additional requirement is the one that laws and policies developed for sustainable development should promote and enforce lack of discrimination (SDG 16 – target 16.b[29]) – this only reiterates that once a central bank intends to develop a CBDC as a sustainable measure, this CBDC needs to offer access on a non-discriminatory basis. There is a different side of the coin here. Social inclusion also means that rights arising from access will be honoured once access is granted broadly. For that reason, a retail CBDC should have a legal tender status (Bossu, 2020), so that persons entitled to it can broadly use it.

However, sustainable development standards go even further as they formulate clear requirements for developing any new infrastructure because when "reliable, sustainable and resilient infrastructure, including regional and transborder" is developed, it should be "affordable" and provide "equitable access for all" (SDG 9 – target 9.1[30]). As a result, accessibility to the CBDC should not be legal (that is, on a non-discriminatory basis), but also this accessibility should be on economic terms. Because of that, costs of the whole CBDC and incurred charges should not be too high (in relative terms).

Those reconstructed elements (concerning social inclusion) clearly show the need for central banks to develop CBDC for general purposes, accessible to everyone, with a close look at the costs (especially for vulnerable social groups).

10.8 CBDC and Its Links to Public Security

Another fundamental issue in regard to the economic and social effects of CBDC is public security, which contains an array of sub-issues, like cybersecurity, business continuity, and operational resilience. This covers matters that build trust towards an architecture of central bank money that CBDC will form. Although it does not stay in visible focus in the literature, including position papers of central banks, as not that many thematize them (Board of Governors of the Federal Reserve System, 2022; G7, 2021), it is an issue that is part of basic function of central banks, because on the one hand we have reputational risk of central banks – on the other – public trust towards this is core function of central banks – that is, to issuing fiat money.

10.9 CBDC and Its Links to Privacy

A further vital area for CBDC, from the perspective of its economic and social effects, forms the issue of privacy. This matter seems well-thematized in the public discussion, in position papers of central banks, and academic literature, but some remarks need to be posed.

On the one hand, discussions on the amount of privacy within CBDC are directly related to fighting financial crime. Central banks are in no position that would allow them to allow CBDC to be used as a platform for illicit activities. Thus one should distinguish privacy from anonymity. Although token-based CBDC could be formed in a way to provide anonymity similar to Bitcoin and Co. (CPMI MC, 2018), one should rather expect that the CBDC will not guarantee anonymity for at least two reasons:

1 To enforce the AML/CFTC regulations, and
2 To verify whether assets in CBDC are being held by eligible persons – in case scope of particular CBDC would be limited (ECB, 2020).

On the other hand, privacy directly relates to the social perception of CBDC and its acceptance. Respondents to the ECB survey directly pointed out to the need for CBDC (digital euro) should have the following particular features: "privacy, security, usability, low cost and accessibility" (ECB, 2021).

There are two dimensions of privacy that need to be distinguished in the context of economic and social effects of CBDC:

1 The amount of data collected by the state and its purpose.
2 Commercialization of the collected data.

Regarding the first dimension, one has to bear in mind that liberal democracies are founded on the assumption that the amount of information that state authorities collect on their citizens should be minimal and always related to public functions that this data retention and data processing serves. This approach serves a clear authoritarianism-preventive purpose. This forms a viable question: What do the state authorities have to amass those amounts of personal financial data, and whether this is necessary? The immediate response would probably always appeal to the enforcement of AML/CFTC regulations. But the amount of intrusion should be assessed on a jurisdiction-by-jurisdiction base by the courts – the same as in the case of telecommunications data retention (Zubik et al., 2021). For that reason, every CBDC project should become its own dedicated legal framework – so that the courts can properly assess the scope of the intrusion into individual privacy.

Regarding the second dimension, consumers' payment data (other than those going through cryptocurrencies) is currently monetized by operators of those payment systems (Bilotta, 2021). Those privacy losses undertaken by private entities intensify with the decrease in physical cash use. The introduction of retail CBDC could be a (mild) game changer in two ways. Firstly, this should spark public discussions regarding the amount of future intrusion into privacy from the side of CBDC and self-reflection regarding the broad invasion of personal privacy by private payment system operators. Secondly, central banks do not have the motive to profit from payment data of consumers (Keister et al., 2021). As a result, all the consumers' payment data will not be monetized (for example, resold for e-marketing purposes) by central banks. In that sense, CBDC might become the first choice for its users that would be willing to stop intrusions into their privacy from private payment operators.

10.10 Conclusions, Future Research Directions, and Policy Implications

CBDC remains at the just-before introduction phase, but it is worth beginning this concluding section by underlining one of the most important features that the concept of CBDC offers. In two (out of three) scenarios, CBDC offers access to central bank money to the general public (mainly for retail payment purposes). This is a big novelty because currently general public uses private entities for electronic payments and is thus exposed to the credit risks of those private entities (which increase along with the decrease of physical cash usage). The scalability of CBDC technology enables central banks to offer a new service to the general public – parallel to providing physical cash. Keeping a fair share of public services within the area of public authorities translates into keeping the sovereignty of particular states in the area of their national economies.

This chapter has assessed whether and how currently developed projects of CBDC include issues of sustainability, public security, and privacy. Research results of this assessment presented in this chapter should encourage central banks to prioritize within their policies the sustainability issue. Broad support for sustainability, public security, and privacy will (positively) influence social acceptance of CBDC. This is important because one of the biggest risks that the central banks are facing is a scenario in which, after launching their (retail) CBDC projects, they will not be able to win over (mass) users (Passacantando, 2021). To address this risk, central banks should include all aspects reconstructed from the broadly understood sustainability in their policies. This includes achieving as low as possible energy usage, ensuring social inclusion by offering broad access to CBDC, significantly lowering remittance costs, and bringing input into fighting financial crime. After weighing cost/benefits, CBDC could also, through its programmable functionality, offer a better implementation framework for green bonds.

What's more, the privacy angles of CBDC will be verified through judicial review. To encourage this process, every CBDC project should become its own, dedicated legal framework – so that the courts can properly assess the the scope of the intrusion into individual privacy.

For those reasons, central banks should appropriately adjust their policies to design their CBDC projects in a way that would be most desired from the perspective of sustainability, public security, and privacy. Adapting CBDC projects following those reconstructed directions will be a step towards decreasing the ecological footprint of CBDC and gaining social acceptance for those projects.

Notes

1 Functioning of DLT technology is based on the circumstance that "DLT enable the direct exchange of digital claims (often referred to as "tokens") without the need for a trusted third party. The system relies on an immutable public transaction record (the "ledger"), which is maintained on different nodes of a peer-to-peer network and updated regularly by means of a consensus protocol. In the extreme case of full decentralization with a "permissionless" ledger, anyone who forms part of the network can certify transactions" (Ahnert et al., 2022).
2 Requirements 7a: "The design of the digital euro should achieve a reduction in the cost of the current payments ecosystem" (ECB, 2020, p. 15).
3 Requirements 7b: "The design of the digital euro should be based on technological solutions that minimise its ecological footprind and improve that of the current payments ecosystem" (ECB, 2020, p. 15).
4 There is a lot of public interest (or even public pressure) in regards to actions that central banks undertake as their input into this global effort.
5 Resolution adopted by the General Assembly on 25 September 2015 'Transforming our world: the 2030 Agenda for Sustainable Development', A/RES/70/1.
6 SDG 1: "End poverty in all its forms everywhere".
7 SDG 5: "Achieve gender equality and empower all women and girls".
8 SDG 8: "Promote sustained, inclusive and sustainable economic growth, full and productive employment and decent work for all".
9 SDG 9: "Build resilient infrastructure, promote inclusive and sustainable industrialization and foster innovation".
10 SDG 10: "Reduce inequality within and among countries".
11 SDG 12: "Ensure sustainable consumption and production patterns".
12 SDG 13: "Take urgent action to combat climate cshange and its impacts".
13 SDG 16: "Promote peaceful and inclusive societies for sustainable development, provide access to justice for all and build effective, accountable and inclusive institutions at all levels".
14 Target 7.3 of SDG 7 foresees: "By 2030, double the global rate of improvement in energy efficiency".
15 Target 8.4 of DG 8 foresees: "Improve progressively, through 2030, global resource efficiency in consumption and production and endeavour to decouple economic growth from environmental degradation, in accordance with the 10-Year Framework of Programmes on Sustainable Consumption and Production, with developed countries taking the lead".
16 Target 12.2 of SDG 12 foresees: "By 2030, achieve the sustainable management and efficient use of natural resources".
17 Target 13.2 of SDG 13 foresees: "Integrate climate change measures into national policies, strategies and planning".
18 Target 13.3 of SDG 13 foresees: "Improve education, awareness-raising and human and institutional capacity on climate change mitigation, adaptation, impact reduction and early warning".
19 Target 7.2 of SDG 7 foresees: "By 2030, increase substantially the share of renewable energy in the global energy mix".
20 Target 13.2 of SDG 13 foresees: "Integrate climate change measures into national policies, strategies and planning".
21 Target 13.3 of SDG 13 foresees: "Improve education, awareness-raising and human and institutional capacity on climate change mitigation, adaptation, impact reduction and early warning".
22 Target 8.2 of SDG 8 foresees: "Achieve higher levels of economic productivity through diversification, technological upgrading and innovation, including through a focus on high-value added and labour-intensive sectors".

23 Target 8.3 of SDG 8 foresees: "Promote development-oriented policies that support productive activities, decent job creation, entrepreneurship, creativity and innovation, and encourage the formalization and growth of micro-, small- and medium-sized enterprises, including through access to financial services".
24 Relevant elements of target 1.4. of SDG 1 foresee: "By 2030, ensure that all men and women, in particular the poor and the vulnerable, have equal rights to economic resources, as well as access to basic services, ownership [...] and other forms of property, inheritance, [...] appropriate new technology and financial services, including microfinance".
25 Relevant elements of target 8.10 of SDG 8 foresee: "Strengthen the capacity of domestic financial institutions to encourage and expand access to banking, insurance and financial services for all".
26 Relevant elements of target 10.3 of SDG 10 foresee: "By 2030, empower and promote the [...] economic [...] inclusion of all, irrespective of age, sex, disability, race, ethnicity, origin, religion or economic or other status".
27 Relevant elements of targets 5.a. and 5.b. of SDG 5 foresee: ""undertake reforms to give women equal rights to economic resources, as well as access to ownership [...] other forms of property, financial services, inheritance [...] in accordance with national laws" (target 5.a) and to "enhance the use of enabling technology, in particular information and communications technology, to promote the empowerment of women" (target 5.b).
28 Relevant elements of target 9.3 of SDG 9 foresee: "Increase the access of small-scale industrial and other enterprises, in particular in developing countries, to financial services [...]".
29 Target 16.b. of SDG 16 foresees: "Promote and enforce non-discriminatory laws and policies for sustainable development".
30 Target 9.1. od SDG 9 foresees: "Develop quality, reliable, sustainable and resilient infrastructure, including regional and transborder infrastructure, to support economic development and human well-being, with a focus on affordable and equitable access for all".

References

Ahnert, T., Assenmacher, K, Hoffmann, P., Leonello, A., Monnet, C., Porcellacchia, D. (2022). The economics of central bank digital currency. *ECB Working Paper Series* No. 2713. https://www.ecb.europa.eu/pub/pdf/scpwps/ecb.wp2713~91ddff9e7c.en.pdf

Allen, F., Gu, X., Jagtiani, J. (2022). Fintech, cryptocurrencies, and CBDC: Financial structural transformation in China. *Journal of International Money and Finance*, 124,102625, 1–13. https://doi.org/10.1016/j.jimonfin.2022.102625

Auer, R., Cornelli, G., Frost, J. (2020). Rise of the central bank digital currencies: Drivers, approaches and technologies. *BIS Working Papers No. 880*. https://www.bis.org/publ/work880.htm

Bansal, R., Singh, S. (2021). China's digital yuan: An alternative to the dollar-dominated financial system. *Carnegie Endowment for International Peace Working Paper* 2021, Carnegie India. https://carnegieendowment.org/files/202108-Bansal_Singh_-_Chinas_Digital_Yuan.pdf

Barontini, C., Holden, H. (2019). Proceeding with caution – a survey on central bank digital currency. *BIS Papers* No. 101. https://www.bis.org/publ/bppdf/bispap101.pdf

Bech, M., Garratt, R. (2017). "Central bank cryptocurrencies. *BIS Quarterly Review* 55. https://www.bis.org/publ/qtrpdf/r_qt1709f.pdf

Bilotta, N. (2021). CBDCs and stablecoins: The scramble for (Controllable) anonymity. In N. Bilotta, F. Botti (Eds.), *The (Near) Future of Central Bank Digital Currencies. Risks and Opportunities for the Global Economy and Society* (pp. 167–180). Peter Lang.

Bilotta, N., Botti, F. (2021). CBDCs: The (Near?) Future of a cashless economy. In N. Bilotta, F. Botti (Eds.), *The (Near) Future of Central Bank Digital Currencies. Risks and Opportunities for the Global Economy and Society* (pp. 15–40). Peter Lang.

Bindseil, U. (2019). Central bank digital currency: Financial system implications and control. *International Journal of Political Economy*, 48, 303–335. https://doi.org/10.1080/08911916.2019.1693160

Boar, C., Holden, H., Wadsworth, A. (2020), Impending arrival – a sequel to the survey on central bank digital currency. *BIS Papers* No. 107. https://www.bis.org/publ/bppdf/bispap107.pdf

Board of Governors of the Federal Reserve System (2022). *Money and Payments: The U.S. Dollar in the Age of Digital Transformation.* Federal Reserve System Washington 2022, https://www.federalreserve.gov/publications/files/money-and-payments-20220120.pdf

Boonstra, W. (2022). CBDC and the international position of the euro. *SUERF Policy Note* 2022, 269. https://www.suerf.org/policynotes/42323/cbdc-and-the-international-position-of-the-euro

Bossu, W., Itatani, M., Margulis, C., Rossi, A., Weenink, H., Yoshinaga, A. (2020). Legal aspects of central bank digital currency: Central bank and monetary law considerations. *IMF Working Paper* 2020, 254, https://www.imf.org/en/Publications/WP/Issues/2020/11/20/Legal-Aspects-of-Central-Bank-Digital-Currency-Central-Bank-and-Monetary-Law-Considerations-49827

Carstens, A. (2018). *Money in the Digital Age: What Role for Central Banks?* Bank for International Settlements, Frankfurt 2018. https://www.bis.org/speeches/sp180206.pdf

Cirasino, M. (2021). CBDC in the broad context of national payments system development. In N. Bilotta, F. Botti (Eds.), *The (Near) Future of Central Bank Digital Currencies. Risks and Opportunities for the Global Economy and Society* (pp. 41–74). Peter Lang.

Chorzempa, M. (2021). China, the United States, and central bank digital currencies: How important is it to be first? *China Economic Journal*, 14, 1, 102–115. https://doi.org/10.1080/17538963.2020.1870278

Committee on Payments and Market Infrastructures, Markets Committee (2018). *Central Bank Digital Currencies.* Bank for International Settlements, Basel. https://www.bis.org/cpmi/publ/d174.pdf

European Central Bank (2020). *Report on a Digital Euro.* Frankfurt am Main, https://www.ecb.europa.eu/pub/pdf/other/Report_on_a_digital_euro~4d7268b458.en.pdf

European Central Bank (2021). *Eurosystem Report on the Public Consultation on a Digital Euro.* Frankfurt am Main 2021. https://www.ecb.europa.eu/pub/pdf/other/Eurosystem_report_on_the_public_consultation_on_a_digital_euro~539fa8cd8d.en.pdf

Gormez, Y. (2019). Central bank digital currency: A historical perspective. In M. Amstad, B. Huang, P. Morgan, S. Shirai (Eds.), *Central Bank Digital Currency and Fintech in Asia* (pp. 251–273). Asian Development Bank Institute.

Group of Seven Nations (G7) (2021). *Public Policy Principles for Retail Central Bank Digital Currencies (CBDCs).* London 2021. https://assets.publishing.service.gov.

uk/government/uploads/system/uploads/attachment_data/file/1025235/G7_Public_Policy_Principles_for_Retail_CBDC_FINAL.pdf

Kahn, C., Van Oordt, M., Zhu, Y. (2021). Best before? Expiring central bank digital currency and loss recovery. *Bank of Canada Staff Working Paper* 2021, 67. https://doi.org/10.34989/swp-2021-67

Kasztelan, A. (2021). On the road to a green economy: How do European union countries 'Do Their Homework'?. *Energies* 14, 5941, 1–16. https://doi.org/10.3390/en14185941

Keister, T., Monnet, C. (2021). Information, privacy and central bank digital currency. In D. Niepelt (Ed.), *Central Bank Digital Currency: Considerations, Projects, Outlook* (pp. 17–22). CEPR Press.

Knoerich, J. (2021). China's new digital currency: Implications for renmibi internationalization and the US Dollar. In N. Bilotta, F. Botti (Eds.), *The (Near) Future of Central Bank Digital Currencies. Risks and Opportunities for the Global Economy and Society* (pp. 145–140). Peter Lang.

Laboure, M., Müller, M., Heinz, G., Singh, S., Köhling, S. (2021). *Cryptocurrencies and CBDC: The Route Ahead.* "Global Policy" 12, 5, 663–676. https://doi.org/10.1111/1758-5899.13017

Lee, S., Park, J. (2022). Environmental implications of a central bank digital currency (CBDC). *Korea Office Innovation and Technology Note Series No. 8*, World Bank Group. http://hdl.handle.net/10986/37702

Office of Science and Technology Policy (OSTP) (2022). *Climate and Energy Implications of Crypto-Assets in the United States.* Washington, DC. https://www.whitehouse.gov/wp-content/uploads/2022/09/09-2022-Crypto-Assets-and-Climate-Report.pdf

Passacantando, F. (2021). The Digital Euro: Challenges and Opportunities. In N. Bilotta, F. Botti (Eds.), *The (Near) Future of Central Bank Digital Currencies. Risks and Opportunities for the Global Economy and Society* (pp. 113–130). Peter Lang.

Rybski, R. (2022). Energy in the European green deal: Impacts & recommendations for MENA countries. *Journal of World Energy Law & Business*, https://doi.org/10.1093/jwelb/jwac033

Sandner, P., Groβ, J., Schulden, P., Grale, L. (2020). Digitaler, programmierbarer Euro, Libra und CBDCs: Auswirkungen digitaler Zahlungsinitiativen auf europäische Banken. *ifo Schnelldienst*, 73, 10, 47–52. https://www.ifo.de/publikationen/2020/aufsatz-zeitschrift/digitaler-programmierbarer-euro-libra-und-cbdcs-auswirkungen

Schnabel, I., Shin, H. (2018). Money and trust: Lessons from the 1620s for money in the digital age. *BIS Working Paper* 698, 2. https://www.bis.org/publ/work698.pdf

Schwarcz, S. (2021). Central bank digital currencies and law. In N. Bilotta, F. Botti (Eds.), *The (Near) Future of Central Bank Digital Currencies. Risks and Opportunities for the Global Economy and Society* (pp. 99–112). Peter Lang.

Sirai, S. (2019). Money and central bank digital currency. In M. Amstad, B. Huang, P. Morgan, S. Shirai (Eds.), *Central Bank Digital Currency and Fintech in Asia* (pp. 11–40). Asian Development Bank Institute.

Spaiser, V., Ranganathanm S., Bali Swain, R., Sumpter, D. (2017). The sustainable development oxymoron: Quantifying and modelling the incompatibility of sustainable development goals. *International Journal of Sustainable Development & World Ecology*, 24, 6, 457–470. https://doi.org/10.1080/13504509.2016.1235624

Stanley, A. (2022). The Ascent of CBDCs. *Finance & Development* 59, 3, 48–49, https://www.imf.org/en/Publications/fandd/issues/2022/09

Wallis, H., Loy, L. (2021). What drives pro-environmental activism of young people? A survey study on the fridays for future movement. *Journal of Environmental Psychology*, 74, 101581. https://doi.org/10.1016/j.jenvp.2021.101581

Ward, O., Rochemont, S. (2019). *Understanding Central Bank Digital Currencies (CBDC)*. Institute and Faculty of Actuaries, London.: https://www.actuaries.org.uk/system/files/field/document/Understanding%20CBDCs%20Final%20-%20disc.pdf

Wehrden, H., Kater-Wettstaedt, L., Scheidewind, U. (2019). Fridays for future aus nachhaltigkeitswissenschaftlicher Perspektive. *GAIA – Ecological Perspectives for Science and Society*, 28, 3, 307–309. https://doi.org/10.14512/gaia.28.3.12

Zubik, M., Podkowik, J., Rybski, R. (Eds.) (2021). *European Constitutional Courts Towards Data Retention Laws*. Springer.

11 Electronic Money Institution as an Example of FinTech Sector Regulation

The Case of Poland[1]

Grzegorz Kuca and Paweł Marek Woroniecki

11.1 Introduction

Technological change has had significant impact on the way of conducting monetary settlements. Particularly, it has allowed the introduction of electronic money, whose transfer became much easier than that of cash (Grodzicki, 2002). It caused the creation of new payment instruments to enable access to capital in a bank account and make settlements effectively, conveniently and safely. Moreover, it contributed to developing more effective payment systems, characterised by the speed of order execution, reliability and accessibility as well as an increase in the scope of the provided services (Cyman, 2013, p. 66).

The basic legal ground for electronic money in Poland is the Payment Services Act[2], binding as of 24 October 2011, which allowed the implementation of the European regulations contained in Directives 2007/64/EC (repealed)[3], 2009/110/EC[4], 2014/92/EU[5] and 2015/2366[6] in the Polish legal order, as well as the implementation in the statutory law requirements stated in Regulation 2015/751[7] and the Commission-delegated Regulation (EU) 2018/389.[8] The implemented legal measures aimed at ensuring a uniform regulation of rules for providing payment services in a manner that promotes the development of the internal market, consumer protection and non-discrimination regarding access to a payment account, as well as regulating the electronic money institution. It is worth noting that the provisions of the said act shall be applied to issuing electronic money in each currency.[9]

More than 10 years of the Polish experience in this scope lead to reflections on initiatives aimed at removing institutional limitations (e.g., both the existing fragmentation of the national legal frameworks and the discrepancy in the effective measures – *inter alia* introducing the minimal unitary in all of the European Union [EU] member states' level of security of such services in the spheres of both public and private laws) (Bajor et al., 2021, p. 17). This chapter aims to conceptualise the notion of the electronic money institution, the rules for transactions using electronic money, its functions in business activities, as well as the rights and obligations of the entities engaged in its functioning. All these issues are discussed as part of FinTech sector

DOI: 10.4324/9781003340454-11

regulation, considering an ontic, praxeological and attributive analysis of electronic money.

11.2 The Statutory Notion of Electronic Money

The statutory definition of electronic money was added to the Polish legal order on 7 October 2013; however, prior to this date, the question of electronic money was also regulated by the act of 12 September 2022 on electronic payment instruments.[10] The latter act indicates that electronic money is a monetary value presenting the electronic equivalent of currency, which shall jointly meet the following conditions: (a) It is kept electronically, including magnetically. (b) It is issued at the disposal under an agreement in exchange for monetary funds of nominal value not less than this value. (c) It is accepted as a legal tender by entrepreneurs other than issuing it at the disposal. (d) It is expressed in monetary units (Article 2 (10) of the said act).

In the current national legislation, the definition of electronic money, which involves a classic construction of *definiendum* – a defining link – *definiens* is based on a mixed objective, functional and subjective criterion based on three elements, which, having jointly met all of them, allow considering a given technological solution with electronic money (Stosio, 2002). The objective criterion concludes that "electronic money is a specified monetary value kept electronically, also magnetically" (thus, various instruments of electronic money can be indicated, e.g., electronic prepaid card, that is, the so-called electronic purse). The functional criterion states that this monetary value remains "issued with the obligation of redeeming it, to make payment transactions". For this reason, electronic money may be issued solely by the entities that were granted proper authorisation for carrying out such types of operations (that is, issuing and redeeming electronic money). The subjective criterion states that this monetary value remains "acceptable by entities other than solely [the] electronic money issuer". Electronic money is issued in exchange for monetary funds allocated for this purpose, subject to the possibility of being redeemed at any time.[11] It is rightly stated that "a clear advantage of electronic money, compared to making payments by payment cards, is the fact that it is not necessary to make a prior authorisation of parties to the transaction by a third party (paying agent)" (Świerczyński, 2010, p. 445).

11.3 Domestic Electronic Money Institutions and Divisions of Foreign Electronic Money Institutions

The electronic money institution emerged in the Polish legal order due to the implementation of the EU provisions. Generally, the electronic money institution is a category of payment service providers whose subject of operation is the issuance of electronic money. However, these institutions are also allowed to provide payment services and additional services, carry out payment schemes, as well as perform other business activities.[12] Considering the place of granting permission to issue electronic money, two categories of electronic money can be distinguished: domestic and European.

A domestic electronic money institution is a legal entity with a registered seat in the Republic of Poland, which was granted permission by the Polish Financial Supervision Authority to operate in the character of an electronic money institution. A European electronic money institution is a legal entity with its registered seat in a member state of the EU or the EEA other than the Republic of Poland, which was granted permission for the issuance of electronic money by the proper supervision authorities. Apart from these two types of electronic money institutions, a foreign electronic money institution is also distinguished, which is not covered by the scope of regulation regarding the institution of electronic money. This conclusion comes from the analysis of Article 2 (10a) of the PSA, under which the electronic money institution shall be considered solely as the domestic and the European institutions of electronic money. Contrary to the case of both domestic and European electronic money institutions, the rule of the uniform licence does not apply to the foreign electronic money institution, which results in the fact that a division of foreign electronic money institution operating within the scope of issuing electronic money in Poland requires permission from the Polish Financial Supervision Authority (Article 132zh of the PSA) (Bajor et al., 2021, pp. 77–78). On one hand, such a division has a statutory right to not only issue electronic money, but it may also provide additional services strictly connected to issuing this money (Article 132zi (1) of the PSA). On the other hand, the Polish legislature forbids the foreign electronic money institution to carry out (under the above-mentioned permission) operations involving issuing electronic money in another country, including cross-border activities (Article 132 zi (3) of the PSA). It is also worth mentioning that based on Article 132zk of the PSA, the European Commission must be informed by the Polish Financial Supervision Authority about each permission granted to a division of foreign electronic money institution.

According to the requirements of European law, business activities by providers on the market of payment services are generally regulated and require permission, which also apply to entities issuing electronic money. As a result, issuing electronic money, as well as delivering payment services in the capacity of a domestic electronic money institution requires permission from the Polish Financial Supervision Authority; however, statutory provisions exclude the possibility to authorise other persons to issue a decision within this scope (Article 12 (2) (5) (a) of the FMSA[13]). The lawmaker created a catalogue of premises conditioning the possibility of withdrawing permission (Article 69 (1) of the PSA). The decision in this matter is immediately enforceable (Article 69 (2) of the PSA). Moreover, if required by users or holders of electronic money, the Polish Financial Supervision Authority may determine the date and the conditions for discontinuing the provision of payment services or the issuance of electronic money by the payment institution (Article 69 (3) of the PSA).

The lawmaker establishes restrictions regarding the possibility of choosing the organisational and legal forms available for undertaking activities in the capacity of a domestic electronic money institution, stating that the permission for such activities may be granted solely to a legal person. However, contrary to previous regulations,[14] it does not indicate the organisational form under which such activities can be conducted (Article 132a (1) of the PSA). Nevertheless, it requires the legal person to have a registered seat in the Republic of Poland (Article 132a (2) of the PSA), which makes it possible for the Polish Financial Supervision Authority to undertake supervisory actions.

One of the essential statutory requirements imposed on an entity applying to be granted the status of a domestic electronic money institution is to have sufficient initial capital, whose minimum amount in PLN shall be equivalent to EUR 350,000.[15] Moreover, as a condition for obtaining permission, the applying entity shall provide relevant organisational establishments directed towards the protection of the monetary funds acquired due to the issued electronic money (Article 132b (4) of the PSA). A significant statutory restriction should also be pointed out, which stipulates that if the electronic money institution is submitted to the process of a merger or a division or if its enterprise is acquired, the previously granted permission is neither taken over by the acquiring entity nor by the newly established entity incorporated as a result of the process of the merger or the division (Article 132h of the PSA).

From the perspective of legal trade security, the lawmaker imposes a particularly significant requirement regarding a reliable and understandable presentation of information connected to an electronic money institution, as well as the latter's activity covering the issuance of electronic money or the provision of payment services, including advertisements spread by this institution, commissioned by this institution or spread on its behalf (Article 132i of the PSA). To ensure the reliability of a domestic electronic money institution's operations, the lawmaker also imposes on such institution the statutory obligation to keep documents concerning its activities involving the issuance of electronic money or the provision of payment services for a period of not less than 5 years, starting from the date when it was created or received (Article 132l of the PSA).

While discussing the question of legal trade security, the issue of securing monetary funds being at the disposal of a domestic electronic money institution cannot be ignored. Namely, the lawmaker provides that the institution protects monetary funds acquired as a result of the issuance of electronic money, based on the following rules: first, not combining the above-mentioned sources, at the time of their keeping, with other monetary funds at the disposal of the domestic electronic money institution; second, investing these funds in a separate bank account designated for this purpose and kept by a domestic bank, a credit institution or a foreign bank branch; and third, investing such funds in assets characterised by their safety, liquidity and low risk, gathered in a separate account designated for this purpose.[16]

The lawmaker orders the institution to secure the monetary funds acquired from its issuance of electronic money not later than on the fifth work day, starting from the day on which the institution had it placed at its disposal (Article 132n (3) of the PSA).[17]

The lawmaker accepts intermediary agents who provide payment services on behalf of a domestic electronic money institution (Article 132s (1) of the PSA). In the case of redeeming electronic money, it is acceptable to be undertaken not only by intermediary agents but also by other entrepreneurs (Article 132t of the PSA). Domestic electronic money institutions have a statutory obligation to guarantee that their divisions that participate in operations, as well as agents and other entrepreneurs intermediating in providing payment services and redeeming or distributing electronic money, provide reliable information concerning that fact to both holders and users of electronic money (Article 132u of the PSA).

The obligation to supervise domestic electronic money institutions is a significant one from the perspective of maintaining their economic stability. For this reason, the domestic electronic money institutions' operations involving the issuance of electronic money and the provision of payment services are subject to the supervision of the Polish Financial Supervision Authority.[18] The lawmaker determined the following goals of the supervision: guaranteeing financial safety to domestic electronic money institutions, ensuring that their operations are conducted in accordance with the law and the permission to do so and securing the interests of entities that are users or holders of electronic money (Article 132z (2) (1–3) of the PSA).[19]

The question of the conditions for the issuance of electronic money requires a separate discussion. Namely, under Article 73a (1) of the PSA, a domestic financial institution, whose initial capital is not less than the amount in PLN equivalent to EUR 125,000, shall be entitled to issue such money. However, the institution may as well provide services that remain in close relation to the issuance of electronic money. Moreover, a domestic payment institution is legally obliged to inform the Polish Financial Supervision Authority in writing about the institution's intent to issue electronic money, as well as to provide (along with the written information) a motion for making an entry in a register concerning electronic money issuance (Article 73a (3) (1) of the PSA).

According to Article 73a (2) of the PSA, a territorial restriction that is established for a domestic payment institution states that it can issue electronic money solely in the territory of the Republic of Poland. Under another restriction to which a domestic payment institution is subjected, it may issue the amount of electronic money whose average value in circulation that is calculated for a given month is equal to the equivalent of a maximum of EUR 5 million. However, in the case of institutions that began their operations involving electronic money issuance, the way of calculating this amount shall be modified accordingly. In accordance with Article 73c (1) of the PSA, if a domestic payment institution fails to comply with the above-stated amount restrictions (that is, exceeds these amounts), it shall be deprived of the right to issue electronic money. However, this rule does not apply immediately but after 30 days, counting from the last day of the period in which the amount restriction was violated (that date is vital because during this period, if the institution adjusts the amount of its issued money to the above-mentioned limit, it will not be deprived of the right to electronic money issuance). At the same time, the lawmaker states that even if a domestic payment institution loses the right to issue electronic money, it will not affect the fulfilment of its obligations and the settlement of its liabilities resulting from the previously issued electronic money (Article 73c (3) of the PSA).

In accordance with Article 73b (1) (1–2) of the PSA, a domestic payment institution is obliged to provide the Polish Financial Supervision Authority with the information concerning both the average value of money in circulation (this information must be submitted not later than the 15th day of each month for each value that is established) and the total amount of electronic money in circulation (this amount is calculated at the end of December of each calendar year, and the information must be submitted by the end of January of the following year).

Under Article 73e of the PSA, the Polish Financial Supervision Authority must inform the European Commission about both the number of domestic payment institutions issuing electronic money and their global amount in circulation – according to the data at the end of each calendar year. At the end of this part of the discussion, it is worth mentioning a domestic payment institution's legal obligation to preserve documents concerning its provision of payment services and issuance of electronic money for a minimum period of 5 years, which should be counted from the date when the documents were created or acquired (Article 75 of the PSA).[20]

A separate type of electronic money institution, which can be distinguished under the criterion of the objective scope of electronic money institutions' operations, is the so-called hybrid electronic money institution, introduced to the Polish legal order as a consequence of the implementation of European provisions.[21] The feature that differentiates this institution from the above-described ones is the permission to conduct other business activities (Bajor et al., 2021, pp. 78–79) – apart from issuing electronic money, providing payment services and services strictly related to electronic money issuance and payment service provision and delivering payment systems. Considering the fact that additional business activities might have a significant impact on the financial stability of this category of a payment institution or could limit the possibilities of supervision performance, the Polish Financial Supervision Authority may order a hybrid payment institution to separate – in legal and organisational terms – the activities within the scope of payment services and electronic money issuance by creating a new entity that will conduct these types of activities.[22]

11.4 Electronic Money Issuers and the Register of Electronic Money Providers and Issuers

The lawmaker precisely determines the entities entitled to issue electronic money, as follows: (1) domestic bank,[23] (2) foreign bank division,[24] (3) credit institution, (4) electronic money institution and electronic money institution division,[25] (5) payment institution, (6) European Central Bank, (7) public administration authority, (8) foreign electronic money institution division, (9) division of an entity that provides postal payment services in an EU member state other than the Republic of Poland, under the law of this country, and is entitled to issue electronic money, in accordance with the law of this country, as well as Poczta Polska SA, and (10) credit union (Article 4 (2b) of the PSA). The entities that are not entitled to perform such activities include a division of an entity providing postal services in an EU member state other than the Republic of Poland, offices of payment services, small payment institutions, as well as entities that solely provide the service of access to information about an account.

In accordance with Polish law, the Polish Financial Supervision Authority keeps an electronic register of domestic electronic money institutions and divisions of foreign electronic money institutions. The register is open and accessible to third parties via the Polish Financial Supervision Authority's website.[26] The register of domestic electronic money institutions includes basic data concerning a particular institution (number in the Polish Financial Supervision Authority Office, type of entity, company name, KRS number and address), issuance of electronic money or provision of payment services and data about its division/divisions as well as agent/agents (company name and address). Electronic money institutions are included in the register within 14 days from the date of being granted permission (Article 138 of the PSA). Moreover, they are obliged to inform the Polish Financial Supervision Authority about each change in the data disclosed in the register and to provide this authority with a motion for amending the data within 14 days from acquiring information about the change (Article 139 of the PSA). Any refusal to make an entry in the register is determined by an administrative decision (Article 140 of the PSA) and can be verified by administrative courts. The Polish Financial Supervision Authority strikes an entity out of the register *ex officio* in case of withdrawal or termination of the permission (Article 142 (1) (1) of the PSA).

11.5 Issuing and Redeeming Electronic Money

In accordance with Article 59j of the PSA, the basic obligation of an electronic money issuer is to issue electronic money with a nominal value corresponding to that of the received monetary funds. The consequence of the above-defined notion of electronic money, whose feature is the possibility of being redeemed (that is, the exchange of electronic money for other monetary funds), is the structure of the agreement for the issuance of electronic money, determining the conditions for redeeming electronic money, as well as the amount of the fee for redeeming it. To protect the acquirer of electronic money, the lawmaker prohibits, under the pain of nullity, applying less favourable terms than statutory ones (Article 8 of the PSA)[27] and requires that the conditions for redeeming and charging fees be stated in a clear and understandable way for an electronic money acquirer (Article 59k (1) of the PSA). These conditions must be presented not later than at the moment of the proposal for agreement conclusion (Article 59k (2) of the PSA). Moreover, an electronic money issuer is obliged to make it possible, at the electronic money holder's demand, to redeem electronic money at any time, according to the nominal value (Article 59l (1) of the PSA) for monetary funds other than electronic money (Article 59l (2) of the PSA). However, before the termination of the agreement for electronic money issuance, the holder may demand the payment in total or in instalments, and after the agreement termination, solely in total (Article 59l (3) of the PSA).

An electronic money issuer may collect a fee for redeeming electronic money only if the agreement provides for such a fee and indicates the date of its termination and if the electronic money holder terminates the agreement before that date or the electronic money holder demands redeeming the electronic money in total before the agreement termination date or after a year from the date of its termination.[28] The amount of the fee cannot exceed the costs incurred by the electronic money issuer in connection to the possibility of redeeming (Article 59m (2) of the PSA) but does not exclude the possibility that the electronic money issuer would deduct tax liabilities from the amount of payment transaction (Article 59m (2) of the PSA). If the agreement for electronic money issuance does not include the above-mentioned provisions, it should be assumed that electronic money is redeemed without any fees. Nevertheless, it is possible to waive the indicated rules for redeeming electronic money as well as the fees collected because of this. Such exception is only possible in the relations between the electronic money issuer and an entity that accepts payment in electronic money, if it is not a consumer.[29] The agreement between an electronic money issuer and an entity accepting electronic money (entrepreneur) may determine other rules for redeeming, particularly different specifications of the allowed dates of redeeming electronic money as well as the type and amount of collected fees.

Claims for redeeming electronic money shall be subject to a time limit of 5 years from the date of termination of the agreement for electronic money issuance (Article 59o of the PSA). The above-stated time limit should be counted from the date of the end of the period in which the agreement was concluded or from the lapse of the termination period. It should be assumed that after 5 years from the agreement termination, the electronic money institution is entitled to liquidate a client's sub-account where the electronic money was deposited. For this reason, representatives of the doctrine of law point out that the demand for redeeming electronic money should be limited by the final date (expiration of the claim for redeeming) rather than the time lapse (Pacak, 2014).

To provide security for electronic money circulation, the electronic money issuer is not allowed to delegate or commission the performance of the activity involving electronic money issuance to agents or other external entities (Article 59p of the PSA).

Moreover, there is a legal obligation to maintain professional secrecy regarding professional activity, that is, the activity involving electronic money issuance (Article 11 (1) of the PSA). The provisions of the act do not define the notion of professional secrecy; thus, it is generally understood that "secrecy means that a given information is not available to the public, but only to a limited group of people" (Krzysztofek, 2010, p. 5). Such understood professional secrecy involves information concerning an electronic money user or holder in connection to the provided payment services, issued electronic money or granted credit and includes specifications of the user's payment account, together with the state of the account, as well as other information related to payment transactions and agreements concluded with the electronic money user or holder if unauthorised disclosure of such information might cause damage to the legitimate interest of the electronic money user or holder whom the information concerns (Article 11 (3) of the PSA). The obligation to maintain professional secrecy lasts even after the termination of the performance of a function, an employment relationship, a commission or other similar (Article 11 (2) of the PSA).

Under the statutory provisions, the electronic money issuer is obliged to provide the National Bank of Poland (Narodowy Bank Polski) with quarterly information about the value of issued electronic money remaining in circulation (Article 14c of the PSA).

The regulation of the Minister of Finance of 15 October 2014 determines the detailed scope and manner of providing information to the National Bank of Poland, which is done by settlement agents, payment instrument issuers and electronic money issuers (Polish Journal of Laws of 2019, item 840 as amended).

In accordance with Article 15 (1) of the PSA, should the activities performed by a provider, an electronic money issuer or an agent of this entity infringe the law, the electronic money user or holder shall be entitled to file a complaint against this provider or issuer's actions to the supervisory authority. In its reply to the complaint, the supervisory authority is obliged to inform the complainant about available procedures enabling out-of-court settlements of disputes (it should particularly indicate the appropriate arbitral tribunal), provided that the complaint concerns a civil-law dispute (Article 15 (3) of the PSA). Moreover, the statutory provisions offer a user the possibility to file a complaint to the Polish Financial Supervision Authority or the appropriate supervisory authority regarding the actions performed by an agent or a provider's division for whom Poland is the host member state in the territory where the entities provide payment services (Article 15

(1a) of the PSA).[30] Based on Article 15 (4) of the PSA, if it is not possible to determine a supervisory authority for a given electronic money provider or issuer, the complaint should be directly filed with this provider or issuer.

The Payment Services Act regulates the issue of claims as well. In accordance with Article 15a (1) of the PSA, a provider is obliged to determine and apply the procedures under which the users' claims related to their statutory rights and obligations will be considered. Based on Article 15a (5) of the PSA, the provider must apply these procedures to users from each member state in the territory where the provider provides its services, except for the situation where there are separate regulations in the law governing the legal relationship, under which the users filed their claims. Moreover, under Article 15a (6) of the PSA, the procedures must be published in the official languages of these member states in the territory where the provider provides a given payment service. However, this requirement will be applied only in the event when the provider and the user, concluding the agreement for providing a service, did not make arrangements regarding applying another language to a payment service execution.

The lawmaker determined that the provider would be allowed 15 workdays – from the date when a claim was filed – to respond to that claim. However, the answer should generally be provided in written form, and another durable medium may be applied only if it was agreed with the user (Article 15a (2) of the PSA). The above-mentioned 15-day limit is not mandatory, as the lawmaker provides for the possibility to waive the time limit if it is impossible to consider the claim within this period and to provide an answer due to a particularly complicated case. Nevertheless, in such a situation, the provider is obliged to give the reason for the delay and the circumstances that are necessary to determine in considering the case, as well as establish the estimated time limit (not more than 35 work days, counting from the date when the claim was filed) within which the claim will be considered and the answer will be given (Article 15a (3) (1–3) of the PSA).

In accordance with Article 15b (1) of the PSA, if the user who files a claim is a natural person, the claim must be considered under the provisions of the act on considering claims by financial market entities and the Financial Ombudsman,[31] with reference to specific provisions of Article 15a (2–4) of the PSA In accordance with this regulation, while considering the claim of a user who is a natural person, the procedures for considering claims resulting from the Payment Services Act (Article 15b (2) of the PSA) should be introduced and applied instead of the provisions of the act on considering claims by financial market entities and the Financial Ombudsman.

Article 15 c (1) of the PSA provides for additional requirements for a provider, which involve the obligation to provide the user with information about the entities that may conduct proceedings regarding out-of-court settlements of consumer disputes.[32] In accordance with Article 15c (2) of the PSA, the provider must also inform the user about the manner and the procedure for obtaining precise information concerning the rules based on which disputes are settled by the above-mentioned entities, which may conduct the proceedings. Based on Article 15c (3) of the PSA, all the above-mentioned information given by the provider must be precise, complete and accessible, both on the provider's website (if the provider has one) and in its division, and in the general condition of the agreement between the provider and the user.

To conclude this part of the analysis, it should also be stated that according to Article 15d of the PSA, the fact that the provider was subjected to administrative sanctions as a consequence of infringing provisions concerning providing payment services may be disclosed to the public by the Polish Financial Supervision Authority (however, such information cannot be made public if this would threaten to unsettle the financial market or would cause excessive damage to the legal interest of the participating parties). The above-mentioned administrative sanctions must be distinguished from penal sanctions. Namely, an illegally conducted activity within the scope of providing payment services or issuing electronic money shall be subject to a fine of up to PLN five million or the penalty of imprisonment up to two years or both. The same penalty may be imposed for the unauthorised use of the name (company name) or the performed business activity or in the advertisement using the phrase "electronic money issuance" (Article 150 (1 and 2) of the PSA).

11.6 Conclusion

The present analysis draws a few conclusions regarding electronic money as part of the FinTech sector regulation (see Czugan, 2017; Kruszewski, 2017; Szpringer, 2017; Folwarski, 2019). First, the lawmaker pays attention to the security of the operations of domestic electronic money institutions, requiring them to have high initial capital (see Article 132b (1) of the PSA) as well as proper organisational establishments (see Article 132b (4) of the PSA). Another aspect that indicates the significance of maintaining the financial stability of domestic electronic money institutions is the introduction of quite restrictive rules for keeping, depositing and investing the financial sources acquired due to the issuance of electronic money (see Articles 132n (1) and (2) (a–b) of the PSA), as well as the statutory obligation of the Polish Financial Supervision Authority to supervise these institutions (see Article 132z of the PSA).

The statutory conditions for the issuance of electronic money similarly indicate that legal and financial security is vital for the Polish lawmaker, particularly in the context of electronic money development (Schweigl, 2018). The following legal measures support this opinion: the obligation of a domestic electronic money institution to have a high minimum initial capital as a condition for being granted the right to issue electronic money,[33] a limited amount of electronic money that can be issued by a domestic payment institution,[34] as well as the fact that a domestic payment institution is required to notify the Polish Financial Supervision Authority about the above-mentioned issues.[35] The question of protection, as well as the security of the market of electronic money, can also be perceived from the perspective of entities using this type of money. In this regard, the Polish lawmaker provides for significant legal measures that ensure the protection of the electronic money acquirer, involving the possibility that the electronic money user or holder would file a complaint, or the user would file a claim.[36]

Notes

1 The publication was funded by the Faculty of Law and Administration of the Jagiellonian University granted within the Priority Research Area FutureSoc under the program "Excellence Initiative – Research University" at the Jagiellonian University in Krakow.
2 The Payment Services Act of 19 August 2011 (Polish Journal of Laws of 2021, item 1907 as amended, hereinafter referred to as the PSA).
3 See Directive 2007/64/EC of the European Parliament and of the Council of 13 November 2007 on payment services in the internal market, amending Directives 97/7/EC, 2002/65/EC, 2005/60/EC. and 2006/48/EC and repealing Directive 97/5/EC (EU Official Journal L 319/1, as corrected and amended, not in force), repealed as of 13 January 2018 by the PSD2 directive (hereinafter referred to as Directive 2007/64/EC).
4 See Directive 2009/110/EC of the European Parliament and of the Council of 16 September 2009 on the taking up, pursuit and prudential supervision of the business of electronic money institutions, amending Directives 2005/60/EC and 2006/48/EC and repealing Directive 2000/46/EC (EU Official Journal L267/7, as corrected and amended).
5 See Directive 2014/92/EU of the European Parliament and of the Council of 23 July 2014 on the comparability of fees related to payment accounts, payment account switching and access to payment accounts with basic features (EU Official Journal L 257/214).
6 See Directive (EU) 2015/2366 of the European Parliament and of the Council of 25 November 2015 on payment services in the internal market, amending Directives 2002/65/EC, 2009/110/EC and 2013/36/EU and Regulation (EU) No 1093/2010, and repealing Directive 2007/64/EC (EU Official Journal L337/35, as corrected).
7 See Regulation (EU) 2015/751 of the European Parliament and of the Council of 29 April 2015 on interchange fees for card-based payment transactions (EU Official Journal L 123/1).
8 Commission-delegated Regulation (EU) 2018/389 of 27 November 2017 supplementing Directive (EU) 2015/2366 of the European Parliament and of the Council with regard to regulatory technical standards for strong customer authentication and common and secure open standards of communication (EU Official Journal L 69/23 of 13 March 2018).
9 Article 5 (4) of the PSA.
10 The act of 12 September 2002 on electronic payment instruments (Polish Journal of Laws of 2012, item 1232, hereinafter referred to as the EPIA).
11 However, it is worth mentioning that the definition of electronic money does not cover cryptocurrencies that are not issued but created, they do not carry any monetary sum, and the entity entitled to cryptocurrencies has no legal claim to buy them out. See Dąbrowska, J. 2017. Charakter prawny bitcoina (Bitcoin's legal status). *Człowiek w cyberprzestrzeni*, 1, p. 61; Zacharzewski, K. 2015. Praktyczne znaczenie bitcoina na wybranych obszarach prawa prywatnego (Practical meaning of bitcoin in a selected sphere of private law). *Monitor Prawniczy*, 4,

p. 194; Prokurat, J. 2015. Podatkowe aspekty obrotu wirtualnymi walutami (Tax aspects of virtual currencies turnover). *Przegląd Podatkowy*, 3, p. 24.
12 According to Article 132j (1) of the PSA.
13 See the act of 21 July 2006 on financial market supervision (Polish Journal of Laws of 2022, item 660 as amended, hereinafter referred to as the FMSA).
14 Under Article 36 of the inapplicable act on electronic payment instruments, the electronic money institutions could operate solely in the form of a joint stock company.
15 This amount is determined by the lawmaker in Article 132b (1) of the PSA.
16 According to Article 132n (1) (2) (a, b) of the PSA.
17 Moreover, according to the statutory requirement, a domestic electronic money institution must immediately inform the Polish Financial Supervision Authority on all significant modifications in the manner of protection of the above-mentioned monetary funds (Article 132n (4) of the PSA).
18 Under Article 132z (1) of the PSA.
19 It is worth adding that domestic electronic money institutions are obliged to make payments to cover the costs of supervision (Article 132ze (1), sentence 1 of the PSA).
20 The five-year period is directly connected to other provisions of the Polish law determining the timing of tax control.
21 At first, there was Directive 2000/46/WE, which was repealed with the effect as of 30.04.2011, and now Directive 2009/110/WE.
22 See Article 68 (1) of the PSA.
23 The notion of a domestic bank is defined in Article 4 (1) (1) of the act of 29 August 1997 Bank law (Polish Journal of Laws of 2021, item 2439 as amended (hereinafter referred to as BLA).
24 The notion of a foreign bank division is defined in Article 4 (1) (20) of the BLA.
25 Articles 4 (1) (17) and (18) of the BLA should be respectively applied to the notions of credit institution and credit institution division.
26 The register of domestic and divisions of foreign electronic money institutions can be found on https://e-rup.knf.gov.pl/
27 According to Article 8 (2) of the PSA, terms of agreements for electronic money issuance that are less favourable for users and holders of electronic money than the statutory ones are invalid; statutory provisions shall be applied instead of such terms.
28 According to Article 59m (1) of the PSA.
29 In accordance with Article 22[1] of the act of 23 April 1964 Civil code (Polish Journal of Laws of 2022, item 1360 as amended, hereinafter referred to as the CC), a consumer is a natural person who enters with an entrepreneur into a legal action that is not directly related to their business or professional activity. In other words, a consumer is a natural person who buys an item or a service from an entrepreneur for his/her private purpose. For more information, see Sadomski, J. 2021. *Komentarz do art. 22[1]* (Commentary to Article 22[1]). In Gudowski, J. (Ed). *Kodeks cywilny. Komentarz, Tom I, część ogólna, cz. 1 (art. 1-55[4])* (Civil code. Commentary, Vol. 1, general part, part 1 (Articles 1-55[4])), Warszawa, pp. 309 ff.
30 It should be stated that under Article 15 (2) of the PSA, the above-mentioned rights to file complaints may be as well executed by consumer organisations and – in the case of refusing to provide payment services or issue electronic money – by natural persons, legal persons, and an organisational unit without a legal personality but with a legal capacity.
31 Particularly, provisions of chapter 2 of the act of 5 August 2015 on considering claims by financial market entities and the Financial Ombudsman will be applied (Polish Journal of Laws of 2022, item 187 as amended).

32 Provisions of the act of 23 September 2016 on out-of-court settlements of consumer disputes shall be applied (Polish Journal of Laws of 2016, item 1823).
33 See Article 73a (1) of the PSA.
34 See Article 73a (4) of the PSA.
35 See Article 73b (1) (1–2) of the PSA.
36 Requirements for a complaint and a claim are regulated in Articles 15 and 15a of the PSA, respectively.

References

Bajor, B. Byrski, J. Zalcewicz, A. (2021). Słowo wstępne In J. Byrski, A. Zalcewicz (Eds.), *Ustawa o usługach płatniczych: komentarz* (pp. 17–18). Wolters Kluwer.

Cyman, D. (2013). *Elektroniczne instrumenty płatnicze a bezpieczeństwo uczestników rynku finansowego*. Wolters Kluwer Polska.

Czugan, M. (2017). Problemy otoczenia regulacyjnego rozwoju sektorze fintech. In W. Rogowski (Ed.), *Regulacje Finansowe FinTech Nowe Instrumenty Finansowe Resolution* (pp. 28–36). C.H. Beck.

Dąbrowska, J. (2019). Charakter prawny bitcoin. *Człowiek w Cyberprzestrzeni*, 1, 54–76.

Folwarski, M. (2019). *Sektor Fintech na europejskim rynku usług bankowych wyzwania konkurencyjne i regulacyjne*. Poltext.

Grodzicki, J. (2002). Karty płatnicze i pieniądz elektroniczny a pieniądz gotówkowy. *Glosa* (pp. 8–14), 1.

Kruszewski, A.K. (2017). Polskie regulacje dotyczące walut cyfrowych. In W. Rogowski (Ed.), *Regulacje Finansowe FinTech Nowe Instrumenty Finansowe Resolution* (pp. 64–69). C.H. Beck.

Krzysztofek, M. (2010). *Tajemnica bankowa i ochrona danych osobowych w praktyce bankowej*. LexisNexis.

Pacak, M. (2014). *Usługi płatnicze. Komentarz*. LexisNexis.

Prokurat, J. (2015). Podatkowe aspekty obrotu wirtualnymi walutami. *Przegląd Podatkowy*, 3.

Sadomski, J. (2021). *Komentarz do art. 221*. In J. Gudowski (Ed.), *Kodeks cywilny. Komentarz, Tom I, część ogólna, cz. 1 (art. 1 –554)*. Wolters Kluwer.

Schweigl, J. (2018). Central bank digital currency – the latest challenge for the theory of monetary law. In E. Lotko, E. Zawadzka-Pąk, M. Radvan (Eds.), *Proceedings of the Conference on Optimization of Organization and Legal Solutions Concerning Public Revenues and Expenditures in Public Interest* (pp. 385–390). Temida2.

Stosio, A. (2002). Pieniądz elektroniczny – cywilnoprawna analiza pojęcia. *Przegląd Prawa Handlowego*, 5, 32–36.

Świerczyński, M. (2010). Aktualne problemy płatności elektronicznych. In E. Gniewek, K. **Górska**, P. Machnikowski (Eds.), *Zaciąganie i wykonywanie zobowiązań. Materiały III Ogólnopolskiego Zjazdu Cywilistów (Wrocław, 25–27.9.2008 r.)*. C.H. Beck.

Szpringer, W. (2017). *Fintech – konkurencja a regulacja na rynku usług finansow*ych. In W. Rogowski (Ed.), *Regulacje finansowe FinTech nowe instrumenty finansowe resolution* (pp. 3–27). C.H. Beck.

Zacharzewski, K. (2015). Praktyczne znaczenie bitcoina na wybranych obszarach prawa prywatnego. *Monitor Prawniczy*, 4, 187–195.

12 Legal Guarantees of Access to a Payment Account – Analysis from the Perspective of the Account Information Service Provider

Jan Byrski and Michał Synowiec[1]

12.1 Introduction

The account information service (AIS) enables obtaining consolidated information on one or more payment accounts maintained with at least one account servicing payment service provider (ASPSP). This service is commonly referred to as a service based on access to a payment account, and this access is crucial not only for the efficient provision of this payment service but also for the general ability of a third (payment)-party (service) provider (TPP) to perform the service. The purpose of this article is, on the one hand, to present the juridical nature of the AIS service along with *de lege ferenda* proposals and, on the other hand, to identify the legal instruments available to providers of this service (account information service providers – AISPs) for the purpose of accessing users' payment accounts. In the light of ASPSPs' inconsistent practice regarding the rules for granting AISPs access to the user's payment account information, it is especially justified to analyse the second of the above issues. In particular, this applies where an ASPSP completely prevents an AISP from gaining access to payment accounts or unlawfully seeks to limit such access.

12.2 Historical Perspective on Implementation of Regulations Regarding So-Called New Payment Services Including the Account Information Service

The common feature of the so-called new payment services introduced by the PSD2 directive,[2] i.e., the payment initiation service (PIS) and the AIS, is that, to perform them, it is necessary for a so-called TPP to access a payment account maintained with an ASPSP. Until the adoption of PSD2, such services were not legally regulated, although they had been performed in the payments market for many years. The reason for this was that in the case of these services, funds were not put at the disposal of TPPs (Byrski, 2018).[3] Thus, those providers could – in their opinion and in line with the prevailing legal publications – benefit from the exemption from the application of provisions of the PSD1 directive and, consequently, from the (Polish) Act on

DOI: 10.4324/9781003340454-12

Payment Services[4] in the wording applicable prior to implementation of PSD2 into the Polish legislation. However, PSD2 made it necessary – as a rule – to obtain authorisation from or to be entered into the register by a supervisory authority (in Poland – the Polish Financial Supervision Authority, hereinafter referred to as the "PFSA") to provide such services (Gradzi, 2019).

TPPs operated in the payment services market and were its active participants before implementation of PSD2. They carried out many payment transactions of very high value (since 2005, Sofort has carried out more than 100 million transactions) (Sofort, 2016). For this reason, PSD2 required that those entities be not discriminated until implementation of its provisions. It is worth noting that the Polish Financial Supervision Authority, prior to the amendment of the Payment Services Act implementing the PSD2 directive, issued warnings against activities of TPPs (Gradzi, 2019).

12.3 Legal Nature of Account Information Service

The definition of "account information service" is provided in Article 4(16) of PSD2, according to which it means an *online* service to provide consolidated information on one or more payment accounts held by the payment service user with either another payment service provider or with more than one payment service provider. The definition has been implemented – in quite similar wording (the words "one or more" have been justifiably omitted because they would not add any substantive value) – into Article 3(6) of the PSA, according to which an AIS is an *online* service to provide consolidated information concerning: (1) a payment account of the user maintained with another provider or (2) payment accounts of the user maintained with another provider or with more than one provider. And not into Article 2 of the PSA, which contains statutory definitions. This seems to result from the fact that the money remittance service (paragraph 3) and the credit transfer service (paragraph 4) had been already defined in Article 3 in the Republic of Poland and, due to implementation of PSD2, [definitions of] the PIS (paragraph 5) and the AIS (paragraph 6) were added. Such step, however, causes some inconsistency, as the acquiring service is not defined at all in a separate paragraph in Article 3 of the PSA, while the legislator introduced the so-called parenthetical definition in Article 3(1)(5) of the PSA (Synowiec, 2023). Thus, the service consists in provision by an entity authorised to provide this service (TPP), at the request and with the consent of the user, of consolidated information regarding the user's payment account or accounts available online, maintained with one or more other payment service providers (ASPSPs) (Leżoń, 2019).

At this point, it is necessary to consider the meaning of the term "consolidated", which so far has not been analysed more extensively in both foreign and Polish publications. According to the accepted meaning, the term "consolidate" *(in Polish: skonsolidować)* should be understood as "unite, combine, fuse" (*in Polish: zjednoczyć, połączyć, zespolić*) (Doroszewski, 1958).

This would mean that provision of consolidated information is a *sine qua non* element of AIS, so either a TPP consolidates the information obtained from an ASPSP or it obtains consolidated information already from the ASPSP. Neither provisions of PSD2 nor regulations of the Payment Services Act explain what the minimum level of this "consolidation" is, so – in our opinion – it should be assumed that for a service to be treated as an AIS a minimum scope of "consolidation" of information is sufficient and it is not necessary to perform complex operations of "combinations, fusions" (*in Polish: połączenia, zespolenia*) of information from the user's payment account or accounts. Furthermore, there is the issue of distinguishing between the so-called pure AIS service and the so-called AIS-premium service (AIS+) which is to additionally provide (supply) the user with additional information (data) – most often the data derived (deduced) from information obtained from an ASPSP by an AISP – or to transfer the information obtained from an ASPSP to a third party (the so-called AISP partner). In our opinion, both forms of AISPs' business are not contrary to provisions of PSD2 and the Payment Services Act, provided that the user gives an explicit consent to such activities of the AISP (although both provisions of PSD2 and provisions of the Payment Services Act state that an AISP shall not use, access or store any data for purposes other than for the performance of an AIS provided based on a contract with the user or the user's consent, this does not mean that it is not allowed to provide an AIS-premium service based on the user's separate, explicit consent – breaking this prohibition – which may be revoked at any time, regardless of provision of an AIS). *De lege ferenda*, we request that rules for provision of the AIS-premium service be explicitly regulated in legislation.

The obligations imposed on an AISP (TPP), i.e., both on an entity providing only the AIS (AISP-only) and on any other payment service provider that provides this service, are set out in Article 67(2) of PSD2 (analogically, in Article 59s(2) of the PSA).

The first condition is that the payment account to be accessed by the AISP must be accessible online. The requirement for such payment account functionality is directly related to the nature of this payment service, which provides for the establishment of a secure communication session between the TPP and the ASPSP. The second condition is that the AISP must – as regards the service provided by it – act only based on the user's consent expressed in an unambiguous manner. In other words, any presumption or implication of consent, including through factual activities, is unacceptable. The extent of such user's consent will be crucial in terms of the scope of data that the AISP should receive from the user's payment account or accounts and present to the user in a consolidated version. The third obligation imposed on the AISP is to duly protect personalised security credentials by not disclosing them to unauthorised persons, i.e., other than the user and the account servicing provider, and by transmitting them through secure and efficient channels. The provision is about the user and provides that personalised security credentials are to be accessible only to the user. This means that a user's personalised security credentials should be accessible exclusively to that user.[5] The fourth obligation imposed on the AISP is to identify itself towards the account servicing provider and securely communicate with it and the user, in accordance with RTS on SCA and CSC (EBA, 2022a). The fifth obligation imposed on the AISP is to limit its access exclusively to information relating to designated payment accounts and the related payment transactions. It follows from this obligation that the user's consent should explicitly indicate individual payment accounts and at least the type or time limits of the payment transactions related to them carried out on those accounts. The sixth obligation imposed on the AISP is not to request sensitive payment data linked to payment accounts. Article 59s(2)(5) of the PSA is worded differently from Article 59r(3)(5) of the PSA, as it refers to the prohibition on requesting – rather than storing – and clarifies that the prohibition applies to requesting sensitive payment data relating to payment accounts, rather than, for example, other accounts maintained with the account servicing provider (Byrski & Zalcewicz, 2021). The last obligation – analogous to that related to the PIS – is the prohibition on using, accessing, or storing data for purposes other than for the provision of the AIS. However, it seems that pursuant to the user's independent, voluntary consent – which may be revoked at any time, regardless of the consent to performance of the service – the AISP may use these data, including personal data, for other purposes that such independent consent will provide for (Byrski & Synowiec, 2017).

12.4 The Rules for Accessing Payment Accounts under PSD2

Upon adoption of the PSD2 directive and its implementation into the legislation of individual Member States, the rules for accessing payment accounts developed in practice by TPPs were strongly formalised (Byrski & Synowiec, 2017). This move was primarily dictated by a desire to increase security standards and intensify protection of payment service users, particularly consumers.

Presently, AISPs may access payment accounts through one of programming interfaces of ASPSPs (so-called APIs – *Application Programming Interfaces*) (Petrović, 2020). As a side note, it is worth mentioning that initially there were many sceptical views as to the effectiveness of solutions based on the so-called open banking model and APIs provided by ASPSPs (Madir, 2019). It is a legal obligation of every ASPSP that maintains online payment accounts for users to provide such interface access (Korus, 2017; Osajda & Dybiński, 2023).[6] This obligation may be fulfilled by creating a special (dedicated) interface or by allowing AISPs to use the interface used for authentication and communication between the ASPSP and the users.[7] The final decision regarding the method to provide TPPs with access to payment accounts lies with ASPSPs,[8] which was not so obvious when the regulatory technical standards underpinning Regulation 2018/389[9] were being developed. The finally adopted solution seems to be an appropriate compromise between the interests of TPPs and ASPSPs. However, it should be kept in view that there are also opinions supporting dedicated APIs as a solution that is generally more secure and enables more effective control over the scope of data made available to TPPs (see the Polish supervisory authority in the Announcement of the Office of the Polish Financial Supervision Authority of 12 January 2018 on selected supervisory expectations for the transition period related to implementation of the PSD2 Directive).[10]

In particular, the interfaces provided by ASPSPs should meet the following six criteria. First, the API used for the purposes of providing services based on access to a payment account should enable the TPP to correctly identify itself towards the ASPSP.[11] Such identification is enabled by using a qualified certificate for electronic seal referred to in Article 3(30) of eIDAS[12] or a qualified certificate for website authentication referred to in Article 3(39) of eIDAS.[13] Importantly, this requirement applies only to TPPs, as none of provisions of PSD2 or Regulation 2018/389 imposes such obligation on ASPSPs as regards their identification towards TPPs.[14] Correct identification is necessary in order to make the ASPSP aware of whether the entity contacting it and establishing a communication session is directly the user or a TPP[15] (which was not the case during provision of services that were the prototype of AISs, based on screen scraping) (Byrski et al., 2019; Leżoń, 2019).

Second, each interface should ensure secure communication between TPPs and ASPSPs,[16] including by establishing and maintaining a secure communication session during which data are exchanged between the payment service providers involved. During a communication session, the ASPSP and the TPP are obliged to securely encrypt data to maintain their confidentiality and integrity.[17] To fulfil this obligation, they should use strong and widely recognised encryption techniques. Notwithstanding the foregoing, both ASPSPs and TPPs should prevent their staff from reading personalised security credentials and authentication codes that are communicated during the established communication session. If personalised security credentials are compromised, it is the responsibility of the relevant provider to inform thereof the user and the issuer of the credentials.

Third, the interface should allow TPPs to rely on authentication procedures provided by ASPSPs directly to users.[18] Providing a dedicated interface, the ASPSP should guarantee the use of the same authentication methods that the user can use via the API providing direct access to the account (without a TPP's involvement).[19] So, for example, if the ASPSP enables the user to use biometric authentication for direct access to the account, this authentication method should also be available in case the user uses a TPP's services (Wolters & Jacobs, 2019).

Fourth, the TPP communicating via the API should be able to instruct the ASPSP to initiate authentication exclusively based on the user's consent.[20] Moreover, there are no grounds to require the TPP to enter into a contract with the ASPSP for the purposes of accessing the account to provide the AIS service.[21] Importantly, the lack of the requirement for entering into a contract between the TPP and the ASPSP results in the decision to grant access to the account actually lying with the account holder and not the ASPSP (Zegers & Nys, 2020). The sole basis for provision of this payment service is the user's consent, which is explicitly confirmed by the wording of Article 67(2)(a) PSD2. Such consent may apply to both single and multiple access to the account (Stanisławska, 2022) and affects the content of the ASPSP's obligation regarding the scope of information to be provided to the AISP (Długosz & Mostowik, 2018; Byrski et al., 2019; Grabowski, 2020).

Fifth, the API should enable establishment and maintenance of a communication session between the user, the TPP and the ASPSP throughout the authentication process.[22] If communication sessions with the ASPSP are maintained in parallel, then the AISP is obliged to ensure that those sessions are securely linked to relevant sessions maintained with individual users. This should enable preventing any misrouting that might occur in the exchange of data or information between the entities involved (Article 35(3) of Regulation 2018/389).

Sixth, the access interface should ensure integrity and confidentiality of personalised security credentials and authentication codes transmitted by or through the TPP.[23] As a matter of principle, the TPP providing the AIS service is obliged to ensure that the user's personalised security credentials are not accessible to parties other than the issuer of those credentials and the user, and that any transmission of such credentials is always done through safe and efficient channels.[24] Regardless of the authentication method used, the AIS provider cannot request sensitive payment data related to payment accounts (e.g., online banking passwords).[25] In general, however, the ASPSP is bound by the obligation to provide the AISP with the same scope of information regarding the designated account and the related payment transactions that would be made available to a user directly accessing the payment account (Article 36(1)(a) *in principio* of Regulation 2018/389) (Byrski et al., 2019).

Notwithstanding the above, it should be noted that pursuant to Article 32(1) of Regulation 2018/389, dedicated interfaces of the ASPSP should ensure the same level of availability and performance, including support, as the interfaces made available to users directly accessing their payment accounts. This means that an ASPSP will be in breach of the regulations if parameters of the dedicated interface put in place by the ASPSP are inferior to those of the interfaces designated for users. As the European Banking Authority (EBA) points out, this also applies to the support services that the ASPSP is obliged to provide to TPPs – if they are guaranteed 24/7 for user interfaces as standard, such parameters should also be guaranteed in the case of the API used to communicate with TPPs (Leżoń, 2019; EBA, 2021).

Importantly, the dedicated interface should not create any obstacles to the provision of services by TPPs.[26] Such obstacles include any arrangement that unreasonably prolongs the process of accessing a payment account through a TPP or hinders the use of the functions available to users as part of a TPP's services (Byrski et al., 2019; Blocher, 2022). It is usually assumed that obstacles within the meaning of Article 32(3) of Regulation 2018/389 include, in particular: verification by the ASPSP whether the TPP has entered into a contract with the user,[27] requesting the TPP to present the user's consent to the ASPSP, imposition by the ASPSP of an additional fee on the TPP for accessing the user's account[28] and the ASPSP's request to the user for confirmation of the user's consent to the TPP accessing the account.[29]

Any ASPSP choosing to provide a dedicated API is, as a rule, also obliged to implement contingency measures for the event that the API does not perform in compliance with the requirements set out in Article 32 of Regulation 2018/389, that the interface becomes completely unavailable or that the ASPSP's systems break down.[30] It is assumed that until the availability and performance of the interface is restored to the level originally assumed, the TPP should be allowed to use the interfaces made available to users for the authentication and communication with the ASPSP. However, under some conditions, competent authorities of the Member States may exempt ASPSPs from the obligation to set up the above-mentioned contingency mechanisms (Byrski et al., 2019).[31]

12.5 Difficulties in Accessing Payment Accounts – An Imaginary Problem or a Real Threat to AISPs' Business?

Providing the TPP with efficient access to the payment account is a key prerequisite for the effective provision of the AIS service and the proper performance by the AISP of its obligation under the contract entered into with the user. When talking about efficient access to the account, it is necessary to concern two dimensions of this issue (Czech, 2023).

On the one hand, it is about ASPSPs' general guarantee that in cases where AIS is provided, the providers of this service will be able to access the user's payment account and obtain information concerning this account and payment transactions made through it. This may apply both to the situation when AISPs are generally denied access to the user's payment account (e.g. some ASPSPs block AISPs from accessing payment accounts maintained for corporate clients) and when the frequency of provision of such access is limited in breach of Article 36(5) of Regulation 2018/389 (Byrski et al., 2019). As a matter of principle, ASPSPs should therefore not unlawfully deny AISPs access to a payment account, thus completely depriving them of the objective possibility of providing the AIS service. Taking measures that are contrary in this respect actually undermines the overall sense of the AIS service and the legislative framework adopted for it.

On the other hand, efficient access to the account should be considered in terms of ensuring that the AISP is able – to the extent required by law – to obtain information about the user's payment account. However, the regulations do not set out an exhaustive list of information that the ASPSP is obliged to provide to the AISP each time the latter is performing a payment service. Moreover, none of the provisions of PSD2 and Regulation 2018/389 in any way defines the term "account information" which in fact is the crux of the AIS service (Wolters & Jacobs, 2019).

Based on recital 28 of PSD2, it seems reasonable to assume that the term "account information" covers all information relating to the payment account that is made available to the account holder when the holder is using the ASPSP's interfaces as part of direct access to the account (Mostowik, 2017; Osajda & Dybiński, 2023). This conclusion is supported by the wording of Article 36(1)(a) of Regulation 2018/389, which requires ASPSPs to provide AISPs with the same information on the payment accounts designated by the user and the related transactions that is made available to the user directly accessing the account, unless this information include sensitive payment data (e.g., online banking passwords).[32] As the EBA pointed out, the AISP should be granted access to the maximum scope of information available to the user regardless of the communication channel used to directly access the payment account (e.g., a website or mobile application)[33] This means that, for example, if the scope of information provided to the user communicating with the ASPSP via the website is broader than that in the case of accessing the account via mobile banking, the scope of information provided to the AISP should match that presented to the user on the website (online banking) (Byrski et al., 2019; Grabowski, 2020).

In practice, ASPSPs' attempts to limit the scope of information provided to AISPs are extremely problematic. Most often, they are manifested through not sharing data such as the account holder's name and address, providing information on operations carried out via the account in a selective manner, not providing a full history of account-related transactions, or refraining from providing information on both parties to payment transactions. Moreover, such approach raises the risk of a number of negative consequences for AISPs' business. By way of example only, it can be pointed out that if the AISP does not know the name of the account holder, the proper fulfilment of AISP-only reporting obligations imposed by the Polish law is significantly hindered. Such providers are obliged to provide the PFSA annually, by 31 January, with information on the number of users to whom the AIS service was provided and the number of accounts to which access was provided during the previous calendar year.[34] Data such as the name of the account holder may, in turn, be important for determining the number of users to whom AIS was provided.[35]

The root cause of the difficulties related to accessing payment accounts is the conflict of interests of AISPs and ASPSPs. After all, each of these categories of service providers seeks to achieve its own goals and build market advantage (Brener, 2019; Petrović, 2020). In fact, they act as each other's competitors which offer, based on account information, their own financial products and services (Kasiewicz, 2018).

However, it should be kept in view that, generally, it is banks and credit institutions that have the ASPSP status while the AISP role is usually played by smaller players in the financial sector, such as payment institutions, electronic money institutions and AISPs-only (FinTechs in the broadest sense). Nevertheless, the established market position and competitive advantage of the former should not justify practices aimed at limiting AISPs' access to payment accounts. Such measures are particularly burdensome for AISPs-only, which are authorised to provide only one type of payment service, i.e., AIS. Therefore, any limitations of access to users' payment accounts have far-reaching consequences for their business, often affecting their overall business profile.

Moreover, it cannot be ignored that, upon the establishment of the legal framework for provision of payment services, such as AIS and PIS, the EU legislator and national legislators implementing PSD2 created a new reality in terms of the rules for accessing and obtaining information from payment accounts, managing such information and requesting the execution of payment transactions. Financial market participants should adapt to these realities, including complying with the legislation that creates a regulatory corset for the phenomenon known as "open banking".

However, past experience shows that the approach to the issue analysed herein varies between individual payment account servicing providers. This is confirmed by two EBA's opinions issued in 2020[36] and 2021.[37] In both documents, the EBA identified a number of irregularities in the rules for providing TPPs, including AISPs, with access to users' payment accounts, and at the same time requested national supervisory authorities to take appropriate supervisory actions to ensure that ASPSPs' activities comply with the law. Despite the EBA's request and the fact that several months have passed since the issue of the last of the above-mentioned opinions, the problem of access to the account seems to be still valid. This is confirmed by another opinion of the EBA, issued in mid-2022, in which the EBA points out that while working on the revision of PSD2, attention should also be paid to removing obstacles to accessing payment accounts (EBA, 2022b, 2022c). Recently, irregularities regarding the scope of information made available via API have also been reported by the UK antitrust authority in its letter addressed to one of the banks operating in the United Kingdom (CMA, 2023).

12.6 Legal Instruments to Protect AISPs against Unlawful Limitation of Access to Payment Accounts

A number of regulations have been adopted at the EU level and in the legislation of individual Member States to regulate access to payment accounts through TPPs, including AISPs. However, as follows from e.g., the above-mentioned positions of the EBA, in the financial market there are many difficulties related to granting such access. This naturally raises the question of how well the legal mechanisms in place protect individual providers as regards their provision of payment services. After all, it would be reasonable to expect that the identified instances of unjustified limitation of access to accounts by ASPSPs should be answered by implementing into the legal system standards that would adequately safeguard the interests of AISPs.

Such expectations may be justified by, for example, the wording of Article 67(3) PSD2.[38] This provision requires the ASPSP not to discriminate account information requests submitted through the AISP, unless this is justified by objective reasons (i.e., in case the AISP is in breach of the law regarding the rules for accessing the account) (Długosz, 2023).

A measure to prevent ASPSPs from ignoring account information requests is a general prohibition of denying an AISP access to a particular account unless there are objectively justified and duly evidenced reasons (the literature rightly points out that, given the assumed rationale, the denial of access to an account must not be motivated solely by the ASPSP's subjective belief that there is a threat of unauthorised or fraudulent access to the account. To justify such decision, it is necessary to have evidence <the substantiation requirement>) (Torończak, 2019) related to unauthorised or fraudulent access to the payment account by the AISP.[39] Any denial of access to the account should involve informing the competent national authorities of such incident, which in such case are obliged to take appropriate actions, including ordering the ASPSP to grant the AISP access to the account if the relevant denial was groundless.

The main drawback of the above-mentioned solution is the procedure according to which the competent authority orders that access to the payment account be granted to the AISP. Under the Polish law, an ASPSP's notification of denial to grant access to a user's account should be treated as a request to initiate official administrative proceedings before the PFSA (Torończak, 2019). These proceedings shall be conducted pursuant to provisions of the Code of Administrative Procedure,[40] meeting all deadlines and observing all forms of handling the case provided for by law. This means that the administrative decision concluding the entire proceedings should be issued without undue delay, but it may as well be issued within a month or even two months if the PFSA considers the case to be particularly complex.

The subject matter of the authority's possible resolution is a separate issue. The decision of the PFSA may concern not so much the general obligation to provide a designated AISP with access to all payment accounts maintained by a particular ASPSP, as ordering the ASPSP to grant the AISP access only to a specific account from which the latter originally wanted to obtain information and was prevented from doing so by the ASPSP. Therefore, this mechanism does not in any way facilitate the resolution of any disputes that would be related to an ASPSP's persistent denial of access to the account requested by a particular AISP. It can only be seen as an antidote to specific instances of an AISP being denied access to a particular payment account of a user. In view of the above, it should not come as a surprise that the solution based on Articles 68(5) and 68(6) of PSD2 is widely criticised – at least in the doctrine of the Polish law (Torończak, 2019; Czech, 2023).

Ordering an ASPSP to grant an AISP access to an account is not the only possible response of competent authorities to unauthorised actions of the ASPSP. In particular, in exercising their supervision powers, they are entitled to use supervisory measures, including those of a disciplinary nature in the form of fines. However, the decision whether to use such sanctions depends on two factors. Firstly, on the national law, which sets out the permissible scope and manner of interference with the sphere of rights and obligations of supervised institutions. Secondly, on the category of the provider that maintains users' payment accounts; after all, the supervisory measures that may be used in relation to ASPSPs that are banks differ from those that may be used in relation to ASPSPs acting as electronic money institutions or payment institutions.

Regardless of public law measures to ensure access to users' payment accounts, AISPs may also use private law instruments.[41] For example – under the Polish law, an ASPSP may be liable in tort (*ex delicto*) to an AISP for damage caused by unjustified denial of access to an account (Czech, 2023). In such case the AISP may, in the course of court proceedings, claim damages from the ASPSP.[42] In such circumstances, an action brought based on competition law cannot be completely ruled out, either (if ASPSP's actions violated the principles of fair competition, the use of appropriate public law measures by competent authorities should also be taken into account). However, similarly as in the case of the grounds for applying public law sanctions by the supervisory authority, pursuing its rights by an AISP in court proceedings depends on the regulations applicable in individual Member States (both substantive and procedural) and, as such, is not subject to harmonisation at the EU law level.[43]

The situation where an ASPSP does not deny an AISP access to the user's payment account but does not provide the AISP with all account information is not less problematic (thus, this is an instance of inefficient account access; cf. comments above). Failure to provide full account information is in fact tantamount to the ASPSP's breach of Article 32(3) of Regulation 2018/389, because the dedicated interface to contact TPPs creates obstacles that hinder the use of functions available to users as part of the AIS service. In such case the AISP is legally obliged to inform the competent authorities about problems with operation of the dedicated API (a similar obligation applies to the ASPSP). Only as a side note, it should be noted that potential liability of an ASPSP to an AISP is autonomous from the potential liability in tort or contract (*ex contractu*) of the ASPSP to the user (account holder). Based on the analysis of the Polish law, T. Czech reaches similar conclusions regarding the ASPSP's contractual liability to the user (Czech, 2023).

Until the appropriate level of availability and performance of the interface is restored, the AISP shall be entitled to use the contingency mechanisms provided by the ASPSP (unless it has been exempted from establishing them). The basis for exempting the ASPSP from the obligation to put contingency mechanisms in place is Article 33(6) of Regulation 2018/389. Under the Polish law, this type of exemption is granted pursuant to an administrative decision issued by the PFSA,[44] which enable communication via the interfaces made available to the users. In such case, the AISP's ability to access the account is subject to the fulfilment of the requirements set out in Article 33(5) of Regulation 2018/389.

The alternative access to the account based on interfaces designed for direct communication and user authentication at the ASPSP may be considered as a means of securing the AISP's interests, provided that the ASPSP provides such contingency mechanism at all, and at the same time it does not limit the scope of account information that is provided to the AISP. Otherwise, it would be difficult to identify any real protection in favour of the AISP. In principle, the resulting impasse may be overcome only because of an interference of competent authorities that decide to take supervisory measures against the ASPSP breaching the regulations.[45] At the same time, the AISP is, in a sense, deprived of other solutions that, according to the letter of the law, would enable immediate response and access to the full scope of account information. Obviously, this conclusion does not compromise the possibility of taking actions aimed at protecting AISPs' interests with the use of private law institutions, as in the case of total limitation of access to users' payment accounts (cf. comments above).

The findings made may be grounds for putting forward a general thesis that the applicable regulations on payment services focus on the protection of AISPs' interests based on follow-up measures, the use of which generally depends on competent authorities taking appropriate actions. At the same time, it is no use looking for legal solutions that would guarantee efficient and smooth provision of access to users' payment accounts to AISPs if the ASPSP limits access to such accounts because of its activities, including by providing incomplete account information.

12.7 Conclusion

Services provided by TPPs have been and continue to be performed in the payment services market. Their rapid growth, and especially that of AIS, is related to their combination with other services provided in the financial market. It should be noted that the regulations on TPPs' activities contained in the PSD2 directive are, on the one hand, still relatively new – no final court rulings regarding them have been issued yet – and on the other hand, quite general. Consequently, it is extremely important to present the correct interpretation of these provisions for the benefit of users of these payment services, ensuring also security of transactions and development of innovation in the payment market.

On the other hand, the analysis carried out leads to the conclusion that, under the current legislation, there are no measures that would allow, on an ad hoc basis, neutralising the difficulties related to ASPSPs limiting access to users' payment accounts. While it is true that the legislation in place provides AISPs with some protection in order to guarantee this category of providers access to accounts, the efficiency of such solutions seems questionable. The problem with effectiveness of current mechanisms results primarily from the manner of their implementation, which, given the dynamic market changes, developing technology and constant emergence of new products on the financial market, significantly hinders conducting business as an AISP.

In the current situation, an ad hoc remedy should be to intensify the efforts of competent authorities regarding verification of ASPSPs' activities and the rules of operation of the interfaces provided by them, used for authentication and communication during the sessions established with the participation of TPPs.

In the long run, however, the possibility of introducing legislative changes that would facilitate AISPs access to users' payment accounts should be considered. One of such solutions could be the establishment of a special (simplified) procedure related to the denial to grant a TPP access to an account. It seems that similar procedures should be created for cases where an ASPSP provides a TPP with account information, but its scope is incomplete. Notwithstanding the foregoing, it should be requested *de lege ferenda* to explicitly allow provision of the so-called AIS-premium (AIS+) service, provided that the user has given an independent, explicit consent to its provision by the AISP.

Notes

1 The publication was co-financed from the subsidy granted to the Cracow University of Economics – Project nr 088/EPG/2022/POT.

2 Directive (EU) 2015/2366 of the European Parliament and of the Council of 25 November 2015 on payment services in the internal market, amending Directives 2002/65/EC, 2009/110/EC and 2013/36/EU and Regulation (EU) No 1093/2010, and repealing Directive 2007/64/EC (OJ of the EU L 337/35), hereinafter referred to as the "PSD2".

3 Article 3(1) of PSD 1 (Article 6(10) of the Polish Payment Services Act (PSA)).

4 Act of 19 August 2011on Payment Services (Journal of Laws of 2011, No. 199, item 1175 with later changes), hereinafter referred to as the "PSA".

5 Article 67(2)(b) of PSD2 and, accordingly, Article 59s(2)(2) of the PSA.

6 See Article 67(1) of PSD2 and Article 30(1) of Regulation 2018/389.

7 Guaranteeing access to payment accounts via a modified interface designed for authentication and communication between the ASPSP and the user is sometimes colloquially referred to as "screen scraping plus", which directly refers to the method of accessing users' payment accounts by TPPs prior to the adoption of PSD2 and Regulation 2018/389 (see comments above).

8 This conclusion is supported by the linguistic interpretation of Article 30(1) of Regulation 2018/389 and the disjunctive alternative between individual options used by the EU legislator.

9 Commission Delegated Regulation (EU) 2018/389 of 27 November 2017 supplementing Directive (EU) 2015/2366 of the European Parliament and of the Council with regard to regulatory technical standards for strong customer authentication and common and secure open standards of communication (Regulation 2018/389).

10 The announcement is available at the following address (in Polish only): https://www.knf.gov.pl/knf/pl/komponenty/img/Komunikat_UKNF_w_sprawie_PSD2_60678.pdf.

11 See Article 30(1)(a) of Regulation 2018/389.

12 Regulation (EU) No 910/2014 of the European Parliament and of the Council of 23 July 2014 on electronic identification and trust services for electronic transactions in the internal market and repealing Directive 1999/93/EC (eIDAS).
13 See Article 34 of Regulation 2018/389.
14 See also EBA in *EBA clarifications to issues VIII to XIII raised by participants of the EBA Working Group on APIs under PSD2*, p. 2 (the answer to question no. XIII).
15 See recital 93 of PSD2.
16 See Article 30(1)(b) of Regulation 2018/389.
17 See Article 35 of Regulation 2018/389.
18 See Article 30(2) of Regulation 2018/389.
19 See EBA in *EBA clarifications to issues XIV to XX raised by participants of the EBA Working Group on APIs under PSD2*, pp. 2-3 (the answer to question no. XV).
20 See Article 30(2)(a) of Regulation 2018/389.
21 See Article 67(4) of PSD2.
22 See Article 30(2)(b) of Regulation 2018/389.
23 See Article 30(2)(c) of Regulation 2018/389.
24 See Article 67(2)(b) of PSD2.
25 See Article 67(2)(e) of PSD2 and Article 36(1) of Regulation 2018/389.
26 See Article 32(3) of Regulation 2018/389.
27 See the EBA's consultation on the guidelines on the conditions to benefit from an exemption from the contingency mechanism under Article 33(6) of Regulation (EU) 2018/389 (EBA/GL/2018/07) – response to question no. 85 to the consultation paper.
28 See the EBA's consultation on the guidelines on the conditions to benefit from an exemption from the contingency mechanism under Article 33(6) of Regulation (EU) 2018/389 (EBA/GL/2018/07) – response to question no. 96 to the consultation paper.
29 See the EBA's position in point 13 of the Opinion of the EBA on the implementation of the RTS on SCA and CSC (EBA-Op-2018-04).
30 See Article 33 of Regulation 2018/389.
31 This area is also the subject of the EBA's guidelines on the conditions to benefit from an exemption from the contingency mechanism under Article 33(6) of Regulation (EU) 2018/389 (EBA/GL/2018/07).
32 The legal definition of sensitive payment data is provided in Article 4(32) of PSD2. This provision has been implemented into the Polish law under Article 2(26c) of the PSA.
33 See point 20 of the Opinion of the EBA on the implementation of the RTS on SCA and CSC (EBA-Op-2018-04).
34 See Article 117b(9) of the PSA.
35 On the other hand, it should be noted that, according to the EBA, the ASPSP is not obliged to provide the AISP with the user's identity data, such as the user's address, date of birth or social security number, as those are not data necessary for provision of AIS; see point 27 of the EBA's opinion on the implementation of the RTS on SCA and CSC (EBA-Op-2018-04). However, this does not apply to the name of the account holder, which is visible to the user directly contacting the ASPSP; see the EBA's position expressed in reply no. 2018_4081 in the EBA's Q&A Single Rulebook.
36 See the Opinion of the EBA on obstacles under Article 32(3) of the RTS on SCA and CSC (EBA/OP/2020/10).
37 See the Opinion of the EBA on supervisory actions to ensure the removal of obstacles to account access under PSD2 (EBA/Op/2021/02).
38 This provision has been implemented into the Polish law under Article 59s(3)(2) of the PSA.

39 See Articles 68(5) and 68(6) of PSD2, implemented to the Polish law by Articles 41(5) to 41(7) of the PSA.
40 Act of 14 June 1960 – Code of Administrative Procedure (Journal of Laws of 2022, item 2000, as amended).
41 Differences in the application of such instruments, including the exact rules for and possible extent of their use, in fact depend on whether we are dealing with common law or a continental legal system. However, due to the nature of this paper, it is impossible to discuss this issue in an exhaustive manner, therefore it is reasonable only to mention it.
42 See Article 415 et seq. of the Civil Code Act of 23 April 1964 (Journal of Laws of 2022, item 1360, as amended).
43 Only as a side note, it should be noted that potential liability of an ASPSP to an AISP is autonomous from the potential liability in tort or contract (*ex contractu*) of the ASPSP to the user (account holder). Based on the analysis of the Polish law, T. Czech reaches similar conclusions regarding the ASPSP's contractual liability to the user; see T. Czech [in:] K. Osajda, J. Dybiński (Eds.), *Ustawa o usługach płatniczych*, 2023, commentary to Article 41, argument 30.1.
44 Announcement of the Office of the Polish Financial Supervision Authority of 1 July 2019 on exemption from so-called fallback option. The announcement is available at the following address (in Polish only): https://www.knf.gov.pl/knf/pl/komponenty/img/Komunikat_Urzedu_KNF_w_sprawie_zwolnienia_z_tzw_opcji_fallback.pdf.
45 *Ex lege*, competent authorities are obliged to ensure that ASPSPs continuously comply with the requirements provided for in Regulation 2018/389 with regard to the implemented interfaces; see Article 30(6) *in principio* of Regulation 2018/389.

References

Blocher, M. (2022). Granice ochrony prawnej dostawców świadczących usługę inicjowania transakcji płatniczej. *Monitor Prawniczy*, 14, 26–30 (supplement).

Brener, A. (2019). Payment service directive II and its implications. In T. Lynn, J. G. Mooney, P. Rosati, M. Cummins (Eds.), *Disrupting Finance. FinTech and Strategy in the 21st Century* (pp. 103–120). Palgrave Macmillan Publishing.

Byrski, J., Juraszczyk, K., Miąsko, M., Synowiec, M. (Eds.) (2019). Najważniejsze zmiany nowelizacji ustawy o usługach płatniczych implementującej dyrektywę w sprawie usług płatniczych (PSD 2) – praktyczny komentarz, Fundacja Rozwoju Obrotu Bezgotówkowego.

Byrski, J., Synowiec, M. (2017). Wybrane zagadnienia charakterystyki prawnej nowych usług płatniczych. *Przegląd Prawa Handlowego*, 12, 304, 34–39.

Byrski, J. (2018). *Outsourcing w działalności dostawców usług płatniczych*. C.H. Beck Publishing.

Byrski, J. Zalcewicz, A. (Eds.) (2021). Ustawa o usługach płatniczych. Komentarz, edit. II, Wolters Kluwer Polska.

CMA (2023). Letter of competition & market authority of 19 January 2023 addressed to HSBC UK Bank plc. https://assets.publishing.service.gov.uk/government/uploads/system/uploads/attachment_data/file/1129899/CMA_letter_to_HSBC_about_breaches_of_the_Retail_Banking_Order.pdf

Czech, T. (2023). In Osajda, K., Dybiński, J. (Eds.). Ustawa o usługach płatniczych. Komentarz Legalis/el. 2023.

Długosz, Z. (2023). In Osajda, K., Dybiński, J. (Eds.) Ustawa o usługach płatniczych. Komentarz, Legalis/el. 2023.

Długosz, Z., Mostowik, M. (2018). Dysponowanie danymi z rachunku w świetle przepisów PSD2 oraz RODO, Monitor Prawa Bankowego 2018, 5, 90, 60–69.

Doroszewski, W. (1958). *Słownik języka polskiego.* https://sjp.pwn.pl/doroszewski/skonsolidowac;5497350.html

EBA (2021). https://www.eba.europa.eu/eba-publishes-clarifications-seventh-set-ssues-raised-its-industry-working-group-application-0

EBA (2022a). https://www.eba.europa.eu/regulation-and-policy/payment-services-and-electronic-money/regulatory-technical-standards-on-strong-customer-authentication-and-secure-communication-under-psd2

EBA (2022b). Opinion of the European banking authority in its technical advice on the review of directive (EU) 2015/2366 on payment services in the internal market (PSD2). https://www.eba.europa.eu/sites/default/documents/files/document_library/Publications/Opinions/2022/Opinion%20od%20PSD2%20review%20%28EBA-Op-2022-06%29/1036016/EBA%27s%20response%20to%20the%20Call%20for%20advice%20on%20the%20review%20of%20PSD2.pdf

EBA (2022c). http://www.eba.europa.eu/eba-replies-european-commission%E2%80%99s-call-advice-%C2%A0-review-payment-services-directive

Grabowski, M. (2020). Ustawa o usługach płatniczych. Komentarz, Warszawa 2020.

Gradzi, M. (2019). Third Party Providers (TPP) – nowi dostawcy usług płatniczych w środowisku internetowym i mobilnym. Przegląd regulacji prawnych i analiza możliwych zagrożeń cyberbezpieczeństwa płatniczej infrastruktury krytycznej, Przegląd bezpieczeństwa wewnętrznego 2019, 19, 10, 126–149.

Kasiewicz, S. (2018). *PSD 2 krytyczny przystanek w drodze do nowej ery bankowości*, Oficyna Wydawnicza SGH.

Korus, K. (2017). *Usługi oparte na dostępie do rachunku w dyrektywie PSD II*, Monitor Prawa Bankowego, 7–8, 80–81, 81–93.

Leżoń, K. (2019). *Otwarta bankowość w świetle wymogów dyrektywy PSD2 – wyzwania i perspektywy rozwoju dla polskiego sektora FinTech*, Pracownia C&C Sp. z o.o.

Madir, J. (Ed.) (2019). *FinTech Law and Regulation.* Edward Elgar Publishing.

Mostowik, M. (2017). Prawna ochrona informacji o rachunku płatniczym w świetle usługi dostępu do informacji o rachunku (AIS). *Monitor Prawa Bankowego 2017*, 7–8, 80–81, 32–43.

Osajda, K., Dybiński, J. (Eds.) (2023). Ustawa o usługach płatniczych. Komentarz, Legalis/el.

Petrović, M. (2020). PSD2 Influence on digital banking transformation – Banks' perspective. *Journal of Process Management and New Technologies*, 8, 4, 1–14.

Sofort (2016). http://prnews.pl/wiadomosci/sofort-wyniki-za-1-polowe-2016-50-sklepow-dziennie-chce-rozpoczac-wspolprace-6553123.html

Stanisławska, M. (Ed.) (2022). *Ustawa o usługach płatniczych.* Komentarz.

Synowiec, M. (2023). Charakterystyka prawna usługi płatniczej acquiringu i umowy łączącej agenta rozliczeniowego z akceptantem (in press).

Torończak, M. (2019). *Nakazywanie przez KNF przyznania dostępu do rachunku płatniczego. Monitor Prawa Bankowego*, 5, 102, 103–112.

Wolters, P.T.J., Jacobs, B.P.F. (2019). *The Security of Access to Accounts under the PSD2. Computer Law & Security Review*, 35, 1, 29–41.

Zegers, A., Nys, E. (2020). Understanding payment services, Droit bancaire et financier (Bank- en Financieel Recht), 2, 105–123.

13 The Role of Blockchain Governance in Banks' Transformation Toward Ecosystem-Based Banking

Piotr Łasak

13.1 Introduction

The digitalization of banking services, with the entrance to the market of new participants (non-bank–FinTech businesses) and the change from supply-driven to demand-driven and customer-oriented approaches, are exerting a significant impact on the new models of banks and the process of transformation of the whole banking industry. Important are the changes from the hierarchical structure to market solutions and the development of banking ecosystems (Gancarczyk et al., 2022; Gancarczyk & Rodil-Marzábal, 2022). They exert a great influence on the mechanisms of bank governance. In turn, internal governance is crucial for bank performance (Williams & Nguyen, 2005). During the last decades, a new type of governance, namely, one, blockchain governance has emerged and become operational alongside apart from the traditional governance modes (contractual and relational governance) (Figuigui & Macrouh, 2020; Lumineau et al., 2021). The new form of bank governance is strictly interconnected with the transformation of banks and banking sectors. It is especially significant for the creation of ecosystem-based banking (Liao et al., 2022). There are considerable research gaps in addressing these transformations, which calls for an investigation of these processes. While the impact of FinTech on banks and banking sectors is still relatively poorly described in the literature, the mechanisms of governance belong to the least explored themes.

The theoretical explanation of the structural changes of industry including the financial sector can be considered using the New Institutional Economics perspective (Williamson, 2000, 2005, 2010). The institutional analysis explains the creation of new formal industrial institutions and governance structures through the interaction of informal transactions and market mechanisms (Williamson, 2000). The model of institutional levels explains the dynamics of changes in banking market structures. Despite the complex theoretical explanation of the mechanisms responsible for the firm's borders, there are many research gaps when considering the processes of the creation of a new banking industry as a consequence of the processes of digitalization (Kleibert, 2020; Lai & Samers, 2021). The New Institutional Economics

DOI: 10.4324/9781003340454-13

theory can help to understand the different mechanisms involved in banking industry transformation. This chapter aims to capture the impact of financial technologies on the changing corporate governance in banking. The impact can be twofold. Firstly, it is related to the development of a new type of banking governance. Second, it embraces the role of the newly created governance in the context of the development of banking ecosystems. The first area and connected tasks relate to the governance between different institutions in the banking industry. There is a need to define and describe in detail the newly created contracts between banks and non-bank institutions. We contribute to the research gap by addressing the question:

> **RQ1:** How does financial technology impact governance in banks and banking sectors, and what is the role of blockchain governance in the context of contractual and relational governance?

The second research gap relates to the relations between incumbent banks and newly created ecosystems. This necessitates defining the actors participating in creating the banking ecosystem and, on that basis, describing their roles. It is important to determine if the newly created start-up ecosystems can be treated as an opportunity or a threat to incumbent banks and further development of their services (like know-your-customer or personal data storage). It is still not clearly defined what the necessary conditions are that would cause incumbent banks to want to partner with start-ups and move to a more open banking system (Svensson et al., 2019). Hence, we formulate the second research question:

> **RQ2:** How does ecosystem structure explain blockchain governance in the provision of banking services?

This chapter is organized as follows. The first part presents the process of banking sector transformation in the context of the New Institutional Economics perspective. According to Williamson's model, the dynamics of the changes in the structure of the financial market can be defined on four layers. The model is presented in this section. The second part refers to collaboration between incumbent banks and FinTech businesses and explains the process of creating the financial ecosystem. The third part defines the three types of corporate governance in banking, namely, contractual governance, relational governance and blockchain governance. Part four defines the role of blockchain governance in the development of the banking ecosystem. The conclusion provides answers to the research questions.

13.2 Three Levels of Banking Sector Transformation

Financial services markets have been changing rapidly since the 2008 global financial crisis (GFC) under the very dynamic processes of digitalization. Digitalization exerts influence on societies and economies but also on individual entities including individual banks and banking sectors. As a consequence, incumbent banks, based on hierarchical structures, gradually give way to new market structures, including emerging ecosystems-based structures. Such processes are currently becoming more advanced and financial technologies play a crucial role creating new, ecosystem-based structures (Omarini, 2022; Resano, 2021).

The literature highlights the process of change from a hierarchical to a heterarchical and market-based structure of banking services (Fenwick et al., 2019). Changes in the banking sector can be theoretically explained by the framework of New Institutional Economics proposed by Williamson. He proposes four levels of institutions, of which three are the most important for understanding the dynamics of the changes in the structure of the financial market (Williamson, 2000):

- Social embeddedness.
- Institutional environment.
- Governance.

The first level represents the informal institutions, customs, traditions, norms and religion. This layer of institutions is based on social mechanisms and is defined by the way how people think about entrepreneurs and how they perceive and respond to individual, legal and administrative factors. The social processes occurring on this level define economic transformations (Dietsche, 2018). Here is also considered the role of networks and relationships that define entrepreneurship mechanisms (Audretsch et al., 2022).

The second level, the institutional environment, represents the formal rules of the game. It embraces the executive, legislative, judicial and bureaucratic functions of powers (Williamson, 2000). This level is responsible for providing formal rules for economic transactions and is responsible for the safety of the market and should not change too frequently (Dietsche, 2018).

The third level, governance, represents the governance structures designed by partners to mediate particular economic relationships (Klein, 1998). In the considered mechanisms of bank and banking sector transformation, the third layer represents the structure of market participants, which embraces incumbent financial institutions but also newcomers that are responsible for changes in the market structure. Previously, banks had a hierarchical structure. As a consequence of the dynamics triggered by financial technology, banking services are now being organized in different structures (heterarchical, contract, etc.).

According to Williamson's analysis, the order of layers is crucial for the creation of an institutional framework. The over-arching role has the first level (social embeddedness), which embeds the lower levels. The same rule is important for the lower layers – in each case, the higher level constrains the lower level, causing the relative cost of abiding to be lower and the cost of evasive action to be higher. In consequence, the lower-level actors conform to the expectations of the higher level (hierarchical interdependence)

(Bylund & McCaffrey, 2017). In our analyses, however, we omit levels 1 (social embeddedness) and 2 (institutional environment) because they are dependent on external conditions, whereas our goal is to focus on the transformation of the banking sector itself. In the case of level 1, a geographical analysis is required, and in the case of level 2, the changes concern the specificity of banking sector regulations. Our analysis concerns only level 3 (governance) and will focus on governance issues in the context of technological changes and the digitization of the banking sector.

13.3 Creation of the Ecosystem from Bank and FinTech Collaboration

Traditional banks are currently undergoing a far-reaching transformation resulting from the impact of financial technology. The process of digitalization of financial markets, institutions and services is exerting great influence on the new shape of financial markets and banking sectors (Scardovi, 2017; Tanda & Schena, 2019; Vives, 2017). As Omarini (2022) highlights, banking is shifting from a vertical paradigm to open banking where open innovation, modularity and ecosystem-based banking business models have become more popular. Financial technologies are treated as external enablers of the transformation of banks' scope (Łasak & Gancarczyk, 2022). Apart from changing bank business models, there are profound changes in banking sectors across different spatial dimensions. The processes of digitalization exert great influence on many aspects of banking sectors. For instance, changes in generic governance modes (from bank governance to firm and markets), from public to private governance and from hierarchical to heterarchical governance. Apart from these processes, banking ecosystems are emerging (Gancarczyk et al., 2022). Usually, in such ecosystems in contrast to privately run and managed traditional banks, the ownership and decision-making is decentralized.

The term financial ecosystem refers to the market structure that encompasses the network of players in the financial system that are involved in the delivery of specific services through both competition and cooperation (Figure 13.1). It happens when a set of distinct but interdependent organizations coordinate their activity without a full hierarchical structure (Jacobides et al., 2018). Usually, there are numerous motives for the development of bank–FinTech ecosystems, but they are built for customers (Drasch et al., 2018). This implies there is a set of actors with different degrees of multilateral, non-generic complementarities that are not fully hierarchically controlled (Jacobides et al., 2018). The elements presented in Figure 13.1 represent only one dimension of the financial ecosystem. The second dimension is the different financial services offered via the ecosystem (e.g., payment, lending, wealth management). The third dimension are different technologies (Artificial Intelligence, blockchain, big data, cloud computing, etc.) (Imerman & Fabozzi, 2020). Only these three dimensions create the whole picture of the FinTech ecosystem. The ecosystem-based model is strictly connected with greater adjustment of banking services to consumer needs. Business ecosystems evolve as a way of acquiring, engaging and retaining customers (Omarini, 2022).

Sometimes the term "ecosystem" is considered as a special type of business model. It comprises a multilateral set of autonomous firms that collaborate to realize a value proposition (Matkovskaya et al., 2022). The term "ecosystem" can be also used to describe innovations around technological platforms. Platforms are based on particular kind of operating system and use particular software applications and hardware, which can capture large shares of the markets they operate in (Leyshon, 2020). When considering financial markets, FinTech ecosystems are especially popular in banking services (Lee & Shin, 2018; Omarini, 2018). The changing pattern of the new digital ecosystem is forcing banks to adapt to business models and better adjust their core activities to customers' expectations. In a time of rapid changes in financial markets, the potential of ecosystem development is great. It triggers the entry of new entities to this market. Some banks become part of external ecosystems whereas others initiate the creation of their own ecosystems (Matkovskaya et al., 2022). In the second case, banks usually are the "platform providers" servicing core functionalities (customers identity, account provision, payments processing, etc.) (Murinde et al., 2022). It is, however, typical that financial ecosystems comprise not only financial institutions, but they also embrace retailers, high-tech companies, social media, crowdsourcing platforms and many other entities that are involved with financial information or transactions (Premchand & Choudhry, 2018).

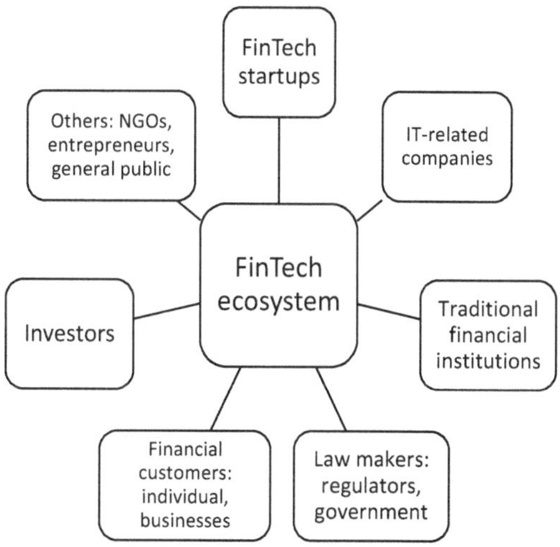

Figure 13.1 The Main Components of the FinTech Ecosystem

Source: Own elaboration on Siddiqui and Rivera (2022).

When considering the nature of financial ecosystems, which embraces a group of entities, most financial ecosystems are dominated by a relatively small number of very large banks or other entities which jointly provide financial services (Zetzsche et al., 2020). Apart from the financial institutions, there are also non-financial participants. Such a division enables the creation of a three-dimensional pattern of banking ecosystems (Figure 13.2). It leads to a change from the bank core activities to the external services situated beyond core banking and pushes the boundaries of existing banks' business models (Khanna & Martins, 2018). The movement from core banking activities to the ecosystem with banking services is crucial as incumbent banks have access to data that provide a more complete view of customer needs, and it enables the extension of existing customer bases and operational capabilities while strengthening engagement. Very often FinTech start-ups participate in providing banking services to retail customers. The further movement towards ecosystem with non-banking participants enables banks' participation in the provision of financial services to other, non-bank activities (like mobile phone services, medical expenses, etc.). Such engagement enables banks to participate in a network of value across different industries and to create their own ecosystems or participate in digital channels or external ecosystems created by another institution.

The process of creating ecosystems as a result of the impact of financial technology on the banking industry triggers changes in modes of governance. The problem of governance becomes especially significant when banking activity goes beyond banks' hierarchical structures and concerns newly created ecosystems. It comes from the more general nature of technology-based

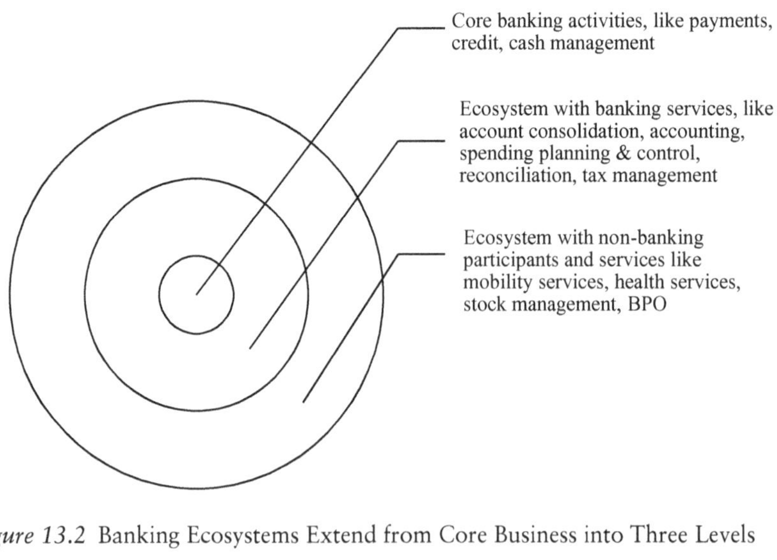

Figure 13.2 Banking Ecosystems Extend from Core Business into Three Levels

Source: Own elaboration on Khanna and Martins (2018).

ecosystems as financial technology enables the creation of such structures where many independent actors act as heterogeneous complementors. The participants act in accordance with stated goals, but to achieve them, they need to apply appropriate governance. Their ability to achieve the desired form of governance creates new challenges because there are significant differences and tensions between the partners that make up the ecosystem. For example, standard – variety, control-autonomy, collective-individual approach (Wareham et al., 2014). Thus, a type of governance is needed which enables the management of undesirable differences between ecosystem co-creators.

13.4 Three Types of Corporate Governance in Banking

Corporate governance is a very important issue in banking, but it should be considered through its own niche related to the specificity of banking industry. As Hagendorff (2014) highlights, corporate governance in banks is greatly different from the corporate governance arrangements of other firms. Accordingly, banks differ from other entities in the share of equity. Moreover, banks' activity is also protected by guarantees provided by regulators and governments. In consequence, these features lead to greater risk, which is usually borne by shareholders and can be harmful for bank creditors. For this reason, regulators should be biased and oriented towards stakeholder protection (Hagendorff, 2014). This is why corporate governance in banking has a contractual dimension – it relies on enforcement by courts or other certificated parties. In the case a breach of contract occurs, the law ensures protection for the injured party. Legal contracts prevent changes in the actions of the parties to an agreement, and at the same time, the parties are dependent on the enforceability of the legal system (Lumineau et al., 2021).

A significant dimension of corporate governance in the banking sector is the relationship between banks and their customers. As highlighted in the literature, the long-term relationship of banks with their clients is considered to have an important corporate governance role, particularly during more difficult times (Nam, 2004). Contrary to the traditional form of corporate governance inside the banking sector, which has a contractual dimension, the relationship between bank and clients has a nature of relational governance.

In contrast to the traditional approach to corporate governance in banking, the digital transformation of the sector triggers new challenges. The process of creating banking ecosystems exerts a great impact on shaping the proper structure of governance in banking. On the other hand, proper governance is critical for the implementation of the basic functions of banks in the new context (Bose et al., 2019). In consequence of these challenges, the traditional corporate governance (responsible for the internal processes in banks) and the relations between banks and their customers are replaced by more complex interdependencies between many participants operating within the new bank models. The adoption of financial technology to banking activities has a significant impact on bank governance. The traditional nodes of governance (contractual and relational) are changing. Apart from traditional forms of governance, a new type of governance, namely blockchain governance is also an important form that can make a significant contribution towards shaping proper relations between the partners creating the ecosystem (Gürünlü, 2019).

13.4.1 *Contractual and Relational Governance in Banking in the Context of Financial Technology*

Changes in the governance of the banking sector have been occurring for the last several years following the rapid development of financial technologies and intensified competition in financial services. They embrace the emergence of dynamic FinTech-driven transformations of governance in banking. This includes, for example, changes from firm governance to market governance, the creation of network governance, to building the governance of markets on a global scale. In the context of banking ecosystem development, the power of the relations is changing from banks as intermediaries towards multi-actor entrepreneurial structures. It is significant, that in some markets (economies) banks prefer to internalize governance functions, whereas in some other markets, these functions could be played together by banks and external partners (Carbó & Williams, 2000). In consequence, governance ecosystem structures emerge (DawnBurton, 2020). Before analysing the FinTech-driven changes in governance modes, we should review the traditional forms of governance in banking.

Banks, like other financial institutions, operate in the context of asymmetric information and risk-taking. These features suggest that the suitable option for organizing proper relations between the participants of banking activity is to formulate a contract and to define the relations between principal(s) and agent(s). For this reason, the first type of governance is contractual (transactional) governance. The transactional approach is expressed by formal contracts which are mechanisms to reduce risk and uncertainty in exchange relationships. It is a type of governance which legally defines obligations and provides exchange parties with an instrument of control and escalation even if there is a great extent of risk. In contractual governance, formal contracts between participating entities are negotiated and signed, performance is monitored and contractual promises are enforced. The contractual agreement has a positive influence on profitability and cost efficiency (Fritsch et al., 2007). Indeed, contractual governance is suitable for the relations between banks and their customers as well as between banks and other businesses (business-to-business relations). Even though sometimes banks have community-based relations with their customers, nowadays, it is a rare situation. The processes of deregulation and technological innovations since the 1980s have mostly replaced community-based banking with more transactional relations. In such situations, creditors can protect themselves through contractual agreements that govern their relations with banks. The same approach characterizes the business-to-business relations of banks. They have stronger motivations to write formal contracts which reflect transactional strategies oriented on short-term goals and opportunistic behavior (Ferguson et al., 2005).

The second type of governance, which has a long tradition in banks and the banking industry is relational governance. This approach was more common in the past and in countries hosting traditional, community-based banking where relationism and social embeddedness or informal self-enforcing governance played a crucial role. It relies on informal structures and self-enforcement of each party. Accordingly, relational governance is an alternative to formal governance regimes like contractual governance (Zobel & Hagedoorn, 2020). Cao & Lumineau (2015) contrapose the contractual governance to relational governance. Under contractual governance, the governance structure in interorganizational relationships is defined by formal and written contract (defining the responsibilities and obligations of each party), relational governance is ruled by social relations and shared norms. Historically relational governance has always played an important role in the banking industry, especially in the bank-oriented, continental model of financial markets. Hill and Scott (2015) highlight the role of relational governance between banks and small businesses. In this case, long-term relations between banks and their clients are important to both sides and they complement market forms of governance. Moreover, the more actively firms create relationships with banks, the greater is the exchange of information between parties. Relational cooperation brings many benefits, such as trust, familiarity, respect and flexibility in the provision of services. Such relations are created especially between small banks and SMEs.

Despite many differences between contractional and relational governance, they can be treated as complementary. Huber et al. (2013) suggest that the relationships between contractual and relational governance oscillate between complementarity and substitution. The authors present arguments for the coexistence of substitution and complementarity in bank-related corporate governance. Similarly, Fischer et al. (2011) argue that both contractual and relational governance have a complementary relationship and that the formal contractual governance is an enabler for relational governance. Rai et al. (2012) suggest that in some business cases, the best options are hybrid strategies which combine both contractual and relational approaches. Thus, there are complex relations between these two forms of governance, and they may complement and substitute each other.

The research on banking governance becomes especially significant when technological innovations are leading to structural changes in banks and banking sectors. Ferguson et al. (2005) highlight that in the past banking was built on a community-based relational approach to clients while nowadays a more transactional approach holds sway. This is the result of greater use of technology and the consequent creation of new business models founded on cooperation between banks and non-banking entities. The changing boundaries between firms raise questions as to how firms govern their relationships with other organizations. Moreover, the widely accepted assumption that current technological changes favor the application of a transactional approach faces many challenges. Zobel and Hagedoorn (2020) argue that relational contracting, characterized by more informal agreements based on flexibility and trust, aligns well with the nature of open innovations. Thus, the rapid changes and new innovations increasing blur the boundaries between entities and consequently contracts shift from written agreements toward more long-term interactive relationships. In addition, financial technology enables the development of a new form of governance – blockchain governance.

13.4.2 Blockchain Governance in Banking

The rapid development of new technologies has triggered the creation of new forms of governance in the banking industry. One example is the governance based on the application of blockchain technology. This technology from its very beginning demonstrated significant value in moving from centralized data management to decentralized management of data, records and transactions (Zutshi et al., 2021). Currently, blockchain technology is considered the key technology to secure the transparent processing of complex transactions within and between organizations and to create interorganizational networks. The advantages of blockchain technology over other types of financial technologies are that it enables decentralization of governance processes (Bokolo, 2022; O'Mahony & Karp, 2022). This approach provides a solution for linking the various participants in the financial ecosystem and ensuring harmony and standardization among them. Therein, stakeholder participation and governance are achieved through consensus mechanisms and autonomous smart contracts. The governance of collaborative networks of different participants is critical for the success of these networks (Mafike & Mawela, 2022) and is especially useful in developed value chains consisting of multiple entities (Chen et al., 2022).

Banks are adopting blockchain to improve their existing products and services. They use the advantages of blockchain, especially its potential to simplify the industry's multifaceted and wide-ranging payment and agreement networks, and in such a way lessen the risks and expenses (Morabito, 2017). Introducing blockchain governance into the banking ecosystem, (e.g., in payment systems), requires the collaborative participation of multiple stakeholders. The governance of these collaborative networks is essential for the success of these networks (Mafike & Mawela, 2022).

The application of blockchain technology and its adaptation as a generic technological solution to the specific needs of governance, which arise in an organizational context, triggers many managerial challenges. The need to manage efficiently and securely the transactions between interconnected networks of customers, partners, subsidiaries, suppliers and regulators has grown together with the development of the interconnected chains of cooperating entities. Choosing the appropriate governance mode is crucial for the success of blockchain-based solutions and blockchain networks. Blockchain technology provides the bedrock of digital network governance and requires careful design; however, as emphasized in the literature, blockchain does not represent an automatic governance mode. It must be complemented by a well-balanced governance structure that addresses the blockchain solution to the desired business needs. When blockchain connects multiple actors, careful consideration of the coordination and control of their activity is needed. Suitable governance is more critical and complex than the decisions to use and implement the technology itself (Goldsby & Hanish, 2022).

Blockchain governance has become very popular and plays an important role in current corporate governance structures (Akgiray, 2019). It represents a self-constrained and autonomous system of formal rules especially useful in the governance in banking. Instead of relying on enforcement through the law (contractual governance) or through the value of future relationships (relational governance), blockchain governance relies on set of protocols and code-based rules (Lumineau et al., 2021). It provides additional functionalities when compared to traditional modes of governance; for example, data privacy, recording user consent, managing APIs and preserving self-sovereign identities (Liao et al., 2022). One of the most important features of blockchain governance is that it can not only simplify the provision of banking services but also enable the coordination of bank and banking sector structures. Blockchain is a technology of decentralization and can aid the evolution of complex systems from centralization to decentralization. Thus, the transformation of banking structures from centralized hierarchical organizations to decentralized markets is much easier with the application of blockchain technology (MacDonald et al., 2016).

Table 13.1 Comparing the Three Types of Governance

	Contractual Governance	*Relational Governance*	*Blockchain Governance*
Defining feature	Enforceable promises defining the rights and obligations of the parties	Set of patterns of behavior to which parties are expected to conform	Self-contained and autonomous system of rules
Regulatory principles	Law	Social norms and "shadow of the future"	Protocols and code-based rules
Mode of enforcement	Enforcement through third parties (court, arbitrator)/ government authorities	Enforcement through the parties themselves	Automatic enforcement by the underlying blockchain-based network
Form	Typically legal prose	Mostly informal	Formal programming language

Source: Lumineau et al. (2021).

Table 13.1 compares the traditional types of governance and blockchain governance. Blockchain governance has many advantages, such as lower cost, shorter time and complexity of payment, clearing and settlement; greater liquidity, more accurate record-keeping and transparency of ownership offered by blockchains (Atzori, 2017; Yermack, 2017). Other advantages of applying blockchain-based governance in the banking sector include reduced need for centralized authorities, automated contractual negotiation, the implementation of smart property and machine-to-machine communication (Morabito, 2017). Thus, blockchain governance can provide services in a potentially more efficient and decentralized way, without having to rely on other forms of governance. In incumbent solutions, some contracts need to be notarized to prove that the parties really did sign the contract in the presence of a legislative officer whilst others must be registered for the transaction to be stored in public records. The application of blockchain technology reduces the need for human intermediation and establishes provenance (Morabito, 2017).

13.5 Application of Blockchain Governance in Banking Ecosystems

The processes of digitalization and the application of advanced financial technology have triggered a deep transformation of the banking industry and are leading to creation of new banking ecosystems (Figuigui & Macrouh, 2020). Blockchain-based applications are an example of solutions which facilitate such changes. They facilitate the offering of novel services like online sales or mobile payments and embrace several participating entities. There are also other financial technologies, such as artificial intelligence, cloud computing and big data, which are used in banking. Banks use and combine these technologies in their operations and create ecosystems linking customers, third-party developers, FinTech companies, suppliers and other partners. Such approaches also create new value and modifies competencies (Zhou et al., 2022).

There are a few phases of the transition from firm-based banking (single bank) to a banking ecosystem. Sironi (2021) identifies three stages that result from digitalization. He contends that a linear activity oriented on goods or services provision in a particular industry should be treated as a simple value chain. In such cases, there is no further connection between consumers or through the business relationships of sellers. When such value chains are enhanced by digital technologies, it can lead to the creation of digital platforms. In doing so, the value is still generated between two parties and the developed platforms are product centric. When the value is generated by allowing the participants to interact through different and complementary contributions, which are facilitated by sharing data and insights about user preferences needs, it leads to the creation of platform-based digital ecosystems (Sironi, 2021). The entrance of the FinTech businesses in financial markets enhances the creation of digital banking ecosystems (Gancarczyk et al., 2022; Gancarczyk & Rodil-Marzábal, 2022). Sometimes it is a more targeted change than simple collaboration between several related institutions which leads to open banking. Such a structure can be defined as a collaborative model between unaffiliated parties in which banking data is shared through APIs to deliver enhanced capabilities to the marketplace (Long et al., 2020). Open banking enables sharing data across organizations and provides new services through the engagement of many entities. It should be emphasized that banking sectors are undergoing a far-reaching transformation and are moving rapidly towards banking ecosystems (Arslanian & Fischer, 2019; Bhatnagar, 2022; Dapp et al., 2015).

Incumbent banks that are operating in the current fast-changing environment are being forced to adapt to customers' expectations and technology-driven behavior. Thus, we can observe a shift in their business models from being based on a single firm to an ecosystem-based model, comprising the firm and its multiple interconnected partners (Vaia et al., 2022). This change from a model in which a business unit lies within a single company to an ecosystem matrix consisting of several institutions suggests the need to change the governance model. Indeed, the contemporary governance in the digitalized financial ecosystem is unbalanced and more balanced governance regime is needed (Tsang, 2017). The increasing focus on governance in banking ecosystems reflects also the need for greater coordination of participants' activities, risk and profit sharing. The development and application of new technologies can enable their implementation to governance as well as other functions of financial activity.

The necessity for a change of governance model is especially important in platform-based ecosystems where the platform orchestrator organizes activities between the participants. They share a ledger which means that both the functional rules and contractual terms must be the same for all participants for the ecosystem to work properly. The emergence of digital governance enhances the agility of participants and the whole ecosystem. The application of digital technologies enables the collaboration of various partners and provides individual benefits to all partners (Bokolo, 2022). In the new structure it becomes necessary to move from internal governance within a particular firm to the external governance setting between the firm and the set of interrelated partners within an ecosystem. The second dimension of governance is made easier by the application of blockchain technology (Vella & Gastaldi, 2021). Zutshi et al. (2021) report that blockchain technology not only has the potential to bring about radical changes in business automation, digital economic models and investment ecosystems, but it also has great potential to transform the governance paradigm by bringing in new models of decentralized participative governance in multi stockholder digital-enabled business ecosystems.

As noted, the firm-oriented banking structure traditionally applied contractual or relational modes of governance depending on the type of financial market. Such government modes are also possible when there is a closed

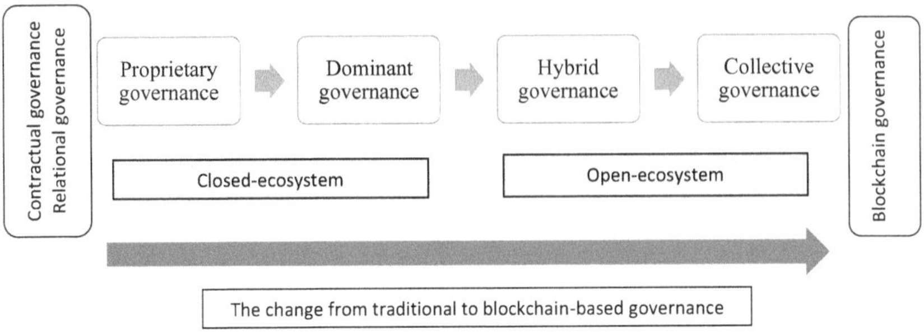

Figure 13.3 The Process of Transition from Proprietary Governance to Collective Governance

Source: Own elaboration on Vaia et al. (2022); O'Mahony and Karp (2019).

ecosystem where incumbent banks are dominant and when the structure includes a small number of participants. Despite the important role of traditional governance in banking activity, the development of ecosystems has triggered a change in bank governance from traditional to blockchain-based governance (see Figure 13.3).

The "proprietary" or "dominant" modes of governance are types where the platform owner and a few firms were granted access to the platform as active users. However, they are limited in how they could participate with the platform. Sometimes a greater number of entities have active access to the platform; while they contribute to the platform, the owner retains the dominant role.

The closed ecosystem and proprietary governance, however, are only the first phase of the transformation of the banking sector. When the community (ecosystem) becomes bigger, governance cannot be efficiently achieved by a series of bilateral contracts between participants. Such an approach would increase governance costs and fail to accommodate all possible contingencies. Thus, it forces the change in the structure of the ecosystem leading to the open ecosystem. This type of ecosystem enables open access for external entities and collective governance. When considering blockchain governance in the context of banking digital transformation and the development of banking platforms and ecosystems, it is especially important to focus on the two features – coordination and control. Coordination focuses on the management of interdependencies that exist within and across organizations. It embraces such aspects as the alignment of interdependent organizations around a common purpose, resource and operations deployment and mutual adjustments. Control embraces participation in information sharing, funding and decision-making and dispute resolution (Goldsby & Hanish, 2022). Coordination can be organized within a particular organization(s) or across the organization(s). Control can be centered on the organization(s) or shared among participating organizations. The intersection of coordination and control leads to the four modes of blockchain governance shown in Figure 13.3: proprietary governance (chief), dominant governance (clan), hybrid governance (custodian) and collective governance (consortium). The higher level of coordination within the organization together with a greater focus on the organization(s) is leading to the application of proprietary (chief) governance. In such cases, blockchain is implemented in-house by one institution and represents the most tightly organized and closed form of blockchain governance. It is especially beneficial for holding companies with many loosely coupled business units that engage in frequent interactions. When the coordination within an organization is high but the focus is shared among organization(s), it leads to the emergence of dominant (or *clan*) forms of governance. Such a type of governance differs from proprietary governance in that it permits shared control over the blockchain network. It is often used when an organization and its subsidiaries, departments or other units share control over functions and activities.

The lower level of coordination within the organization(s) and greater coordination across the organization(s) together with a higher level of control centered on the organization(s) is responsible for the development of hybrid (*custodian*) governance. This type of governance occurs when one company wants to coordinate its blockchain-related activities with other network participants. It characterizes the movement from an ecosystem with banking services to an ecosystem with non-banking participants (mobility services, health services, etc.). However, the crucial aspect is that the leading company wants to retain control over the blockchain's governance. Such type of governance occurs when the platform (ecosystem) initiators want to hold a steering role, but many of the governance functions become decentralized. Greater connections across organizations (lower coordination within the organization(s)) together with shared control among organization(s) can lead to the creation of a collective (*consortium*) mode of governance. It occurs when different organizations come together to jointly control activities for a blockchain network within the whole ecosystem. It represents the most open and collaborative governance approach. Consortium favors consensus-based decisions made among all participating entities (Goldsby & Hanish, 2022). It is the closest mode of governance to full blockchain-based governance.

The different types of blockchain governance together with different structures of banking platforms and ecosystems define the types of governance. The newly created blockchain-based ecosystem first must consider what form of governance mode best suits a particular activity or business structure. Secondly, the dynamics of blockchain governance also play an important role. A good governance structure should allow the ecosystem to attract and retain new members. The growing number of participants may lead to further changes in ecosystem governance. It means that no one type of blockchain governance is the best, and they change according to the dynamics of banking sector transformation. Usually, this infers movement from a more centralized form of governance to a more decentralized form. The decentralized forms seem to be more effective in blockchain-based platform ecosystems. Commentators suggest the most important behavioral drivers of blockchain governance embrace the following: access rights, decision rights, incentives, accountability and conflict resolution (van Haaren-van Duijn et al., 2022). This implies the possibility to participate in the ecosystem, to control the platform (ecosystem), to contribute to the quality of the ecosystem and to be responsible for the process, as well as possibility for conflict resolution. Usually, the blockchain-based ecosystem changes from the initial stage, when the consortium is created, through the achievement of an efficient operational level, to the opening of the ecosystem to external partners.

More open bank ecosystems mean that the relationships and governance in such ecosystems should occur through a platform interface that automates the elements of coordination, control and monitoring procedures (O'Mahony & Karp, 2022). Under such conditions, blockchain governance can be a better alternative to contractual or relational governance. Its biggest advantage is that it eliminates opportunism on the one hand and human errors on the other (Shanti & Elessa, 2023). Blockchain governance enables the coordination across organizational boundaries and control of relations between actors (activities) participating in the organization's network (Goldsby & Hanisch, 2022). A tool that enables the implementation of blockchain-based governance into the banking ecosystem is a special decentralized application. The application enables users, banks, third-party service providers and regulatory authorities to use various open banking ecosystem functionalities to achieve consortium blockchain co-governance, user identity integration, secure data sharing and other functions (Liao et al., 2022). Blockchain governance might be implemented at entities operating in the market due to smart contracts, which are one of the forms of blockchain applications in banking. A smart contract is a computerized protocol (fragments of computer programs encoded on blockchain) that executes the terms of a contract. Their application can overcome moral hazard problems and reduce the costs of verification and enforcement (Yermack, 2017). Smart contracts have encoded conditions which are very precise and specific. There is no room for interpretation and contestation – if the detailed conditions are not met, the transaction is not executed and the parties have no obligations to each other. Contracts are strictly rule-based and not allowing for discretion; the main idea is to reduce the governance costs and to leave no room for exceptions and for intervention (Pietrewicz, 2019).

13.6 Conclusion

The dynamic transformation of banks and banking sectors suggests the need for research focused on governance mechanisms applied in the emerging models and structures of banks and banking sectors. Blockchain technology is of particular importance in this context. This technology not only enables the development of banking services but also triggers the development of a new form of corporate governance. This chapter has provided a theoretical study dedicated to these problems and it provides answers to the formulated research questions.

The first research question pondered how does financial technology impact governance in banks and banking sectors, and what is the role of blockchain governance in the context of contractual and relational governance? Financial technology enables the process of digitalization of financial markets and is continuing to stimulate a far-reaching transformation of banks and banking sectors. Currently, banking is shifting from a vertical paradigm to open banking where open innovation, modularity and ecosystem-based banking business models have become more popular. The emerging new shape of banking sector structures requires also new forms of governance. The traditional, contractual and relational governance modes are less efficient and can be replaced by new modes. Financial technology enables the creation of such structures in banking where many independent, non-banking entities become heterogeneous complementors. Such structures require a new form of governance. One of the most adequate governance modes is blockchain governance. The application of blockchain technology reduces the need for human intermediation and can improve existing banking products and services. It also improves governance in banking.

The second research question is how does the ecosystem structure explain blockchain governance in the provision of banking services? It can be concluded that the ecosystem structure is leading the change of governance from traditional governance modes (contractual and relational governance) to blockchain governance. When banking services are provided within firm level or in a closed ecosystem, the accepted governance mode is based on contract or relations governance. The further development of ecosystems and creation of ecosystems with non-banking participants and services appear suitable for the blockchain governance mode. The more open is the bank and banking ecosystem, the more likely is the change from traditional forms of governance towards blockchain governance.

These answers are only a starting point for further research on shaping corporate governance in banking as a response to the development of financial technologies. There is need for a detailed comparison of blockchain governance and the traditional (relational and transactional) forms of governance in banking, involving the presentation of case studies of this form of corporate governance in the banking sector, as well as further quantitative research on this topic. The theoretical basis of this chapter is the New Institutional Economics perspective of Oliver Williamson. This research, however, has focused only on the one level, namely, governance. Thus, future research should examine the other levels and address the broader processes of the transformation of banks and banking sectors.

References

Akgiray, V. (2019). *The Potential for Blockchain Technology in Corporate Governance*. OECD. https://doi.org/10.1787/ef4eba4c-en

Arslanian, H., Fischer, F. (2019). *The Future of Finance: The Impact of FinTech, AI, and Crypto on Financial Services*. Springer.

Atzori, M. (2017). Blockchain governance and the role of trust service providers: The TrustedChain® network. *Available at SSRN 2972837*. http://dx.doi.org/10.2139/ssrn.2972837

Audretsch, D. B., Belitski, M., Caiazza, R., Desai, S. (2022). The role of institutions in latent and emergent entrepreneurship. *Technological Forecasting and Social Change, 174*, 121263. https://doi.org/10.1016/j.techfore.2021.121263

Bhatnagar, S. (2022). Technological evolution and emergence of new banking models. *IUP Journal of Bank Management*, 21, 2, 7–15.

Bokolo, A.J. (2022). Investigating the decentralized governance of distributed ledger infrastructure implementation in extended enterprises. *Journal of the Knowledge Economy*, 1–30. https://doi.org/10.1007/s13132-022-01079-7

Bose, S., Dong, G., Simpson, A. (2019). *The Financial Ecosystem*. Springer.

Bylund, P.L., McCaffrey, M. (2017). A theory of entrepreneurship and institutional uncertainty. *Journal of Business Venturing*, 32, 5, 461–475.

Cao, Z., Lumineau, F. (2015). Revisiting the interplay between contractual and relational governance: A qualitative and meta-analytic investigation. *Journal of Operations Management*, 33, 15–42.

Carbó, S., Williams, J. (2000). Stakeholder value in european savings banks. In L. Schuster (Ed.), *Shareholder Value Management in Banks* (pp. 134–166). Palgrave Macmillan UK. https://doi.org/10.1057/9780333981740_8

Chen, W., Botchie, D., Braganza, A., Han, H. (2022). A transaction cost perspective on blockchain governance in global value chains. *Strategic Change*, 31, 1, 75–87. https://doi.org/10.1002/jsc.2487

Dapp, T.F., Slomka, L., Hoffmann, R. (2015). Fintech reloaded–Traditional banks as digital ecosystems. *Deutsche Bank Research*, 261–274. https://www.dbresearch.com/PROD/RPS_EN-PROD/PROD0000000000451937/Fintech_reloaded_%D0_Traditional_banks_as_digital_ec.PDF?undefined&realload=6lOkYREF0AQmDjr3hKZVWE~FvGwiHIEnygbB0Jzjj6Spu~lrlz2qoSwRFl1~a4gj

DawnBurton. (2020). Digital debt collection and ecologies of consumer overindebtedness. *Economic Geography*, 96, 3, 244–265.

Dietsche, E. (2018). Political economy and governance. *Extractive Industries. The Management of Resources as a Driver of Sustainable Development*, 114–136. https://library.oapen.org/bitstream/handle/20.500.12657/28349/9780198817369.pdf#page=147

Drasch, B.J., Schweizer, A., Urbach, N. (2018). Integrating the 'Troublemakers': A taxonomy for cooperation between banks and fintechs. *Journal of Economics and Business*, 100, 26–42. https://doi.org/10.1016/j.jeconbus.2018.04.002

Fenwick, M., McCahery, J.A., Vermeulen, E.P.M. (2019). The end of 'Corporate' governance: Hello 'Platform' governance. *European Business Organization Law Review*, 20, 1, 171–199. https://doi.org/10.1007/s40804-019-00137-z

Ferguson, R.J., Paulin, M., Bergeron, J. (2005). Contractual governance, relational governance, and the performance of interfirm service exchanges: The influence of boundary-spanner closeness. *Journal of the Academy of Marketing Science*, 33, 2, 217–234.

Figuigui, B., Macrouh, F. (2020). Banking governance in the era of digital transformation. *Journal of Research in Administrative Sciences (ISSN: 2664-2433)*, 9, 2, 10–16.

Fischer, T.A., Huber, T.L., Dibbern, J. (2011). Contractual and relational governance as substitutes and complements – Explaining the development of different relationships. In A. Heinzl, P. Buxmann, O. Wendt, T. Weitzel (Eds.), *Theory-Guided Modeling and Empiricism in Information Systems Research* (pp. 65–83). Physica-Verlag HD. https://doi.org/10.1007/978-3-7908-2781-1_4

Fritsch, M., Wahrenburg, M., Hackethal, A., Wüllenweber, K. (2007). The impact of business process outsourcing on firm performance and the influence of governance: A long term study in the German Banking industry. *Available at SSRN 1076422.*

Gancarczyk, M., Łasak, P., Gancarczyk, J. (2022). The fintech transformation of banking: Governance dynamics and socio-economic outcomes in spatial contexts. *Entrepreneurial Business and Economics Review (EBER)*, 10, 3, 143–165.

Gancarczyk, M., Rodil-Marzábal, Ó. (2022). Fintech framing financial ecologies: Conceptual and policy-related implications. *Journal of Entrepreneurship, Management and Innovation*, 18, 4, 7–44.

Goldsby, C., Hanisch, M. (2022). The boon and bane of blockchain: Getting the governance right. *California Management Review*, 64, 3, 141–168. https://doi.org/10.1177/00081256221080747

Gürünlü, M. (2019). Blockchain as a disruptive technology reshaping corporate governance and finance. In *Global Challenges in Development, Finance and Education* (Vol. 5, p. 115). IJOPEC Publication Ltd. https://doi.org/10.1016/j.ijinfomgt.2019.10.014

Hagendorff, J. (2014). Corporate governance in banking. In A. N. Berger, P. Molyneux, J. O. S. Wilson (Eds.), *The Oxford Handbook of Banking* (pp. 139–159). Oxford University Press. Second Edition.

Hill, J., Scott, J. (2015). Knows Me and My Business: The Association between Preference for Relational Governance and Owners' Choice of Banks, *Journal of Small Business Management*, 53(S1), 174–192. https://doi.org/10.1111/jsbm.12193

Huber, T.L., Fischer, T.A., Dibbern, J., Hirschheim, R. (2013). A process model of complementarity and substitution of contractual and relational governance in is outsourcing. *Journal of Management Information Systems*, 30, 3, 81–114. https://doi.org/10.2753/MIS0742-1222300304

Imerman, M.B., Fabozzi, F.J. (2020). Cashing in on innovation: A taxonomy of FinTech. *Journal of Asset Management*, 21, 3, 167–177. https://doi.org/10.1057/s41260-020-00163-4

Jacobides, M.G., Cennamo, C., Gawer, A. (2018). Towards a theory of ecosystems. *Strategic Management Journal*, 39, 8, 2255–2276.

Khanna, S., Martins, H. (2018, April 13). *Six Digital Growth Strategies for Banks.* McKinsey. https://www.mckinsey.com/capabilities/mckinsey-digital/our-insights/six-digital-growth-strategies-for-banks

Kleibert, J.M. (2020). Unbundling value chains in finance: Offshore labor and the geographies of finance. In J. Knox-Hayes, D. Wójcik (Eds.), *The Routledge Handbook of Financial Geography* (pp. 421–439). Routledge.

Klein, P.G. (1998). New Institutional Economics. *Available at SSRN 115811.*

Lai, K.P.Y., Samers, M. (2021). Towards an economic geography of FinTech. *Progress in Human Geography*, 45, 4, 720–739. https://doi.org/10.1177/0309132520938461

Łasak, P., Gancarczyk, M. (2022). Transforming the scope of the bank through fintechs: Toward a modularized network governance. *Journal of Organizational Change Management,* 35, 1, 186–208. https://doi.org/10.1108/JOCM-05-2021-0147

Lee, I., Shin, Y.J. (2018). Fintech: Ecosystem, business models, investment decisions, and challenges. *Business Horizons*, 61, 1, 35–46. https://doi.org/10.1016/j.bushor.2017.09.003

Leyshon, A. (2020). Financial ecosystems and ecologies. In J. Knox-Hayes, D. Wójcik (Eds.), *The Routledge Handbook of Financial Geography* (pp. 122–141). Routledge.

Liao, C.-H., Guan, X.-Q., Cheng, J.-H., Yuan, S.-M. (2022). Blockchain-based identity management and access control framework for open banking ecosystem. *Future Generation Computer Systems*, 135, 450–466.

Long, G., Tan, Y., Jiang, J., Zhang, C. (2020). Federated learning for open banking. In Q. Yang, L. Fan, H. Yu (Eds.), *Federated Learning. Privacy and Incentive* (pp. 240–254). Springer.

Lumineau, F., Wang, W., Schilke, O. (2021). Blockchain governance—A new way of organizing collaborations? *Organization Science*, 32, 2, 500–521.

MacDonald, T.J., Allen, D.W., Potts, J. (2016). Blockchains and the boundaries of self-organized economies: Predictions for the future of banking. In P. Tasca, T. Aste, L. Pelizzon, N. Perony (Eds.), *Banking Beyond Banks and Money* (pp. 279–296). Springer.

Mafike, S.S., Mawela, T. (2022). Blockchain design and implementation techniques, considerations and challenges in the banking sector: A systematic literature review. *Acta Informatica Pragensia*, 11, 3, 396–422. https://doi.org/10.18267/j.aip.200

Matkovskaya, Y.S., Vechkinzova, E., Biryukov, V. (2022). Banking ecosystems: Identification latent innovation opportunities increasing their long-term competitiveness based on a model the technological increment. *Journal of Open Innovation: Technology, Market, and Complexity*, 8, 3, Article 3. https://doi.org/10.3390/joitmc8030143

Morabito, V. (2017). *Business Innovation through Blockchain*. Springer International Publishing.

Murinde, V., Rizopoulos, E., Zachariadis, M. (2022). The impact of the FinTech revolution on the future of banking: Opportunities and risks. *International Review of Financial Analysis*, 81, 102103. https://doi.org/10.1016/j.irfa.2022.102103

Nam, S. (2004). *Relationship Banking and Its Role in Corporate Governance* (Working Paper No. 56). ADBI Research Paper Series. https://www.econstor.eu/handle/10419/111151

O'Mahony, S., Karp, R. (2022). From proprietary to collective governance: How do platform participation strategies evolve? *Strategic Management Journal*, 43, 3, 530–562.

Omarini, A. (2022). The changing landscape of retail banking and the future of digital banking. In Heckel, M., Waldenberger, F. (Eds.) *The Future of Financial Systems in the Digital Age* (pp. 133–158). Springer, Singapore.

Omarini, A.E. (2018). Fintech and the future of the payment landscape: The mobile wallet ecosystem - A challenge for retail banks? *International Journal of Financial Research*, 9, 4, Article 4. https://doi.org/10.5430/ijfr.v9n4p97

Pietrewicz, L. (2019). Token-based blockchain financing and governance: A transaction cost economics approach. *Studia i Materiały Wydziału Zarządzania UW, 2/2018*(28), 126–139. https://doi.org/10.7172/1733-9758.2018.28.11

Premchand, A., Choudhry, A. (2018). Open banking & APIs for transformation in banking. *2018 International Conference on Communication, Computing and Internet of Things (IC3IoT)*, 25–29.

Rai, A., Keil, M., Hornyak, R., Wüllenweber, K. (2012). Hybrid relational-contractual governance for business process outsourcing. *Journal of Management Information Systems*, 29, 2, 213–256.

Resano, J.R.M. (2021). *Regulating for Competition with Bigtechs: Banking-As-A-Service and 'Beyond Banking'* (SSRN Scholarly Paper No. 3982500). https://doi.org/10.2139/ssrn.3982500

Scardovi, C. (2017). *Digital Transformation in Financial Services*. Springer International Publishing. https://doi.org/10.1007/978-3-319-66945-8

Shanti, A.A.M., Elessa, M.S. (2023). The impact of digital transformation towards blockchain technology application in banks to improve accounting information quality and corporate governance effectiveness. *Cogent Economics & Finance*, 11, 1, 2161773. https://doi.org/10.1080/23322039.2022.2161773

Siddiqui, Z., Rivera, C.A. (2022). Fintech and fintech ecosystem: A review of literature. *Risk Governance and Control: Financial Markets & Institutions*, 12, 1, 63–73.

Sironi, P. (2021). *Banks and Fintech on Platform Economies: Contextual and Conscious Banking* (1st edition). Wiley.

Svensson, C., Udesen, J., Webb, J. (2019). Alliances in financial ecosystems: A source of organizational legitimacy for fintech startups and incumbents. *Technology Innovation Management Review*, 9, 1, 20–32.

Tanda, A., Schena, C.-M. (2019). Bank strategies in the light of the digitalisation of financial activities. In A. Tanda, C.-M. Schena (Eds.), *FinTech, BigTech and Banks* (pp. 51–81). Springer International Publishing. https://doi.org/10.1007/978-3-030-22426-4_4

Tsang, C.-Y. (2017). Balancing the governance of the modern financial ecosystem: A new governance perspective and implications for market discipline. *Houston Journal of Internatinal Law*, 40, 531.

Vaia, G., Arkhipova, D., DeLone, W. (2022). Digital governance mechanisms and principles that enable agile responses in dynamic competitive environments. *European Journal of Information Systems*, 31, 6, 662–680.

van Haaren-van Duijn, B., Bonnín Roca, J., Chen, A., Romme, A.G.L., Weggeman, M. (2022). The dynamics of governing enterprise blockchain ecosystems. *Administrative Sciences*, 12, 3, 86.

Vella, G., Gastaldi, L. (2021). Blockchain platform ecosystem: An empirical analysis on the Italian banking sector. *28th Innovation and Product Development Management Conference (IPDMC)*, 1–12.

Vives, X. (2017). The impact of FinTech on banking. *European Economy*, 2, 97–105.

Wareham, J., Fox, P.B., Cano Giner, J.L. (2014). Technology ecosystem governance. *Organization Science*, 25, 4, 1195–1215.

Williams, J., Nguyen, N. (2005). Financial liberalisation, crisis, and restructuring: A comparative study of bank performance and bank governance in South East Asia. *Journal of Banking & Finance*, 29, 8–9, 2119–2154.

Williamson, O.E. (2000). The New Institutional Economics: Taking stock, looking ahead. *Journal of Economic Literature*, 38, 3, 595–613.

Williamson, O.E. (2005). The economics of governance. *American Economic Review*, 95, 2, 1–18.

Williamson, O.E. (2010). Transaction cost economics: The natural progression. *American Economic Review*, 100, 3, 673–690.

Yermack, D. (2017). Corporate governance and blockchains. *Review of Finance*, 21, 1, 7–31.

Zetzsche, D.A., Arner, D.W., Buckley, R.P. (2020). *Decentralized Finance (DeFi)* Social Science Research Network. https://doi.org/10.2139/ssrn.3539194

Zhou, L., Shi, C.X., Chen, S.L., Di Liu, Y. (2022, June 17). Research on the development of open banking in China under the background of internet finance. *Proceedings of the International Conference on Information Economy, Data Modeling and Cloud Computing, ICIDC 2022*.

Zobel, A.-K., Hagedoorn, J. (2020). Implications of open innovation for organizational boundaries and the governance of contractual relations. *Academy of Management Perspectives*, 34, 3, 400–423.

Zutshi, A., Grilo, A., Nodehi, T. (2021). The value proposition of blockchain technologies and its impact on digital platforms. *Computers & Industrial Engineering*, 155, 107187.

Index

Note: **Bold** page numbers refer to tables; *italic* page numbers refer to figures and page numbers followed by "n" denote endnotes.

FSC
www.fsc.org
MIX
Papier | Fördert gute Waldnutzung
FSC® C083411

Kolibri 360 GmbH
Ferdinand-Jühlke-Straße 7
99095 Erfurt, Deutschland
produktsicherheit@kolibri360.de